War In Peace

Volume 4

War In Peace

The Marshall Cavendish Illustrated Encyclopedia of Postwar Conflict.

Editor-in-Chief
Ashley Brown

Editorial Board
Brig-Gen. James Collins Jr (USA Retd.)
Vice-Admiral Sir Louis Le Bailly KBE CB
Ian V Hogg; David Floyd
Professor Laurence Martin
Air-Vice Marshal SWB Menaul CB CBE DFC AFC

MARSHALL CAVENDISH
NEW YORK, LONDON, TORONTO

Reference Edition Published 1985

Published by Marshall Cavendish Corporation
147 West Merrick Road
Freeport, Long Island
N.Y. 11520

Printed and Bound in Italy by L.E.G.O. S.p.a. Vicenza.

British Library Cataloguing in Publication Data

Brown, Ashley
    War in peace : the Marshall Cavendish
    illustrated encyclopaedia of post-war conflict.
    1. History, Modern—1945-   2. War—History
    —20th century
    I. Title   II. Dartford, Mark
    909.82   D842

    ISBN 0-86307-293-3
        0 86307 297 6   vol. 4

Library of Congress Cataloging in Publication Data

Main entry under title:

War in peace.

    Includes bibliographies and index.
    1. Military history, Modern—20th century.   2. Military
art and science—History—20th century.   3. World politics—1945-
I. Marshall Cavendish Corporation.
U42.W373 1984   355'.009'04   84-19386
ISBN 0-86307-293-3
        0 86307 297 6   vol. 4

Editorial Staff

Editor	Ashley Brown
Editorial Director	Brian Innes
Editorial Manager	Clare Byatt
Editorial Editors	Sam Elder
	Adrian Gilbert
Sub Editors	Sue Leonard
	Simon Innes
Artwork Editor	Jonathan Reed
Artwork Buyer	Jean Morley
Picture Editor	Carina Dvorak
Picture Consultant	Robert Hunt
Design	EDC

Reference Edition Staff

Editor	Mark Dartford
Designer	Graham Beehag
Consultant	Robert Paulley
Indexers	F & K Gill
Creation	DPM Services

Editorial Board

Contributors

David Blue served with the CIA in various countries of Southeast Asia, including Laos, and is a writer on and a student of small wars.

Gordon Brook-Shepherd spent 15 years in Vienna, first as lieutenant-colonel on the staff of the British High Commission and then as a foreign correspondent for the *Daily Telegraph*. A graduate in history from Cambridge, he is currently Chief Assistant Editor of the *Sunday Telegraph.*

Jeffrey J. Clarke is an expert on recent military history, particularly the Vietnam War, and has written for the American Center of Military History.

Major-General Richard Clutterbuck OBE has been Senior Lecturer in politics at Exeter University since his retirement from the army in 1972. His works include *Protest and the Urban Guerrilla, Guerrillas and Terrorists* and *Kidnap and Ransom.*

Alexander S. Cochran Jr is a historian whose area of research is modern Indochinese affairs with particular reference to the war in Vietnam since 1945. He is at present working in the Southeast Asia Branch of the Center of Military History, Department of the Army.

Colonel Peter M. Dunn is a serving officer in the USAF. His doctoral thesis is on the history of Indochina during the mid-1940s.

John B. Dwyer served both with the infantry and with armoured units in Vietnam. He was editor and publisher of the Vietnam veteran's newsletter *Perimeter* and has been a writer and correspondent for *National Vietnam Veteran's Review* for the past few years. His particular interest are Special Forces and Special Operations.

Brenda Ralph Lewis has specialised in political and military history since 1964. She s a regular contributor to military and historical magazines in both Britain and the United States.

Hugh Lunghi served in Moscow in the British Military Mission and the British Embassy for six years during and after World War II. He was interpreter for the British Chiefs of Staff at the Teheran, Yalta and Potsdam conferences, and also interpreted for Churchill and Anthony Eden. He subsequently worked in the BBC External Services and is a former editor of *Index on Censorship.*

Charles Messenger retired from the army in 1980 to become a fulltime military writer after 21 years service in the Royal Tank Regiment. Over the past 10 years he has written several books on 20th century warfare, as well as contributing articles to a number of defence and historical journals. He is currently a Research Associate at the Royal United Services Institute for Defence Studies in London.

Billy C. Mossman is a well-known American writer and historian. He is currently working on a volume on the Korean War for the US Army Center of Military History.

Bryan Perrett served in the Royal Armoured Corps from 1952 to 1971. He contributes regularly to a number of established military journals and acted as Defence Correspondent to the *Liverpool Echo* during the Falklands War. His recent books include *Weapons of the Falklands Conflict* and *A History of Blitzkrieg.*

Chapman Pincher is one of England's leading authorities on international espionage and counter-intelligence. He is the author of political novels and books on spying, the most recent of which is *Their Trade is Treachery*, which deals with the penetration of Britain's secret services by the Russian secret police.

Yehoshua Porath is a noted scholar at the Hebrew University in Jerusalem. He has made a special study of the Palestinian problem and is the author of two books on the subject, the most recent of which is *The Palestinian Arab National Movement 1929—39*, which was published in Britain in 1977.

Contributors

Antony Preston is Naval Editor of the military magazine *Defence* and author of numerous publications including *Battleships, Aircraft Carriers* and *Submarines.*

Brigadier-General Edwin H. Simmons, US Marine Corps, Retired, is the Director of Marine Corps History and Museums. At the time of the Inchon operation and the Chosin Reservoir campaign, he, as a major, commanded Weapons Company, 3rd Battalion, 1st Marines. Widely published, he is the author of *The United States Marines.*

Ronald Spector is an expert on Vietnam and has recently completed a book on that subject for the Center of Military History in the United States.

Andres Suarez served in the Cuban ministry of education from 1948—1951, took part in the Cuban revolution, and served in the ministry of housing from 1959. From 1965, he has been Professor of Latin American Studies at the University of Florida. Other publications include *Cuba and the Sino—Soviet Rift.*

Sir Robert Thompson KBE, CMG, DSO, MC is a world authority on guerrilla warfare, on which he has written extensively. He was directly involved in the Emergency in Malaya in the 1950s and rose to become permanent Secretary for Defence. From 1961 to 1965 he headed the British Advisory Mission to Vietnam and since then he has advised several governments, including the United States, on counter-insurgency operations Sir Robert Thompson is a Council member of the Institute for the Study of Conflict, London. His books include *Defeating Communist Insurgency and Revolutionary War in World Strategy, 1945—69.*

Patrick Turnbull commanded 'D' Force, Burma during World War II. His 29 published works include a history of the Foreign Legion.

Contents of Volume

IRA revival

A new generation and a new campaign

The IRA has its roots in an ancient Anglo-Irish historical problem. This is at its most intractable in northeastern Ireland where, since the Battle of the Bóyne in 1690 (an event still commemorated by the descendants of the victorious Protestants who followed King William of Orange) and in particular the subsequent plantation of Protestants on Catholic land, sectarian feeling has been intense. The Catholics in the area are still largely nationalist in sentiment and the Protestants strongly in favour of close links with the United Kingdom. In the 20th century there have been two major peaks of violence. The first of these was the 'Anglo-Irish War' of 1918-21, which ended with the independence of the 26 southern counties, and the second was the 'troubles' in Northern Ireland of the 1970s and 1980s. But these two periods are closely related; they form part of a chain, and the link between them is provided by a smaller, but important episode: the border war of the 1950s.

The salient point about the campaigns of the Irish Republican Army (IRA) in the 1950s is that they represented, in republican terms, the gospel of having a 'rising in every generation', which had been part of the physical-force tradition for centuries. But the IRA leadership faced considerable problems in achieving this. Ireland had been neutral during World War II and the IRA had been weakened in that period, hamstrung by internment in both North and South, riven by internal feuds, and decimated by harsh sentences including, in some cases, executions.

A number of factors helped the small coterie of IRA men, Micksie Conway (now a Cistercian lay brother), Cathal Goulding, Tony Magan, Sean MacCurtain and others, who began to regroup the movement after World War II when the prison camps emptied.

The absence of postwar benefits such as Marshall Aid for example meant that the Irish Republic had remained literally insular, cut off from western Europe's economic recovery. High unemployment led to massive emigration, but because of the high

Violence has been a part of Irish politics throughout the 20th century.
Above: British troops stand by as an armoured demolition vehicle clears burning debris from the streets in Northern Ireland in the 1970s.

Below: Troops man a hastily built barricade in preparation for an attack by Irish rebels during the Easter Rising in 1916.

Below right: Eamon de Valera, accompanied by his aide-de-camp, Colonel Sean Brennan (right), inspects troops on parade in Dublin in 1966 during anniversary celebrations of the Easter Rising. Far right: A constable of the RUC, armed with a Sten sub-machine gun, stands guard outside a police station. Far right below: An Orange Day parade of Irish Protestants; religious divisions have been institutionalised in Northern Ireland.

birth rate there was a large pool of young men and women to draw upon when once more the republican spark ignited. On the constitutional front the most decisive circumstance was the emergence of a new political party led by Sean McBride. This was the Clan na Poblacta (Republican Clan), which proved the vital element in a coalition which in 1948 overthrew Eamon de Valera and his Fianna Fail government after 16 years of power.

McBride, former Chief of Staff of the IRA and son of the Irish nationalist leader Major John McBride (executed in 1916), now holds both the Nobel peace prize and Lenin peace prize. He was a romantic figure, who, as a lawyer, had successfully cheated the gallows or the firing squad for his IRA clients on a number of occasions during World War II. An anti-partition campaign was launched after he came to power and the 26 counties declared themselves a republic on 18 April 1949. This declaration had important results, for the government of Great Britain felt impelled to safeguard the position of the Ulster Unionists and affirmed that no change in the status of Northern Ireland could occur without the consent of the Protestant majority.

All of this generated a great deal of publicity, and pro-republican sentiment was heightened by the return of the bodies of those men who had died or been executed in Portlaoise prison under de Valera. But in practical terms the IRA consisted of a largely weaponless, spent force, whose principal activity consisted of a few dedicated organisers cycling around the country preaching either to the converted or to the few, the very few, new recruits. In 1945, the IRA could scarcely have called on 400 active volunteers in the whole of Ireland and it would have been very hard put to arm more than a dozen of these.

Between 1949 and 1956, however, a number of different activist groupings within the republican spectrum began to come to life, and provided the

basis for a new campaign. There was Laochra Uladh (Warriors of Ulster), Saor Uladh (Free Ulster) and a grouping known as Arm na Saoirse (Army of Freedom) which ultimately became part of the IRA.

The principal new grouping of the period was, however, a breakaway wing of volunteers who followed Joe Christle, a law student with a considerable following in the University College Dublin student fraternity. Christle organised IRA actions of a student 'rag' nature such as taking a picture from the Tate Gallery in London. But he also favoured an activist 'forward' policy against Northern Ireland and drew off many of the painstakingly assembled cadre of volunteers from the more conservative-minded leadership of the older IRA.

By the early 1950s the IRA was run by Tony Magan, Patrick MacLogan and Thomas MacCurtain; the latter had narrowly escaped being executed during World War II and his father, the Lord Mayor of Cork, had been murdered by a British assassination squad in the Anglo-Irish war of 1918-21. Under the 'Three Macs', as the trio were known, the IRA had (unknown to Christle) adopted a plan for 'attacking the North'. This was largely the work of Sean Cronin, a former army officer and a journalist, who had returned from a stay in America, and Charlie Murphy, a brewery worker. Unlike the 'Three Macs', who were veterans of imprisonment in the 1940s, Murphy and Cronin had come into the IRA well after World War II and could be taken as representative of the new generation which, interested in the Irish language, history and culture, also took a keen interest in the activities of guerrilla movements in other countries.

The plan called for a number of flying columns, 12 in all, to attack targets in the border area – customs posts, police barracks and, above all, the British Army. A principal flaw in this strategy, however, was that it was based on experiences of the 1918-21 period, when communications were primitive and helicopters unknown and it was possible to spend as much as two days attacking a barracks before relief need be expected. Another great flaw was that most of the attackers were young southerners attacking in unfamiliar terrain among a largely apathetic Catholic population and a very actively hostile Unionist one.

Abortive attacks

The declared intention of having a crack at the British Army was largely frustrated by the strength of the Unionist B Specials, the armed militia, and by the armed Royal Ulster Constabulary (RUC). The attacking groups never succeeded in penetrating these outer defences to hit the soldiers. The only successes the movement had against the army came in 1954-55 in a series of daring raids against Gough, Omagh and Armagh Barracks in the North, and even these attacks were not without drawbacks, although they did provide the IRA with a certain amount of publicity.

The raids in Northern Ireland and in England, at Arborfield Barracks (August 1955) and Felsted School Officers' Training Corps (July 1953), also left the IRA with a number of their best men in jail. As a result there were several abortive attempts at jail breaks during the period which drew off a good deal of the IRA's planning and resources. But despite the splits, the jailings, the diversions of the attempted jail breaks and, most woundingly, police crackdowns in the South, the IRA was sufficiently reorganised and regrouped to launch attacks along the border from the end of December 1955.

These raids, chiefly against RUC barracks and customs posts, generated enormous publicity, and for a time some alarm and tension between Belfast, Dublin and London. One of the later attacks, that at Brookeborough on 1 January 1957 was a fiasco militarily, but an emotional success of the first order for the IRA. A combination of the hostile forces ranged against the IRA in the North, however, and the fact that the Catholic population did not rise in sympathy with the assaults – in stark contrast to today, for instance, there were no IRA activities in Belfast because of the difficulty of conducting operations there – the loss of volunteers through attrition and the continuing crackdown of Southern authorities meant that the campaign was losing momentum by the end of 1956.

Actions virtually ceased in 1957 on de Valera's return to power, for he reintroduced internment without trial and to all intents and purposes stamped out the IRA for another generation. Only a handful of isolated killings, bus burnings and bombings took place afterwards, and these had no significant military effect. The campaign was formally wound up in 1962.

An important and lasting carryover effect for the IRA, however, was that those who decided to carry on the torch of the 1950s men by forming the Provisional IRA in the late 1960s and early 1970s had the opportunity of both learning from their mistakes and drawing inspiration from the fact that there had been a rising in the previous generation. Another link in the emotional chain of Irish nationalism had been forged.

Tim Pat Coogan

Border war
The 1950s raids by the IRA

After the failure of the bombing campaign by the Irish Republican Army (IRA) in the late 1930s, its activities quietened down during World War II. Although a number of arms raids occurred on both sides of the border, as well as attempts to cooperate with the Germans, the widespread detention of IRA suspects, both in Northern Ireland and the South, restricted its operations. In 1949 the Republic of Ireland withdrew from its limited association with the British Commonwealth, forcing the British government to amend its Irish legislation, which was done through the Ireland Act of the same year. Among the clauses forming the 1949 Ireland Act was one which stated that Northern Ireland remained part of the United Kingdom and that it would not cease to do so 'without the consent of the Parliament of Northern Ireland'. In effect, therefore, the republic's gesture had strengthened rather than weakened the position of Ulster within the UK.

Meanwhile, the IRA was lying low. It was short of weapons, many of its arms dumps having been captured during the war, and so it concerned itself with trying to build up numbers, running weekend training camps south of the border. In terms of new recruits, selection was on the basis of having a proven record of discretion and sobriety. Anyone who had a criminal record or had been interned during the war was excluded. After 1949, however, the feeling grew that another military campaign would have to be launched against the border, which now seemed even more permanent than before. The first necessity was to obtain sufficient arms through raids on police and military establishments.

On 12 June 1954, masked men carried out a raid on the Royal Irish Fusi-

Above: The result of an IRA bomb attack against the Territorial Army HQ at Enniskillen in 1957. Below: An RUC policeman mans a Bren gun at a border crossing point in Ireland.

liers at Gough Barracks, Armagh, and successfully made off with some rifles. Further such operations were to follow, though not all were successful. An alert sentry at the barracks at Omagh, home of the resident British armoured car regiment in Northern Ireland, foiled an attempt on 17 October and most of the raiding party were captured. In a later attempt to capture weapons the IRA blew a hole in the wall of Rosslea police barracks on 26 November 1955, and were about to enter when they were driven back by a police sergeant armed with a Sten gun.

As a result of this violent compaign, the Royal Ulster Constabulary (RUC) and its part-time counterpart, the Special Constabulary or B Specials, stepped up their patrols. Correspondingly, in an effort to gain maximum publicity and to demonstrate their strength, the IRA hatched a plan to blow up the main symbol of Protestant domination in Northern Ireland, the parliament building at Stormont. But the plot misfired when, on 4 July 1955, the time bomb blew up prematurely, wrecking the car in which it was being carried and killing the driver.

In spite of achieving only partial success in their early military operations, the IRA could seek some comfort and encouragement on the political front. The British general election of 1955 saw two Republican candidates, Thomas Mitchell and Philip Clarke, returned for Ulster constituencies, although neither could take up their seats since both were serving 10-year sentences in the Crumlin Road gaol in Belfast for their part in the abortive arms raid at Omagh. Indeed, no less than 23.5 per cent of

The reaction in Northern Ireland to the IRA actions was swift, the Special Powers Act being reactivated and some 200 prominent Republicans being interned in Crumlin Road. Furthermore, the Irish general election in March 1957 saw the veteran Eamon de Valera returned to power. Although four Sinn Fein members were returned, there was a noticeable fall in their share of the vote. De Valera had made his feelings plain in 1956 when an IRA deputation, keen to enlist his support for the military campaign, was told by him that any attempt to do away with partition through armed insurrection was bound to fail and would merely cause unnecessary suffering. It was not surprising that once back in power he acted quickly, arresting a number of Sinn Fein leaders and interning them in the Curragh with little public protest. Public support for the IRA was lacking, especially since the revelation of their plans had turned the bulk of Roman Catholic opinion against them in Ulster.

Attacking morale

The IRA then channelled their energies into terrorist attacks against members of the RUC and B Specials with the object of lowering their morale. Two typical incidents involved Sergeant Arthur Ovens and Corporal Norman Anderson of the RUC. At 2300 hours on 17 August 1957, Sergeant Ovens, while on duty at his police station in County Tyrone, received an anonymous telephone call saying there was suspicious activity at an unoccupied house not far away. He took a party to investigate, and discovered that a light was burning inside, but the windows had been painted white to prevent anyone seeing inside. He decided to enter. Finding the front door unlatched, he stepped across the threshold. No sooner had he done so than he was blown to pieces by a booby trap. Although this type of action caused concern among the families of policemen, it also caused the police to increase their vigilance and stiffened their determination to eradicate the threat.

As for Anderson, he left his car on the Northern Ireland side of the border late on 27 January 1961 and crossed over to see a girl friend in the republic. He

the votes in Northern Ireland were cast for Sinn Fein, the political wing of the IRA. Furthermore, the government in Dublin, although on the surface condemning the IRA's policy of violence, took no active steps to curtail it. IRA leaders, particularly Sean Russell, who had controlled its activities during the war, believed that popular support for the IRA's aims on both sides of the border was growing.

It was not until December 1956 that a full military campaign got underway. Following their previous policy, the IRA decided that no attacks were to be made on the police or army of the republic; efforts would be concentrated against the RUC and B Specials. The aim was to draw into action the British Army in Ulster, then merely a brigade group (39th Infantry Brigade) of three infantry battalions and an armoured car regiment, and thereby create an atmosphere of British repression. This, it was hoped, would lead to a massive popular movement for reunification on both sides of the border. Yet the IRA was woefully ill-equipped to carry out this campaign, having no more than 200 acitivists in its ranks.

On the night of 12 December 1956, the IRA launched a number of simultaneous attacks on police barracks and military depots. Although the security forces were initially taken by surprise – one example being that half the B Specials' rifles in South Derry were away for their annual overhaul – the IRA achieved little. Indeed, five of its members were captured that night, three on an abortive raid on the Torr Head radar station and two at Gough Barracks, Armagh. During the next two weeks further attacks were mounted: six border customs posts were destroyed and a BBC relay station was blown up.

There was then a lull over Christmas, but on 8 January 1957 the IRA suffered a serious blow when the Garda Siochana, the republic's police force, captured documents giving details of the IRA's plan of campaign. They showed that the operations were to be conducted in three phases. First, there were the attacks on installations; these were to be followed by a month's build-up; and finally phase three was to see continuation of the struggle 'onto a higher level when we can coordinate on a more perfect communication basis'. The documents also spoke of hoping 'to liberate large areas, that is, areas where the enemy's writ no longer runs'.

Above: Rail repair gangs in Northern Ireland set about rebuilding a section of track severely damaged by IRA bombs. These assaults against installations were soon to be superseded by terrorist attacks against members of the RUC and B Specials.

The six counties

Ballycastle
Coleraine
Ballymoney
IRISH SEA
Limavady
ANTRIM
Londonderry
LONDONDERRY
Ballymena
Larne
DONEGAL
Swatragh
Strabane
NORTHERN IRELAND
Ballyclare
Cookstown
Antrim
Lough Neagh
Belfast
Omagh
Pomeroy
Lisburn
River Mourne
Dungannon
Lurgan
DOWN
Portadown
TYRONE
Enniskillen
Armagh
Banbridge
LEITRIM
FERMANAGH
Downpatrick
Rosslea
ARMAGH
Newry
MONAGHAN
REPUBLIC OF IRELAND

wore a mackintosh over his uniform. On his return, he was unable to start his car. The IRA had, in fact, immobilised it and were waiting for him. They seized him immediately, dragged him up a narrow lane and forced him to lie face down while they emptied 30 rounds from a sub-machine gun into his back. They then departed, leaving a note on his body to say that he was a spy, 'executed' by them.

The IRA continued its attacks on barracks and military installations. One of the most spectacular was the blowing-up of the new Territorial Army Centre at Dungannon two days before it was due to be officially opened. Perhaps the biggest attack, however, was against the police barracks at Swatragh in South Derry on the night of 14 January 1958. No less than 70 IRA insurgents volunteered for the operation. Before making the actual attack they tried to seal off the town with 11 roadblocks. The barracks itself was defended by six B Specials. When it came under attack the sound of automatic fire alerted neighbour-

---

Daily Mirror
FORWARD WITH THE PEOPLE
No. 16,851
MON FEB 17 1958

BIG LONDON POLICE SWOOP AFTER—

CALL-UP BOYS FIGHT I.R.A.

Recruit shot as six gunmen bind and gag the camp guard

DAILY MIRROR REPORTER

NINE soldiers were bound and gagged and a National Service man was shot in a raid by six Irish Republican Army gunmen on Blandford Army Camp, Dorset, yesterday.

Two of the soldiers who fought with the raiders were clubbed unconscious with pistol butts.

The condition of the shot sentry, who was hit in the stomach, was stated last night to be "not serious."

He is Private John Francis, 21, who had been in the Army only three weeks.

A VITAL CLUE

The object of the raiders, who struck at 1.30 a.m., was the camp armoury—but they got away with nothing. They are believed to have panicked because of the shooting.

The area was sealed off by the police after the raid but the raiders escaped in a car and a van. The car was later abandoned.

A vital clue the I.R.A. men left behind in the abandoned car is a slip of paper with a name and address on it.

A senior detective said: "I'm sure whoever left that bit of paper, didn't mean to."

Last night Scotland Yard Special Branch officers swooped on a number of addresses in North London.

None of the sentries at the camp was armed. Lieutenant-Colonel E. G. Hollis, C.O. of the raided REME unit which trains National Servicemen, said: "The lads were too inexperienced to have ammunition. They put up a good fight in the circumstances."

FULL STORY AND MORE PICTURES—SEE CENTRE PAGES

Lieutenant-Colonel Hollis—he said his men had no ammunition.

I.R.A. raiders used their pistols to club Private John, 21, and Corporal Brian ... who clothing ... running across landscape yesterday.

Clubbed

OHILLS — CLONES 7 A·34

APPROACHING BORDER

Top left: The IRA bring their fight to England as this newspaper from February 1958 illustrates. Above: In an attempt to reduce cross-border operations, air patrols were regularly flown along the border between Eire and Northern Ireland. These aircrewmen are being given pre-flight briefing on the areas to be covered.

Left: Security on the ground was maintained by border patrols. In this picture members of the RUC search the contents of a cart as it crosses the border.

ing police stations. Reinforcements had little difficulty breaking through the roadblocks, but by the time they arrived the attack had been beaten off, the only casualty being one B Special with a splinter in the eye. They did, however, capture one gunman speeding away by car.

Apart from guarding police stations and important installations, the security forces were mostly involved in constant patrolling of the countryside, particularly at night, setting up roadblocks in order to search cars and restrict IRA movements, and house searches. These operations were conducted very much with the RUC in the van, the army being used only in support to supplement mobile patrols and provide cordons for searches. Much of the night work was undertaken by part-timers, and there is no doubt that their Protestant fervour did, on occasion, make them over-enthusiastic and allegations arose of brutality being committed against Catholics.

The security force operations were successful and by mid-1958 there had been a noticeable fall-off in IRA incidents. The number of 'safe' houses available to them in Northern Ireland also declined, and they were often forced to bury their arms caches and hide in the countryside. Indeed, the only external support which they received was from elements of the radical left, both in Ireland and on the British mainland. This began to draw them away from straightforward nationalism and towards the politics of the left, a tendency which was accelerated by the failure of Sinn Fein to secure any seats in the British election of 1959. The cross-border dialogue initiated after 1959 by Viscount Brookeborough in the North and Sean Lemass in the South also eroded the IRA's position.

On 29 February 1962 in an official communique, the IRA called a halt to its campaign. In just over five years there had been some 600 incidents resulting in £1,000,000 damage to property. Six members of the security forces, all policemen, had been killed and 32 wounded. The IRA had lost nine, with 46 languishing in gaol for terrorist offences. Lack of military resources and little popular support had been the main cause of failure. The IRA now concealed their remaining arms and began to develop strategies for the future.   **Charles Messenger**

Top: A reconnaissance aircraft patrols border airspace in Ireland.
Above: Much of the work performed by the security forces involved the collection and collation of intelligence. Here an IRA suspect is interrogated by members of the RUC.

Right: A patrol of the Royal Warwickshire Regiment, armed with rifles, a Bren gun and Sten sub-machine guns, moves cautiously through the streets as civilians look on.

Brookeborough

The raid that created a martyr

One of the most important ingredients in the continuation of the tradition of violence in the cause of Irish nationalism of which the Irish Republican Army (IRA) is today's embodiment has always been failure – preferably glorious and heroic. Out of failures in the past, such as the 1916 revolution, came eventual triumph and vindication, and the 1955-62 border campaign was no exception to this historical precept.

The most glorious failure of that era was the Brookeborough ambush of 1 January 1957, in which two IRA men were killed, a number wounded and the rest, exhausted and suffering from exposure, lucky to escape with jail sentences when they had re-crossed the border.

Led by Sean Garland (now a member of the executive of the Workers Party, which has gone constitutional and has members in the Irish Parliament), the 12-man flying column involved in the Brookeborough assault had been in the Fermanagh area for some days. It had been laying ambushes for RUC and B Special patrols (none of which passed its way) when news of a relatively successful raid on the RUC Barracks at Derrylin in December reached the column. Brookeborough had not been reconnoitred and did not figure on GHQ's list of targets, but it did contain an RUC barracks similar to Derrylin and, after days of frustration, it was decided to attack it.

Arrival at the barracks

A lorry was commandeered and two home-made mines with a battery attachment were placed aboard the truck. The 12 men were armed with a variety of weapons, including a Bren gun, some Thompson sub-machine guns and a few hand grenades. Brookeborough is a strongly Protestant town; the bulk of the raiders were Catholics from the South, and though Vincent Conlon who drove the truck was from Armagh in the North, none of the party had any local knowledge of the area. Two lookouts were posted in the town prior to the assault. Among their duties was the task of keeping women and children off the road out of harm's way. The truck drove into Brookeborough on 1 January 1957 as night was falling, so as to take advantage of the dark, and pulled up a little way past the barracks so that it was enfiladed.

It had been intended to use the truck as a shield while the mines were placed and then detonated with the aid of a battery. The idea was that the barracks would be reduced instantly to rubble and those RUC men inside who were not killed would surrender. However, one of the policemen on duty, Sergeant Kenneth Cordner, was just stepping into the street as the truck stopped. His appearance was greeted by a blast of gunfire which missed; the station was now alerted and the element of surprise immediately lost. It then transpired that the truck was wrongly situated, and the Bren gun's fire could not reach above the sand-bagged first floor. Next the mines failed, although Daithi O'Connell – later to become a found-

er member of the Provisionals – sprayed them with his Thompson.

In a set-piece engagement resembling the days of the OK Corral and the Wild West rather than modern guerrilla warfare, the IRA party and the barracks defenders fired at each other from almost point-blank range, Sergeant Gardner replying with Sten-gun fire from an upstairs window to the Thompsons in the street below. The IRA's hand grenades proved something of a liability to them when they bounced off the cast iron window frames and fell back into the street.

Inevitably several of the IRA party were hit with two, Fergal O'Hanlon and Sean South, being mortally wounded. Vincent Conlon was wounded in the leg as was Phillip O'Donoghue. Paddy O'Regan survived, as he said later, because of the Geneva Convention, which meant that bullets supplied to conventional armies were designed only to wound. O'Regan was hit twice, once by a ricochet which lodged in his body but miraculously did no serious injury.

The truck became a colander but Conlon managed to get it started. Unfortunately it was of the tip-up variety and the shooting had damaged the mechanism. The result was bizarre and macabre: every bump in the road caused it to tip up sufficiently to send the entire party, including the wounded and dying into a sprawling bloodstained heap.

Sean South and O'Hanlon had to be abandoned in a small outhouse in the bleak mountain area above Brookeborough, and Sean Garland, badly wounded in the thigh, had to be dissuaded from staying behind with his dead and dying comrades to fight to the last. In an exhausted condition, the party somehow made their way through the sleety, freezing night, past patrols of thousands of Army, B Specials and RUC men, and made it across the border into the republic

Below: Two B Special constables examine the battered exterior of the tip-up lorry used in the Brookeborough raid.

Below: A newspaper report a few days after the assault on the RUC barracks at Brookeborough describes the raid. Bottom: Brookeborough High Street, scene of the action, showing the RUC barracks (by the telephone box).

where they were picked up by the Irish security forces.

Practically the only thing the column got right during the whole affair was to dump all arms before capture. Subsequently, however, the public funerals of the dead men and a ballad, 'Sean South of Garryowen,' brought enormous publicity and many new recruits into the movement. The ballad contained the following lines:

'No more he'll hear the seagull cry o'er the murmuring Shannon tide,
For he fell beneath the North sky, brave Hanlon at his side.
He had gone to join that gallant band of Plunkett, Pearse and Tone,
A martyr for old Ireland,
Sean South of Garryowen.'

The ballad in its entirety became one of the most popular in Ireland and was one of the more lasting mementoes of the 1956 era, particularly as it drew attention to South's career and beliefs. He was a remarkable figure, a Gaelic speaker, a devout Catholic and a noted musician. Before leaving for the border on his final mission he had written in his Irish language magazine, *Ah Gath*: 'Jacta Alea Est. There is an end to foolishness, the time to talk is ended.' A great number of young men were to follow in his footsteps.

The ballad is still sung today and the attack on Brookeborough serves as an important stepping stone in the IRA's gospel of continuity, from the great republican uprisings of 1798 to the 19th century, to 1916 and the Anglo-Irish War, and to the present day. Brookeborough was, in any practical assessment, a dismal failure; but it became another layer of the emotional swaddling around a fervent nationalism, and so, in a sense, no failure at all. **Tim Pat Coogan**

THE FERMANAGH HERALD, SATURDAY, JANUARY 5, 1957

o Men Die in Attack on Barracks
chine-gun battle in Brookeboro' street
dy and Dying Man found by Police

Second Attack on Derrylin Police Barracks
Constable Sean Scally fatally wounded

National Liberation

Minorities fighting for independent statehood

When President Woodrow Wilson said in 1917, 'No people must be forced under a sovereignty under which it does not wish to live,' he believed he was expressing a simple truth. He probably did not foresee the extent to which the principle of self-determination would spread, complicating and exacerbating the world's problems. For the demand for national rights has been the single largest cause of war since 1945; initially in the struggle to throw off colonial rule, but secondly because many nation states have within them considerable national minorities that demand rights incompatible with the continued integrity of the state in which they find themselves. This has given rise to some of the most intractable and bloody wars of the modern age.

There is now hardly an area of the globe that is free from the demands of a minority group for greater political freedom. In the European democracies, there are currently campaigns being conducted for the rights of the Basques, the Bretons, the Welsh, Northern Irish Republicans, Scots, Catalans, Lapps, Sicilians, Corsicans, Walloons and the German-speaking peoples of Alsace-Lorraine and the South Tyrol. The problems of minorities are, if anything, even more acute in central and eastern Europe, where the wholesale redrawing of borders after World War II and the interpenetration of many linguistic groups have combined to create difficulties such as the large Hungarian minority in Romanian Transylvania, or the Albanian minority in Yugoslavia.

The Soviet Union is beset with similar problems, particularly where nationalistic sentiment combines with general political dissent. There are Muslim and Jewish minorities and over 92 recognisably different national groups in the USSR. Soviet intervention in Afghanistan in 1979 was partly caused by anxiety over the effects of political and religious upheaval there (and in Iran) on the three Soviet Central Asian Republics. The Georgian and Ukrainian national movements have always been ruthlessly clamped down on by the Soviet authorities, as have all representatives of nationalism in the Baltic states – Latvia, Lithuania and Estonia. During 1975, leaders of the Estonian dissident movement were placed on trial, accused partly of plotting the independence of Estonia, and in 1978 one of the founders of the Ukrainian Workers and Peasants Union, which campaigns for greater autonomy and respect for Ukrainian culture, was jailed for 10 years and exiled for a further five.

In Asia there are the problems of the Shans in Burma, the Nagas in India and the Naxalites in East Bengal, the Muslims in the Philippines and the struggles of the peoples of West Irian and East Timor. There were revolts by Tibetans against

Far left: Demonstrations followed the arrest of Sheikh Mujibur Rahman, who had championed autonomy for East Pakistan.
Below: Women rebels demonstrate their support for the West Somali Liberation Front. Below inset: Filipino Muslim rebels who fought against the Christian administration in 1977.
Left: Refugees are a major problem during civil war.

Chinese rule in 1954 and 1959, Muslim unrest in Sinkiang and Yunnan provinces in 1975, and a simmering conflict between China and the Khamba tribesmen of eastern Tibet that continued into the 1980s.

Even in the New World, Canada remains troubled by the demands of French-speaking separatists, and in the United States the demand for greater autonomy is raised by native Indians and occasionally by American blacks.

In Africa the difficulties are probably at their greatest. Tribal boundaries were not necessarily considered in the carve-up of the continent by the colonial powers in the 19th century, and the new states created on colonial boundaries are often riddled with latent or overt tribal conflicts. The Berbers in Algeria, the Somalis, the Oromo and Tigre in Ethiopia, the Ewe in Ghana and the Ibo in Nigeria are merely the most well known of the tribal minorities who have demanded autonomy.

Some minorities, like the Kurds and the Nagas, have been fighting for autonomy for hundreds of years, but the development of minority struggles has more recently been fuelled by two factors. First is the general acceptance of the principle of the right to self-determination, which has given the educated members of all racial and linguistic groups a simple, popular cause to espouse. The concept of self-determination has been taken as one of the central human freedoms, and other social, religious or economic problems can be conveniently yoked to it to form a potent basis for violence. The second factor lies in the nature of the modern state, particularly the modern states that have replaced the former colonial regimes all over the world. Colonial rule tended to be rather loose and maintained by a general class of white administrators. But the attempt to modernise and centralise newly independent nations in the 1950s and 1960s suddenly highlighted the linguistic or racial differences that had been glossed over by the old paternalist rulers. Africa provides the best examples: the Somali tribal lands had been divided between Italian Somaliland and British East Africa and

Ethiopia by taking convenient geographical markers, such as the Juba River, as a border. This began to create large-scale problems only when Ethiopia, Somalia and Kenya tried to become unitary states within the old colonial borders. Similarly, in both Nigeria and Uganda, the educational and economic power of certain tribes – the Ibo and Baganda respectively – only became a critical problem when there was no colonial power to mediate or provide a common enemy.

Minority struggles have little in common with each other and encompass wide differences in aims. At times the demand is simply for a level of autonomy or the preservation of a cultural tradition. In some instances, for example the creation of the new canton of the Jura in Switzerland or the official recognition of minority rights as in Canada, the grievances of the minority may be defused. On the other hand, demands may not be satisfied until, as in Biafra or the Ogaden, there is attempted secession from the existing state. Demands often fluctuate with circumstances. A Kurdish leader is reported to have said, when asked what his goal was, 'We have never given a definition. It depends on our strength and that of our enemy.'

Reasons for resentment

As with aims, so also there are a great variety of background causes. At times religion, ethnic origin, language and cultural tradition have fuelled conflicts over minority rights. Yet there is often an underlying economic relationship between the minority and the majority which fosters resentment. The separatist movement of the Ibos, who declared Biafra independent from Nigeria in 1967, was hastened by the massacre of thousands of Ibos resident in the north. And there had been continual conflicts between the Ibos of the eastern region, the Hausa and Fulani of the north and the Yoruba in the west. All were separated not only by culture and language, but also by religion, the Ibos being predominantly Christian, and the Hausa and Fulani being Muslim. But everything was intensified because, under British rule, the

Below: While two men maintain a lookout for enemy units, other Eritrean guerrillas prepare an anti-aircraft gun. Despite the apparently well-uniformed appearance of these guerrillas, supplies of weapons and equipment were limited and great emphasis was placed on the preservation of all war material and the capture of enemy equipment.

Ibos made more rapid progress educationally and economically than the rest of Nigeria. The northern and western regions were constantly threatening secession, before and after independence, and there was continued resentment in other regions at what was seen as Ibo domination. This resentment overflowed during the massacres into the killing of any easterner, Ibo or not. Also, the north was alarmed at the threat of a successful secession by the east in case the north was left as a landlocked state surrounded by hostile countries. So the roots of the three-year civil war (1967-70), causing hundreds of thousands of deaths, went far beyond simple tribal differences and racism.

Similarly, an allegedly religious conflict leading to the creation of the Muslim state of Pakistan was, in fact, much more complicated. The Muslim League was formed in 1928, but the campaign for separate national status crystallised during World War II when Britain agreed to advance self-rule for India. In 1946 a referendum was held to test opinion, and the Punjab and Bengal voted overwhelmingly for a separate existence as Pakistan. Upon the creation of Pakistan, the Muslim minority became a majority in the new country. But this religious-based nationalism was merely a pretext for the subjugation of one nationality by another. The two wings of Pakistan were radically different from each other, with the eastern wing being predominantly agricultural and discriminated against in favour of the commercial economy of the west. Also, the East Pakistanis spoke an entirely different language, Bengali, which was not given any official status until 1956. By 1954 the Awami League was calling for a separate state of East Pakistan, but this was not achieved until 1971, when Bangladesh became independent.

Bangladesh raises one of the most important points about the struggles of minorities – that is, their relationship to other states. Rarely do struggles for self-determination by minorities avoid becoming embroiled in regional inter-state conflicts, or pawns in superpower diplomacy. So important is the attitude of other states that it can determine the success of failure of the campaign. In this regard, it is instructive to examine the fate of two neighbouring secessionist movements – the Nagas of Assam and the Muslims of East Bengal.

The state of Bangladesh was created because in 1971 the Indian Army invaded East Pakistan and defeated the Pakistani Army. Without this interven-

Above: An Indian soldier, during the attack on East Pakistan in 1971. Indian intervention was the most important single military factor in the eventual independence of Bangladesh. Below: Polisario guerrillas stand around an abandoned enemy tank in the Sahara.

tion, Bangladesh would probably never have come into existence. But the Indians themselves were resolutely determined to prevent the Nagas acquiring independence. The Nagas are situated on the northeast frontier of India between Assam and Burma. Originally eight or more totally diverse tribes, the Nagas were united by British rule and their total dissimilarity to the Hindus and Muslims of the plains.

By 1947 the Naga National Council had been formed to plead the cause of separation. In 1950 a plebiscite was organised and called for a separate sovereign state. Although prepared to offer some concessions on autonomy, the Indian government adamantly refused to allow secession, and in 1955 fighting broke out between Naga separatists and the Indian Army. By 1967 the Nagas were receiving arms from China and Pakistan as, incidentally, had the secessionists of the Mizo district of Assam. However, with the creation of Bangladesh in 1971 the Nagas lost a safe base area for their guerrillas, and the Indian Army could strengthen its presence in Nagaland. By November 1975 the Nagas opened discussions to end hostilities. In a sense, the Indian Army had prevented in Nagaland what it had brought about in Bangladesh.

Overseas intervention

Foreign involvement in minority struggles is best demonstrated by the history of the Somali and Kurdish conflicts. The five parts of the greater Somali nation are Somalia, the contiguous area of Djibouti, the Ethiopian areas of the Ogaden and Haud, and the Northern Frontier District of Kenya. In the 19th century the area was colonised by the British, the French and the Italians. After the defeat of Italian forces by Ethiopia in 1896, the British and Italians ceded traditional Somali grazing grounds in the Haud and Ogaden to Ethiopia.

In 1946 the British government proposed that the various Somali territories should be amalgamated into a trusteeship. This was rejected by Ethiopia, and in 1954 Britain handed over to Ethiopia the region of the Haud, which had reverted to British control during World War II. There were immediate protests in Somalia at this action. Britain further angered Somali opinion by refusing to cede the Northern Frontier

District of Kenya to Somalia, despite the result of a plebiscite held in the region. In 1963 Kenya gained independence, with the Northern Frontier District intact.

Border clashes developed between the Somalis and Ethiopian troops, and in 1964 there was serious fighting along the border, with Ethiopian jets bombing targets well inside Somalia. There were also clashes with the Kenyan Army and police. The United States started to supply arms to Ethiopia, to suppress the Somali revolt in the Ogaden. And by now, Soviet interest in the region had become intense. The provision of arms and advisers to both the Ethiopian and Somali governments led to an extension of Soviet influence. By 1977 all US military aid to the region had stopped. Unable to make any headway in negotiations with Ethiopia, the Somalis decided to change to the US camp; they expelled Soviet advisers, in anticipation of US aid, and invaded Ethiopia. The Soviet Union then stepped up its support for the Ethiopian regime, and by 1978 Soviet weapons and Cuban troops had driven out the invading Somalis. The interests of the Somali tribesmen had been buried in the diplomatic struggle for influence in the area.

Just as cynical was the manipulation of the Kurds at the hands of the Shah of Iran and the CIA. The Kurds inhabit an area covering parts of Iraq, Iran, Syria, Turkey and the Soviet Union. In 1925 the League of Nations granted Mosul province (inhabited by the Kurds but previously under Turkish rule) to Iraq, and stated that regard must be paid to the desires of the Kurdish race for the administration of their country.

Until 1975 the Kurds received arms from the United States via the Iranian government. The two governments preferred that the insurgents should continue a level of hostilities sufficient to sap the resources of Iraq, a revolutionary force in Middle East affairs and a traditional foe of Iran, but insufficient to force a conclusion of the struggle in favour of the Kurds. In 1975, when a rapprochement was reached between Iraq and Iran, this policy of support for the Kurds ended. The Iraqis stepped up their military operations using tanks, planes and artillery. Large numbers of Kurds were killed or forced to leave their homes in the mountains. There is also now a significant Kurdish refugee population in Lebanon, while in 'Kurdistan' the revolt rumbles on.

Conflicts involving minorities are constantly developing. In 1974, for example, the Secret Army for the Liberation of Armenia launched its guerrilla campaign for recognition of the Armenian language and the creation of an autonomous republic in eastern Turkey.

Yet despite the proliferation of the struggles for self-determination by minority peoples, very few have achieved success. What recognition of their status there has been has normally occurred only in the more developed world, where the recognition of cultural or linguistic rights (as in the case of the French-speaking Canadians) can be accommodated within the structure of the state. In the Third World, only Bangladesh stands as an example of a successful secession, and there were very advantageous international and geographical factors at work there. If the principle of self-determination for many of the world's minorities were to be accepted, then the question of definition of a minority would become so complex as to threaten to destroy many states – certainly most of those of black Africa. Until the problem of minorities is settled, however, it can only continue to cause trouble, to be a major cause or contributory factor to a depressing cycle of violence over much of the world.

Mike Rossiter

Above: Members of the Secret Army for the Liberation of Armenia (masked for security reasons) with an Armenian language newspaper.

Below: An Eritrean guerrilla keeps a vigil from his machine-gun post in the mountains. Inset: Kurdish rebels, prepare for an operation. The desire for an independent Kurdistan has been a contentious factor in Middle-Eastern politics ever since 1945.

Key Weapons
The
A-4 SKYHAWK
part 1

Developing the A-4

Known affectionately as the 'Bantam Bomber', the Douglas Aircraft Company's diminutive A-4 attack bomber began life during the Korean War. The company's chief designer, Ed Heinemann, worried by the ever growing size, complexity and cost of combat aircraft, wanted to see if it was possible to reverse the trend and create a small, simple fighter with a performance capability the equal of any.

The initial work was carried out as a private company exercise without government funding and a draft proposal was submitted to the Bureau of Aeronautics in January 1952. The US Navy was impressed with what it saw but, as it was already committed to a number of new fighter designs, asked that the concept be applied to a jet-powered, carrier-borne attack bomber. Such an aeroplane was required to have a top speed of not less than 805km/h (500mph), a combat radius of 555km (345 miles) with a 908kg (2000lb) weapons load and a maximum take-off weight of no more than 13,600kg (30,000lb).

Two weeks after the initial discussions, Douglas re-presented the design optimised for the attack role. If the speed of the response was surprising, the aircraft proposed was astonishing. The calculations laid before the Navy chiefs envisaged an airframe weighing under half the figure specified, with a maximum speed and combat radius well in excess of the original requirements. Not surprisingly, the proposal was viewed with scepticism, but the thought that the aircraft might, in reality, come close to the paper outline gained Douglas authorisation to proceed with detailed design work.

Previous page: Trainer Skyhawks of the US Marines maintain formation while on exercise. Above: Although only one example of the XA4D-1 was built, this Skyhawk prototype was the first in a line that was to become a major success story in American aviation history.

Right: The assembly line at Douglas's El Segundo factory showing the various stages of manufacture of the early model Skyhawks.

By the time inspection of a mock-up took place, the Skyhawk had crystallised into a 12.01m (39ft 4¾in) long fuselage housing a pilot, fuel systems and a licence-built Armstrong Siddeley Sapphire jet engine mated to a modified delta wing, spanning just 8.38m (27ft 6in) and a stalky tricycle undercarriage. On 21 June 1952, Douglas was given the go-ahead to produce a flying prototype and by October that year 19 Skyhawks were on order.

In June 1954 the first Skyhawk took to the air from Edwards air force base, California. Flight trials showed up a number of minor aerodynamic problems but the basic design more than vindicated itself when the second pre-production aircraft set a new 500km

Above: The A-4E represented an important advance in the Skyhawk's capability: a new, more powerful Pratt & Whitney engine was fitted, a Doppler radar and new radar altimeter installed and provision was made for two extra weapon points.

Left: One of the 638 A-4C Skyhawks which were manufactured for the US Marines and Navy as limited all-weather attack aircraft.

A-4A Skyhawk

Type Single-seat nuclear attack aircraft
Dimensions Span 8.38m (27ft 6in); length 12.01m (39ft 4¾in); height 4.57m (15ft)
Weight Empty 3810kg (8400lb); loaded 6747kg (14,875lb)
Powerplant One 3493kg (7700lb) Wright J65-W-4 or -4B turbojet

Performance Maximum speed at sea level 1069km/h (664mph)
Range 740km (460 miles)
Ceiling 14,935m (49,000ft)

Armament Two 20mm Mk 12 cannon; centreline and wing pylons for a maximum of 2268kg (5000lb) external stores

A4-E Skyhawk

Type Single-seat attack aircraft
Dimensions Span 8.38m (27ft 6in); length 12.23m (40ft 1½in); height 4.62m (15ft 2in)
Weight Empty 4469kg (9853lb); loaded 7355kg (16,215lb)
Powerplant One 3856kg (8500lb) Pratt & Whitney J52-P-6A turbojet

Performance Maximum speed at sea level 1083km/h (673mph)
Range 1865km (1160 miles)
Ceiling 11,795m (38,700ft)

Armament Two 20mm Mk 12 cannon; centreline and underwing pylons for a maximum of 3719kg (8200lb) external stores

Below: An A-4B (originally designated A4D-2) of the US Navy takes off, complete with drop tank.

A-4M Skyhawk

Type Single-seat attack aircraft
Dimensions Span 8.38m (27ft 6in); length 12.29m (40ft 3¾in); height 4.57m (15ft)
Weight Empty 4747kg (10,465lb); loaded 11,600kg (25,575lb)
Powerplant One 5080kg (11,200lb) Pratt & Whitney J52-P-408A turbojet

Performance Maximum speed at sea level 1167km/h (725mph)
Range 2872km (1785 miles)
Ceiling 15,850m (52,000ft)

Armament Two 20mm Mk 12 cannon; centreline and underwing pylons for a maximum of 4127kg (9100lb) external stores

(310 mile) closed-circuit world speed record of 1118km/h (695mph) on 15 October 1955. The first production model, designated the A4D-1, was cleared for operational service in September 1955, so beginning a service life which continues to the present day.

The A4D-1, or A-4A as it became known in 1962, was powered by a single Wright J65-W-4 or W-4B turbojet and carried an internal armament of two 20mm cannon. Up to 2268kg (5000lb) of external stores could be carried on a fuselage and two wing racks which could, alternatively, support three drop tanks with a capacity of 3028 litres (800 gallons) to increase range. Production continued until 1957, by which time 165 had been built.

The next model, the A-4B (A4D-Z), appeared during 1956. It was powered by a Wright J65-W-16A engine, had a redesigned rudder, a revised cockpit layout and gunsight and provision for air-to-air refuelling. A total of 542 were produced. A-4C (A4D-2N) appeared in 1959. Essentially similar to its predecessor, the A-4C was optimised for all-weather operations and was equipped with terrain-following radar, an autopilot, a low-altitude bombing system and an improved ejector seat. Initial production machines received the W-16A engine but later aircraft incorporated the W-16C model. Production of the A-4C ended in 1962, a total of 638 having been built.

The next two models were not proceeded with and production continued with the A-4E (A4D-5). The new aircraft differed from the A-4C in being powered by the Pratt & Whitney J52-P-6A engine, having a further improved ejection system and two additional wing racks which increased the maximum offensive load to 3719kg (8200lb). The use of the J52 engine improved the type's combat radius by virtue of its lower fuel consumption compared with the previously used J65. Most importantly, the A-4E marked the end of the Skyhawk as a nuclear bomber; this model and all subsequent ones were optimised for conventional bombing and ground attack work. The A-4E remained in production from 1961 until 1966, by which time 499 had been built.

Like the A4D-3 and A4D-4, the A4D-6 remained a paper project. The next Skyhawk to appear was the TA-4E trainer version, two of which were built during

Above: The A-4F, with its characteristic saddleback hump, was the first Skyhawk to embody combat improvements suggested by pilots in Vietnam. Bullpup missiles flank the standard bomb load on this Navy Skyhawk.

Right: An overhead view of the tandem two-seat TA-4F Skyhawk. As well as acting primarily as a trainer aircraft the TA-4F was also 'combat-capable' and served in Vietnam on visual reconnaissance missions.

1965. The TA model featured a 0.76m (2ft 6in) increase in fuselage length to accommodate a second seat and a reduction in fuel capacity but was otherwise similar to the single-seater upon which it was based.

The next single-seat sub-type, the A-4F, appeared in 1966 and was destined to be the last combat model to be supplied new to the US Navy. The improved J52-P-8A engine was used, there was a 'zero-zero' ejector seat, a steerable nose wheel and a dorsal 'hump' fairing to house additional avionics. This last feature was also retrofitted to a number of A-4Es. A two-seat training version was produced under the designation TA-4F, a few of which were later re-equipped for the electronic warfare role under the designation EA-4F. Total production of the A/TA-4F series amounted to 385 units of which 147 were single-seaters and 238 the trainer model.

With completion of the F series, Douglas turned to the US Marine Corps and foreign air forces as its chief markets for the Skyhawk. The next model, the A-4G,

Below: The Skyhawk had the longest production run of any US military aircraft. This A-4M was delivered to the US Marines in February 1979. The aircraft is specially painted with the insignia of the seven countries that ordered the Skyhawk: Singapore, New Zealand, Kuwait, United States, Israel, Australia and Argentina; though the Skyhawk's overall colours are that of the US Blue Angels display team.

was built for the Australian Navy. Eight were produced and were generally similar to the A-4E but were powered by the J52-P-8A engine. The Australian single-seaters were accompanied by two trainers, designated TA-4G, which were generally similar to the US Navy's TA-4F.

At the same time as the Australian aircraft were being produced, Douglas began building the A-4H for Israel, a country which was to become the second largest user of the Skyhawk after the USA itself. The Israeli aircraft were also based on the A-4E but optimised for operations from land bases rather than carriers. The 90 A-4Hs that were built were powered by J52-P-8A engines and featured a new square-tipped fin, a braking parachute housing below the rear fuselage and 30mm DEFA cannon in place of the normal 20mm weapons. Many aircraft of this type were later modified to carry an F-type avionics 'hump' and were fitted with extended jet pipes as a counter to heat-seeking missiles. The single-seat aircraft of this type were accompanied by 10 trainer versions which were designated as TA-4Hs.

The success of the two-seat Skyhawks as trainers led to the development of the next model to be built, the TA-4J, which flew from 1966. Unlike the earlier TA-4F, the J carried only a single 20mm cannon armament and had much operational equipment removed. Power was provided by a J52-P-6 engine. The US Navy's Air Advanced Training Command received a total of 293 such aircraft.

Following soon after was the A/TA-4K, produced for the Royal New Zealand Air Force. Similar to the A-4H, 10 A-4Ks and 4 TA-4K trainers were delivered in 1970. During the same year, Douglas began delivery of the A-4M to the US Marine Corps. This model may be considered as the culmination of the Skyhawk line, featuring as it did major improvements over all previous models; as one American publication put it,

Above: A Marine 'Skyhawk II' tests its armaments on a training mission. The 'Skyhawk II' (A-4M) was developed for the Marine Corps from the A-4F but with an improved operational capability and a number of design changes.

Below left: An A-4A Skyhawk of the US Marines in flight. Below right: A pre-production YA4D-1 (later YA-4A) showing modified tailpipe configuration, wing-root guns and arrester hook. The YA-4A was used for the initial carrier qualification trials on USS Ticonderoga in September 1955.

the M model was '100 per cent more manoeuvrable, 50 per cent faster in the climb, faster in level flight and needed 305m (1000ft) less runway than any other Skyhawk'. Power for this 'super' A-4 was provided by the J52-P-408A engine and the type incorporated a redesigned and enlarged cockpit canopy, double ammunition capacity for the 20mm cannon, the square-tipped fin and dorsal avionics 'hump', a revised electrical system, an onboard starter motor and a redesigned refuelling probe. Production of the A-4M ended in 1978; 30 such aircraft had been transferred to Israel during the Yom Kippur War of 1973.

The emergence of the A-4M added new impetus to the export model Skyhawks, acting as a basis for the A-4N, the A-4KU and providing elements for the A-4S. The first of these, the A-4N or Skyhawk II, was the second model built for Israel. Employing the M's basic airframe and engine, the model N featured a new navigational and weapons delivery system including a head-up display and a built-in armament of two 30mm DEFA cannon. First flown in 1972, a total of 129 A-4Ns were built, most of which have received the elongated jet pipe modification. Another notable feature is the addition, in Israel, of a fin top fairing to house a radar warning system.

The A-4KU appeared two years after the A-4N and a total of 30 were supplied to Kuwait. The KU was similar to the M with the addition of a braking chute housing below the rear fuselage. In addition to the single-seaters, Kuwait purchased six trainers under the designation TA-4KU.

The appearance of the A-4S in 1972 neatly tied together the remaining strands of the Skyhawk's development history. As well as incorporating elements such as the refuelling probe from the A-4M, the S represented the final product of Douglas's 'new from old' refurbishing programme. Ordered by the

Left: The crowded cockpit of the A-4F, as seen from above with the pilot's seat removed. Originally designer Ed Heinemann had tried to keep the business of flying the Skyhawk as simple as possible, but as the weapons and flight systems became more advanced and numerous so the consoles and instrument panels of later variants became inevitably more complex.

Singapore government, the A-4S had a re-worked, ex-US Navy A-4B airframe incorporating a redesigned cockpit, solid state electronics, the ventral braking parachute housing, 30mm Aden cannon in place of the original weapons, and overhauled and up-rated J65 engines. Forty such aircraft were produced, complemented by seven TA-4S trainers. These aircraft differed from all other two-seat Skyhawks in having two separate crew positions rather than the normal tandem seating arrangement covered by a continuous canopy.

The first refurbished Skyhawk model appeared during 1965 under the designation A-4P, which was to become familiar in the UK 17 years later when the Argentinian Air Force used the type against the British Task Force during the 1982 Falklands War. Production totalled 75 units, the aircraft being an overhauled A-4B or A-4C. Work on the type was undertaken by Douglas (50 aircraft) and Lockheed (25), the Lockheed machines being originally A-4Cs and fitted with the Ferranti D126R Isis weapons sighting system. Sixteen extra A-4Bs were supplied to the Argentinian Navy under the designation A-4Q for use aboard the carrier *Veinticinco de Mayo*.

The most recent model is the A-4L, which is another 'new from old' type. Based on the A-4C, it is powered by the J65-W-16C engine, features improved instrumentation, the dorsal avionics 'hump' and is used by US Naval Reserve Squadrons.

Many of the 23 operational variants of the basic design remain in service, over a quarter of a century after the US Navy received its first Skyhawk. Such a record more than vindicates Heinemann's original concept and the design team's ability to translate the dream into a working reality. McDonnell-Douglas is still scanning the world for customers and Israel Aircraft Industries are offering, with typical business acumen, a $1.5 million package of improvements – head-up display, extra stores stations, extended jet pipe, 30mm cannon, a radar warning suite and the WDNS-141 navigation/attack system – to any Skyhawk user with the money.

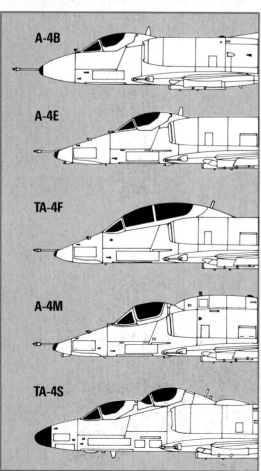

A-4B

A-4E

TA-4F

A-4M

TA-4S

Left and right: One of the outstanding features of the Skyhawk was its capacity to incorporate design changes to keep it a step beyond obsolescence. The major modifications to the Skyhawk's fore section and tail end are shown here.

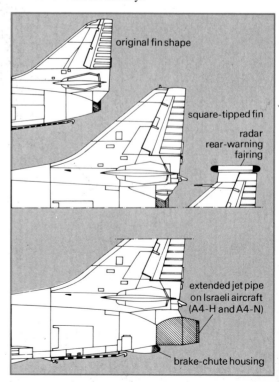

original fin shape

square-tipped fin

radar rear-warning fairing

extended jet pipe on Israeli aircraft (A4-H and A4-N)

brake-chute housing

Controlling the straits

The strategic importance of the Persian Gulf

The strategic importance of the Arabian (Persian) Gulf derives entirely from the fact that it is a broad arm of the sea which reaches deep into the richest oil-bearing region of the world. Altogether, approximately 30 per cent of the world's oil consumption, or 18 million barrels a day, leaves the Gulf in tankers which must pass through the narrow Strait of Hormuz before reaching open water. Interruption of this flow has the immediate effect of raising international oil prices; and as the world's economy is largely based on oil, prolonged stoppage can lead to inflationary pressures and the de-stabilisation of national economies. If the Strait of Hormuz were to be closed for any reason, the economic and military consequences for the West would be momentous.

Unfortunately, the whole area is inherently unstable. Alongside national rivalries exist racial and religious tensions. The Iranians, for example, are of Aryan stock whereas their neighbours around the Gulf are Arabs; all are Muslims, but while Shi'ites form the majority of believers in Iran, they are in a minority in the remaining Gulf states, who favour the Sunni persuasion. Again, the move towards Islamic fundamentalism has had a profoundly unsettling effect in recent years. There is, too, an incessant conflict between the principles of revolutionary (often Marxist) republicanism and those of absolute monarchy.

For the better part of a century British influence was paramount in the Gulf. This arose directly as a consequence of Russian expansion into central Asia, which Britain viewed as a threat to India. During the latter half of the 19th century the British strove, successfully, to preserve Afghanistan and Persia (as Iran was then called) as buffer states between India and the czar's newly acquired territories. The Persian government, grateful for support against its mighty neighbour, tended to view British commercial enterprises with favour.

In 1907 Britain and Russia, seriously alarmed by

Above: A British pilot patrols the Strait of Hormuz; a closure of the strait for any period of time could result in the economic destabilisation of the Western world. Below: The threat to stability in the Gulf comes from many sources; here Omani rebels man a jeep-mounted heavy machine gun.

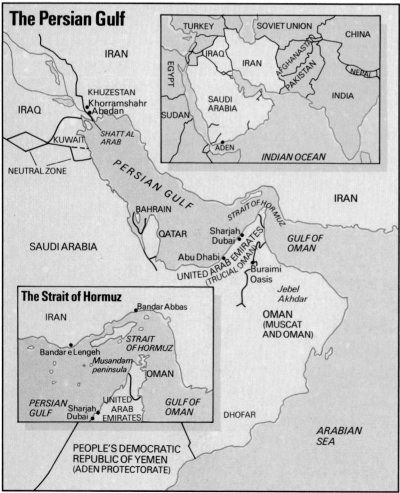

the threat posed by Germany, concluded an agreement which divided Persia into a Russian sphere of influence in the north and a British sphere of influence in the south. This agreement was deeply resented by the Persians. Ill feeling was intensified in both world wars when their country was twice invaded by British and Russian forces in order to deny Germany and her allies access to the oil fields.

Persia's oil resources had been developed during the early years of the 20th century by the Anglo-Persian Oil Company, in which the British government took a majority shareholding in 1914. In due course it changed its name to the Anglo-Iranian Oil Company and continued trading successfully until 1951, when a coup brought Dr Mohammed Mossadegh to power as premier of Iran. Mossadegh, an emotional man of extreme views, believed that Anglo-Iranian was stripping his country of its assets. Although the company was in the process of negotiating a profit-sharing agreement with his government, he nationalised the oil industry and refused to submit the dispute to arbitration.

Anti-British feeling ran high, and three British subjects were killed at the refinery in Abadan. The cruiser HMS *Mauritius* was sent to lie off the port and British troop movements were reported. Mossadegh responded by closing British consulates in Iran and severing diplomatic relations with the United Kingdom in 1952. However, countermeasures by the international oil community reduced the flow of Iranian oil revenues to a trickle and the country's economy soon lapsed into chaos. Mossadegh was ousted by Shah Mohammed Reza Pahlavi in 1953, being subsequently tried and imprisoned. Diplomatic relations were restored the following year and Anglo-Iranian (now British Petroleum) received compensation, joining an international consortium which had been formed to operate the Iranian oil industry.

Elsewhere in the Gulf, British policy since World War II has sought to preserve the status quo among the other states lining its shores – Iraq, Kuwait, Saudi Arabia, Qatar, Oman and the seven United Arab Emirates. In 1952 a Saudi invasion of the Buraimi Oasis was repulsed by British-led troops of the sultan

of Oman, and in 1961 the despatch of British naval reinforcements to the Gulf effectively deterred a threat by Iraq to annex Kuwait.

Oman, while lying outside the Gulf, possesses the Musandam peninsula which forms one side of the Strait of Hormuz and is therefore a vital element in the security of the area. Elements of the British Army have fought two successful campaigns there, the first in 1957-59 against internal dissidents and the second between 1965 and 1975 against communist guerrillas who infiltrated the Dhofar region from the Marxist Republic of South Yemen. The latter campaign included numerous small-scale actions and, on 18 July 1972, a full-scale battle at the town of Mirbat which ended in the complete rout of the invaders.

The British withdraw

From 1971 Britain began to withdraw from the Gulf and the role of peacekeeper devolved upon Iran, which possessed large armed forces equipped by Western powers. This role was never fully accepted by the other Gulf states, however. The position changed radically with the Iranian revolution of 1979. The Shah and his regime were replaced by an Islamic fundamentalist administration led by the Ayatollah Khomeini. The quality of the country's armed services dropped dramatically as its officer corps was ruthlessly purged or fled abroad. The president of Iraq, Saddam Hussein, was not slow to take advantage of the situation: hoping to resolve a long-standing dispute with Iran, he launched an invasion on 12 September 1980.

The dispute centred on the precise position of the border in relation to the Shatt al Arab waterway. Iraq had once formed part of the Turkish Empire, which had never adequately settled the question of its boundary with Persia. A 1937 treaty fixed the frontier on the eastern bank of the Shatt, save off Abadan and Khorramshahr, where it ran in midstream. This treaty was abrogated by the Shah in 1975 and a fresh treaty was signed whereby, in return for the withdrawal of Iranian support for the Kurdish nationalists within Iraq, the latter conceded that the centre of the entire deep-water channel should form the frontier. In 1980, by military means, Saddam Hussein sought to restore the Iraqi position as well as to secure several other disputed areas, and in so doing to humiliate the Ayatollah Khomeini, whom he detested.

The Iraqi offensive was directed at the oil province of Khuzestan and successfully overran both Khorramshahr and Abadan. The Iranian Army did not collapse, however, and by the autumn of 1980 it had managed to contain the penetration. Since then a state of attritional stalemate has been maintained, neither side being able to strike a conclusive blow, although both countries have committed substantial reserves to the struggle. The conflict has shown both sides to be seriously deficient in training, staff work and inter-service cooperation – and unable to handle the sophisticated weapons systems that have been purchased. The war is causing acute strain on the economies of both countries and although the remaining Gulf states, anxious to procure the downfall of Khomeini, are providing Iraq with financial assistance, there are signs that this will not be continued indefinitely.

In terms of power politics, the Gulf provides only shifting sand instead of the bedrock on which alliances can be usefully constructed. The Baghdad Pact in 1955 consisted of Great Britain, Iran, Iraq,

Far left: The Ayatollah Khomeini (centre), whose Islamic administration replaced the Shah and his regime in 1979. Below left: Oil tanks burn fiercely after an attack during the Gulf War between Iraq and Iran in 1980. Oil installations have been a major target for both sides.

Below: Iraqi troops jubilantly wave their AK assault rifles in celebration of a victory over the Iranians.

Pakistan and Turkey, thus forming a southern defensive front against Russian expansion. But in 1959 Iraq withdrew from the alliance, which was re-named the Central Treaty Organisation (Cento), and placed herself within the Soviet sphere of influence. The Iranian revolution has now virtually destroyed Cento. On the other hand, Saudi Arabia and the smaller Gulf states remain pro-Western in policy.

By and large the Gulf states, although aware of the existence of a power vacuum in the region, are not anxious to see an increase in America's influence there, believing that this will induce a Soviet reaction. Nonetheless, the United States has declared the Gulf to be an area of vital interest to its security and maintains a large fleet in the Indian Ocean.

The Soviet intervention in Afghanistan in December 1979 brought Russian troops to within striking distance of the Strait of Hormuz. It provoked such a strong American reaction that Moscow was forced to realise that Afghanistan was as far as she could penetrate. It is even likely that the Kremlin now believes its apparently open-ended commitment in Afghanistan to have been a serious miscalculation. It is also probable that, for the present, the Soviet leaders have no desire to become involved in the Gulf; they certainly have no wish to expose their own substantial Muslim population to the de-stabilising influences of Islamic fundamentalism. Equally important is the fact that the Soviet Union will herself join the ranks of the oil-importing nations quite shortly. It is inadvisable to try and predict the future of this region, for in the politics of the Gulf the only constant factor is change. **Bryan Perrett**

Outposts of empire

Britain's involvement in the Arabian Peninsula

British involvement in the Arabian (Persian) Gulf and the Arabian peninsula was a consequence of the conquest of India. British communications with the Indian empire ran through the Mediterranean and Red Sea, and it was believed that the Arabian peninsula and the Persian and Arabian shores of the Gulf were essential outworks for the defence of India. Therefore Aden, seized in 1839 and Britain's first foothold in south Arabia, was governed from India until 1937 when the Colonial Office took over. The Gulf was a bailiwick of the government of India until 1947, when India became independent and the Foreign Office assumed responsibility. Then the discovery of oil in the Gulf states and in Muscat and Oman soon after the end of World War II made the region of paramount importance to Britain and the West.

The RAF was the predominant British service in the Arabian peninsula from 1928 until the early 1950s. The tribes, who were frequently at war with each other, were kept in order by air control. Those who failed to obey the orders of government were bombed into submission. The air strike would be preceded by an ultimatum and if this was ignored the tribe was given time to evacuate. Casualties were few and houses, if knocked down, could be easily rebuilt since they were of mud-brick. Air control was simple in conception and economical in execution but it meant that the government did not bother to construct roads; there were, for example, no tarmac roads outside the boundaries of the colony of Aden after more than a century of British rule. This made it difficult to open up the tribal areas where tribe fought with tribe and every man went armed.

However, the chain of landing grounds which the RAF used between Iraq and Aden had to be defended.

Above: A unit of the Trucial Oman Scouts carries out a patrol in the desert. This largely Bedouin force was first raised in the early 1950s to protect British oil interests.

Below: Villagers in a mountainous region of Aden stand by as British military personnel unload a truck-borne water tank from an RAF Blackburn Beverley transport aircraft. Air mobility gave the British a tremendous advantage in this type of operation, maximizing the potential of Britain's limited resources.

This was done by locally-raised forces led by officers on loan from the British Army and RAF Regiment. In Aden and the Western Protectorate the force was called the Aden Protectorate Levies (APL) until 1961 when it was re-named the Federal Regular Army (FRA); it was about 4000 strong. There was also a paramilitary force called the Government Guards (GG), re-named the Federal National Guard (FNG) after 1961. There were only two British officers in the FNG but the Levies contained 100 or more. In the Eastern Protectorate there was the Hadhrami Bedouin Legion (HBL) modelled on the Arab Legion of Jordan and mostly Bedouin in content. It was about 1000 strong and had only three British officers. The tribesmen of south Arabia made good soldiers, being both tough and proud to bear arms, but they were fanatical Muslims and were often involved in blood feuds which made them difficult to handle. Mutinies were not uncommon.

Controlling the mountains

Little or no attempt was made to control the mountainous hinterland which lay between Aden and the Yemen until after 1945. The Imam of the Yemen, who laid claim to Aden on historical grounds, meddled with the tribes and actually invaded the Western Aden Protectorate (as the tribal areas were known) in the early 1950s. He was driven out by a combination of air strikes and land operations by the APL. By 1957 it was decided that the British Army should take over from the RAF and the APL was greatly expanded, re-equipped and the provision of a larger British element led to improved training.

In 1958 the British persuaded the tribal rulers to come together in a federation which was eventually joined by the colony of Aden in 1962. It might have worked had there not been a revolution in the Yemen

in September of that year when the imam was driven out and a republic set up. However the imam survived the attempt to kill him and took to the mountains where the Royalists, supported by Saudi Arabia and Jordan, fought a long war against the Republicans, who were supported by Egypt.

This war spilled over into the Western Protectorate and a series of minor campaigns took place between 1957 and 1964, culminating in a major operation in the Radfan which began on 4 January 1964 and lasted for nearly two years. British troops were involved in most of these operations, largely artillery and armoured car squadrons in support of the APL/FRA; one battery of Royal Horse Artillery and one armoured car squadron from the British regiment stationed in Aden were placed in support of the local force.

After the withdrawal from Suez in 1956 Aden became the main British base on the Indian Ocean. Headquarters Middle East Command was established there in 1961. This was a joint command, the commander-in-chief coming from each of the three services in turn. Under him were three single-service commanders of major-general rank or equivalent, with their own staffs. Their responsibilities extended far beyond Aden, of course, and the headquarters had no sooner been established than it was put to the test by events in Kuwait, then under British protection. The Iraqis threatened to invade Kuwait in August 1961. The 24th Infantry Brigade under Brigadier D. G. T. Horsford was flown to Kuwait from Kenya. No fighting occurred but the weather was unusually hot and there were several casualties from heatstroke. The commander-in-chief and his subordinate commanders controlled the operation from a warship lying off Kuwait. It was basically a political problem but undoubtedly the speed of the British reaction prevented what could otherwise have been a very serious situation.

Aden was never a popular garrison. The climate

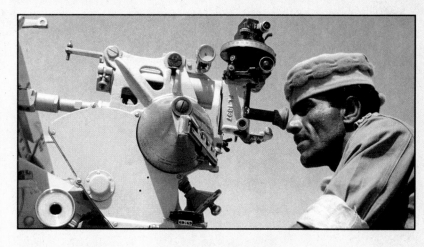

Above: Soldiers of the Sultan of Muscat and Oman's armed forces sight an artillery piece. Much of the skill of the SAF can be attributed to British training in the 1950s.

Below: Royal Marines of 42 Commando prepare to climb aboard a helicopter on the flight deck of HMS *Bulwark* in 1961 during the operations in support of Kuwait against Iraqi threats.

was oppressive and the requirement to restrict the troops and their families to the narrow confines of Aden colony itself made the place remarkably claustrophobic. Conditions within Aden began to deteriorate from 1963 onwards when the Egyptian-financed National Liberation Front (NLF) began a campaign of assassination and terrorism. The campaign in the neighbouring Radfan mountains, beginning in January 1964, eventually involved the 39th Infantry Brigade, flown out from Britain, although originally it was intended to let the FRA handle it.

Loss of control

In Aden itself matters went from bad to worse, culminating in a mutiny by the South Arabian Army (as it had been re-named) in June 1967. Several British soldiers were killed in an ambush and for a few days control over the Arab quarter was lost. This was restored by the Argyll and Sutherland Highlanders, under the command of Lieutenant-Colonel Colin ('Mad Mitch') Mitchell. The British government, however, had had enough of Aden and its intractable people and the last British soldier was withdrawn on

was owned partly by the Sultan of Muscat and Oman, and partly by the sheikh of Abu Dhabi, but the Saudis insisted it lay within their boundaries. The real reason was, of course, their belief that there was oil beneath Buraimi's sand dunes and palm groves. After three years of diplomatic negotiations, which proved fruitless, the TOS drove out the Saudis in 1955, losing only two soldiers killed. Buraimi has since disappeared from the world's news – probably because no oil has yet been discovered there.

There was no permanent garrison of British troops (apart from the RAF at Sharjah) during the 1950s and 1960s. The TOS were responsible for controlling the interior in the Trucial States while the Sultan's Armed Forces (SAF) looked after the sultanate of Muscat and Oman. There was a small British headquarters at Bahrain where the Political Resident Persian Gulf was based; he was responsible to the Foreign Office. In order to deter any attack from Iraq a squadron of tanks, and their administrative support, was based in Bahrain after 1961, half the squadron being embarked on an LST and at instant readiness. It was not a popular assignment at the height of the hot season.

Oil and opulence

From the mid 1950s onwards the discovery of oil, inland and off-shore, transformed the economies of the Gulf states. First in Qatar, Abu Dhabi and Dubai, and later in Oman, oil brought undreamed-of riches to a region which had formerly been one of the poorest on earth. By 1971, when the British finally withdrew from the Gulf, the entire region had been transformed. A new federation had been set up, largely as a result of British urging, which is now known as the United Arab Emirates (UAE), and the TOS was handed over to the new government and re-named the Union Defence Force (UDF); only Abu Dhabi and Oman (not a member of the UAE) retained their own separate forces. British officers were gradually re-

29 November 1967 with no regrets and hardly a backward glance.

British involvement in the Gulf has been a happier story than that of south Arabia. The British went there originally to put down piracy and made little or no attempt to control the desert interior until oil was discovered in the early 1950s. It then became essential to protect the oil exploration teams and a local force was raised for this purpose. Based on the Arab Legion it became known eventually as the Trucial Oman Scouts (TOS) and was largely Bedouin in composition, led by officers on loan from the British Army.

This force was first put to the test in 1952 when the Saudis occupied the important oasis of Buraimi. This

Above: British troops brew up while taking a rest from patrol. The gun in the foreground is a 75mm pack howitzer.

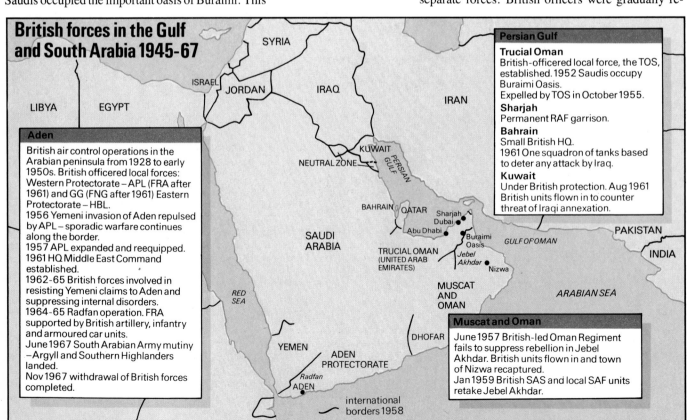

British forces in the Gulf and South Arabia 1945-67

Aden
British air control operations in the Arabian peninsula from 1928 to early 1950s. British officered local forces: Western Protectorate – APL (FRA after 1961) and GG (FNG after 1961) Eastern Protectorate – HBL.
1956 Yemeni invasion of Aden repulsed by APL – sporadic warfare continues along the border.
1957 APL expanded and reequipped.
1961 HQ Middle East Command established.
1962-65 British forces involved in resisting Yemeni claims to Aden and suppressing internal disorders.
1964-65 Radfan operation. FRA supported by British artillery, infantry and armoured car units.
June 1967 South Arabian Army mutiny – Argyll and Southern Highlanders landed.
Nov 1967 withdrawal of British forces completed.

Persian Gulf
Trucial Oman
British-officered local force, the TOS, established. 1952 Saudis occupy Buraimi Oasis.
Expelled by TOS in October 1955.
Sharjah
Permanent RAF garrison.
Bahrain
Small British HQ.
1961 One squadron of tanks based to deter any attack by Iraq.
Kuwait
Under British protection. Aug 1961 British units flown in to counter threat of Iraqi annexation.

Muscat and Oman
June 1957 British-led Oman Regiment fails to suppress rebellion in Jebel Akhdar. British units flown in and town of Nizwa recaptured.
Jan 1959 British SAS and local SAF units retake Jebel Akhdar.

international borders 1958

Top: Scottish soldiers go through fire drills with their .303in water-cooled Vickers machine guns during operations in Aden, 1957. A Ferret armoured car is parked in the background. Above: The Sultan of Muscat and Oman's fort at Buraimi in 1957, where a garrison was stationed to deter the Saudis from further invasion.

placed by their Arab counterparts as the latter were trained and given experience. There were, however, two campaigns involving British troops which took place within the frontiers of the sultanate of Muscat and Oman in the 1950s. These were the operations on the Jebel Akhdar (Green Mountain) in 1957 and 1959.

The protagonists in this conflict were the sultan of Oman and the rebel forces under the command of the religious leader, the Imam of Oman. The 1957 campaign proved a disaster for the sultan: his British officered forces were badly mauled in an ambush near the Jebel Akhdar and as a result his rule over Oman lay in jeopardy. Assistance, however, came in the shape of British intervention. A mixed force of British Army and RAF units were despatched to Oman, firstly to prevent the collapse of the sultan's rule and, secondly, to put down the rebellion. During 1958 the British consolidated the sultan's position, retraining the Omani troops and rebuilding their morale. In January 1959 a major assault was launched against the imam's rebel forces on the Jebel Akhdar itself. A triumph of inter-arms cooperation, the British and Omani troops routed the rebels so that for the first time in years the sultan's word was law on the Jebel Akhdar.

Despite the oppressive heat, high humidity and lack of amenities, service in the Gulf was more popular with the British soldier than service in Aden. Unlike Aden there was no colonial tradition and to that extent relations were easier with the locals. There was no popular liberation movement such as gave the British so much trouble in Aden. Also, oil had brought untold wealth in the short space of 20 years; everyone knew this and, apart from in southern Oman, there was relatively little discontent. When the British finally left Bahrain in January 1971, handing over to the Abu Dhabi and Union Defence Forces, which still contained British officers serving on loan, they left in much better heart than they had left Aden three years previously. Some of them even remained there, serving with the local forces until the next decade. **James Lunt**

Assault on the Jebel Akhdar

Civil war in Muscat and Oman

Between June 1957 and January 1959 the Sultanate of Oman, in the southeastern corner of the Arabian peninsula, was in the throes of civil war. The authority of the sultan, Said bin Taimur, was threatened by a coalition of tribes and factions intent upon his overthrow and the establishment of a republic under their religious leader, the Imam of Oman. In terms of contemporary world politics the conflict appeared to have little significance, but in retrospect the defeat of the rebels, achieved largely as a result of British military assistance to the sultan, may be seen as crucial. For Oman, by virtue of its possession of the Musandam peninsula, controls the southern shores of the Strait of Hormuz, through which so much of the world's crude oil is delivered. The sultan's victory ensured that the state – and the oil route – remained firmly in the Western camp.

The roots of civil war ran deep in Oman. Despite a history of independent rule, the power of the sultan

was effectively restricted to the thin coastal fringe of the northeast, protected by the mountains of the Hajar. Elsewhere, in the desert wastes of the interior, the Arab tribesmen were fiercely independent, owing allegiance to local sheikhs and the imam. Conflict between the rival factions was endemic, leading successive sultans to seek outside aid. From as early as 1798 this was provided by Britain, aware of Oman's importance as a centre of trade and communications, although attempts were made to persuade the sultan and imam to sink their differences. In 1920, by the Treaty of Sib, some progress was made, with the imam agreeing to recognise the sultan's primacy in exchange for increased autonomy for the tribes of the interior, but the details were vague and the prospects for lasting peace uncertain.

When the old imam died in 1954, his elected successor, Ghalib bin Ali, enjoyed a number of new advantages. Disputes over the sultan's right to grant

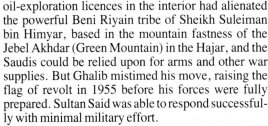

Far Left: Trucial Scouts
prepare to defend a
fortified position against an
imminent rebel attack. Left:
The Sultan of Muscat and
Oman – he called on the
British to crush the rebels.
Bottom: The commanding
view from Jebel Akhdar.
Such hilly approaches
were easily defended by
resolute troops. Bottom
right: A Trucial Oman
Scout aims at a rebel from
a watchtower.

oil-exploration licences in the interior had alienated the powerful Beni Riyain tribe of Sheikh Suleiman bin Himyar, based in the mountain fastness of the Jebel Akhdar (Green Mountain) in the Hajar, and the Saudis could be relied upon for arms and other war supplies. But Ghalib mistimed his move, raising the flag of revolt in 1955 before his forces were fully prepared. Sultan Said was able to respond successfully with minimal military effort.

The settlement was only temporary. In June 1957 Ghalib's younger brother, Talib bin Ali, landed on the northeast coast with about 80 armed followers and moved inland towards the Jebel Akhdar. The sultan hurriedly despatched his Oman Regiment to Hamra in an effort to cut the rebels off from the interior, but Sheikh Suleiman seized the opportunity to rise again in support of the imam. The Oman Regiment, faced with encirclement, withdrew in some disorder, abandoning the key towns of Nizwa and Firq.

In desperation the sultan turned to Britain for aid, and in late July a small force (comprising one company of the Cameronians and one troop of the 15th/19th King's Hussars) arrived in Oman under Brigadier J.A.R. Robertson. He faced a chaotic and potentially disastrous military situation but responded well, committing his force to the recapture of Nizwa as first priority. The operation, carried out in August with support from the Royal Air Force, elements of the British-officered Trucial Oman Scouts and the remnants of the Sultan's Armed Forces (SAF), was a success but, as the British contingents had to be withdrawn before the onset of the 'hot season' in September, Robertson could not exploit his victory. The SAF, weak and poorly equipped, was left to contain the rebels in the Jebel Akhdar, a fertile and easily defended plateau atop precipitous cliffs with only a limited number of difficult approach routes. Stalemate ensued.

But the threat to the sultan's power remained, manifested throughout 1958 in a series of rebel attacks against the SAF which, although not major battles, imposed a steady drain on morale and resources. A long-

term solution was essential and, once again, it was the British who stepped in. In January 1958 the sultan was persuaded to introduce much-needed civil reforms in exchange for British assistance in training and expanding the SAF. Three months later a regular British officer, Colonel David Smiley of the Royal Horse Guards, arrived in Oman as chief of staff to the SAF and he began to reorganise the force with the declared aim of defeating the rebels.

By the end of the year the main rebel strongholds on the Jebel Akhdar had been pinpointed – on the northern edge of the plateau at Aquabat al Dhafar and in the centre around the villages of Habib, Saiq and Sharaijah – and SAF patrols had penetrated to the foot of the cliffs at Hijar in the north and Tanuf in the south. With the rebels, estimated to consist of about 700 armed tribesmen, blockaded and running short of supplies, Smiley's next step had to be a direct assault.

Planning the assault

The SAF, however, was clearly unsuited to such a task and in October 1958 Smiley was forced to request more specialised aid. He was given D Squadron of the 22nd Special Air Service (SAS) Regiment, returning to Britain from active service in Malaya, and as soon as they arrived in late November they began to patrol out of Hijar and Tanuf, determined to probe for usable routes to the top of the plateau. In late December an unsuccessful assault was mounted towards Aquabat al Dhafar and Smiley had to reassess his plan. He asked for more reinforcements.

These arrived in early January 1959 in the form of A Squadron, 22 SAS, supported by a TAC HQ under the regiment's commanding officer, Lieutenant-Colonel Tony Deane-Drummond. He reconnoitred the Jebel Akhdar from the air and decided that his men would be used more profitably in a less direct attack, designed to capture the villages of Habib, Saiq and Sharaijah, without which the main rebel positions to the north would be untenable. A steep but climbable route was discovered, following a ridge-line between Wadi Kamah and Wadi Sumeit to the east of Tanuf, and patrols established that the line was unguarded.

Between 18 and 22 January diversionary attacks were mounted against Aquabat al Dhafar and around the Tanuf and Izki areas, designed to tie down the main rebel force. They were remarkably successful, enabling the SAS/SAF to move out of Kamah on the evening of the 26th to face a 9½-hour climb over difficult terrain. Progress was slow and just before dawn the leading SAS troops were forced to dump rucksacks and make a dash for the plateau top. At first light, as an RAF air-strike came in, the summit was reached against desultory opposition and the approaches to the villages were seized. The SAS and SAF proceeded to clear the villages, unearthing caches of arms and documents which guaranteed complete rebel defeat. By late March, when the British contingents were withdrawn, the sultan was in full control of his state.

John Pimlott

War in the desert

Technical, logistic and combat problems

Desert regions are usually defined as areas where annual rainfall is less than 255mm (10 inches) and they account for well over a third of the land surface of the globe. It would be a mistake, however, to assume that desert is always composed of sand dunes. Apart from sand desert, there are at least five other major surface types, including: uneven rocky surfaces; soft rock ridges; dust and gypsum surfaces; salt flats; and 'pavement' desert, where winds have blown away the sand to reveal a gravel and pebble patchwork. Sinai, over which major campaigns have been fought in 1956, 1967 and 1973, has a flat central expanse of sand and loess ringed with white limestone hills, while the southern part of the peninsula rises in mountains 2000m (6500 feet) high.

The desert has a constant capacity to surprise, as in the Dhofar region of Oman where British and Omani forces were involved in campaigns against guerrillas between 1965 and 1975. Most of southern Arabia is a grim wasteland of barren mountains and the massive sand sea of the 'Empty Quarter', yet the 920m (3000 feet) Dhofari mountains immediately inland from the coast are annually transformed between June and September into a lush almost jungle-like terrain by monsoon winds from the Indian Ocean. Rainfall is not unknown in the desert, but it frequently comes suddenly and torrentially, flash floods turning dried-up river beds into dangerous obstacles.

The desert is unyielding and provides few if any resources, so all necessities for forces fighting in the desert have to be transported. The nature of the problem is perhaps best illustrated by the experience of Rommel's Afrika Korps during World War II. It was not that supplies were failing to reach the German forces' base at Tripoli that caused shortages of petrol and other commodities at the front, just the sheer physical difficulty of transporting those supplies across 1600km (1000 miles) of desert. At least 10 per cent of available fuel was required to transport the remainder. Since all other supplies also had to be sent forward, possibly as much as 50 per cent of all fuel landed in North Africa was used up before it reached the German front line. Moreover, a 3200km (2000 mile) round trip for transport vehicles resulted in at least a third being constantly out of repair.

Modern armies still need to carry all their requirements in such terrain. In the 1956 Sinai campaign the Israeli 9th Infantry Brigade advancing on Sharm el Sheikh carried sufficient food for five days, enough fuel for a 600km (375 mile) trip and was accompanied by 18 water tankers – yet the actual distance to be covered was only 298km (185 miles). In 1967 Israeli armoured formations entered Sinai with sufficient resources for 72 hours, but the difficulty of resupplying an unexpectedly rapid advance was such that the leading tanks of Colonel Avraham Yoffe's division had to be towed into the Mitla Pass through lack of fuel. Furthermore, the leading reconnaissance jeeps and tanks reached the Suez Canal only because other units gave up their own fuel supplies. Even with the advantage of total air superiority and superior military capacity, the Israelis could cover no more than 65km (40 miles) per day during the 1967 campaign with tanks capable of making at least 24km (15 miles) per hour. It is a good example of the difficulty of actually traversing desert.

The advance on Sharm el Sheikh between 29 October and 5 November 1956 is a similar example, since the 9th Brigade could not have returned once it set out because the inclines on the narrow coastal road ran north to south and could only be easily traversed downhill. The first 98km (62 miles) were covered at 11km/h (7mph) but the next 14km (9 miles) were crossed at an average speed of only 4km/h (2½mph), and the following 48km (30 miles) at 9km/h (6mph) with liberal use of dynamite to blast a way through the rocky terrain.

In northern Sinai in 1956 the Israeli 202nd Para-

Left: A unit of Israeli M48 tanks cross the Sinai desert in pursuit of Egyptian targets. Inset left: An Israeli armoured patrol use signalling flags to identify themselves to other units while patrolling desert areas.

Below: The rigours of desert warfare are particularly telling on infantry who have to fight in intense heat and sand. These Iranian troops rest in their foxholes between engagements.

chute Brigade's advance towards the Mitla Pass was also held up by the terrain. The brigade had expected to be able to use 153 trucks, but only 46 became available; and as there was no netting or steel slats for difficult sand stretches, any vehicles that broke down had to be abandoned. It took 28 hours to travel 305km (190 miles), with only seven of the brigade's original 13 tanks reaching the first objective and only two participating in the first action.

Crossing the dunes

In both 1956 and 1967 the Israelis' willingness to attempt to bypass roads and tracks frequently achieved tactical surprise – as on 5 June 1967 when Yoffe's division crossed the sand dunes to the north of Abu Aweigila, which the Egyptians considered impassable, and cut off the Egyptian 7th Division. The Egyptians generally refused to leave the roads unless forced to do so, and tended to rely on static fortified positions in the belief they could not be bypassed. In 1967 their general unpreparedness for the conditions in Sinai was illustrated by the fact that they had brought Soviet-supplied wood-burning decontamination vehicles with them.

The Israelis themselves have, however, not always been able to solve problems in the Sinai. They were forced to rely on existing asphalt roads for bringing up supplies in non-tracked vehicles and this occasionally resulted in spectacular traffic jams, as in 1967 when

the Gaza operations were held up by congestion behind General Israel Tal's front. In the Yom Kippur War of 1973, General Avraham Adan's intended counter-attack on the Egyptians planned for 7/8 October was delayed by traffic jams and on 15 October the advance of General Ariel Sharon's division along the Akavish road brought hundreds of vehicles into a bumper-to-bumper traffic jam over a distance of 20km (12 miles). The delays, particularly in getting bridging equipment through, resulted in serious consideration being given to postponement of the Israeli crossing of the Suez Canal.

After the 1973 war Adan criticised Israel's failure to modernise its half-tracks, since the old American M3 half-tracks of World War II vintage had been unable to cross soft sand and were, in any case, too slow to keep up with modern tanks. During one counter-attack against the Egyptians on 9 October 1973, an Israeli brigade had had to leave its infantry support behind because the half-tracks could not traverse the sand around Hamutal, with the result that 17 of the 24 unsupported Israeli tanks were hit. Relatively few of the new fully-tracked American M113 Zelda armoured personnel carriers were in service with the Israelis when the war began.

Driving a wheeled vehicle on sand requires considerable experience and the ability to judge the surface texture and the probable shape of dunes. In British operations in Muscat and Oman in 1957 it was

recognised that the capacity of the ubiquitous Land-rover had to be related to the maximum weight it could successfully carry over soft dunes. Eight 4½-gallon jerry cans of petrol (equivalent to 163 litres) and two cans of water were about the maximum possible with three men in the front. Tyres had to be deflated for soft sand to as little as 13lbs pressure, risking punctures if stony surfaces were suddenly encountered.

Even tracked vehicles are not without problems in desert terrain. One of Sharon's reasons for not being able to support Adan's counter-attack in the Sinai on 8 October 1973 was that his tanks had had to cross hundreds of kilometres of desert on their own tracks in the absence of sufficient tank transporters and needed many repairs. In 1956 the Israelis had calculated that they would need at least 670 spare sets of tracks for their armoured formations in order to conduct the campaign at all.

More significant is desert heat, which can affect engines adversely. The Centurion, which provided the nucleus of the Israeli armour from 1960 onwards, was originally disliked in the Israeli Army because of its tendency to overheat, which was believed to be inevitable. It was only subsequently discovered that this could be avoided by scraping the radiator every day to prevent the accumulation of oil and dust. Dust can shorten an engine's life, the Afrika Korps calculating that the North African desert reduced tank engine life from 2250-2575km (1400-1600 miles) to as little as 480-1450km (300-900 miles).

Tanks can, however, be adapted to desert conditions. After the 1967 Sinai campaign the Israeli Centurions were fitted with a longer range diesel engine to increase battlefield endurance. The new Israeli Merkava tank, brought into service in 1979, not only has front wheel drive but also lacks the high acceleration rate common in most contemporary tanks because this would kick up too much dust in the desert.

Visibility is indeed a major problem in desert warfare. In deserts like the Sinai, wind strength invariably increases during the afternoon and brings dust or sand storms, while the definition produced by a low sun in the mornings is completely lost in the heat of midday. Mirages are also common. In such conditions it may be difficult to remain orientated or to

Top: A Polisario guerrilla takes advantage of a piece of rising ground from which he can command a wide arc of fire across the desert. Above: Royal Marines camouflage a desert patrol base. Below: Egyptian jets hit an Israeli convoy as troops take cover.

distinguish other formations. On 3 November 1956 the tanks of the Israeli 7th Armoured Brigade fired on those of the 37th Mechanised Brigade, putting eight out of action, as a result of dust clouds obscuring vision. In 1967 one company of the Israeli 7th Armoured Brigade became so disorientated during the attack on Rafah Junction that it blundered into an Egyptian tank battalion. Units of Adan's division found it particularly difficult to distinguish one another once they had crossed to the featureless Aida

Plain on the west bank of the Suez Canal in October 1973. Indeed, it has often been alleged that the relatively high casualty rate among Israeli tank commanders is due to their habit of riding in open turrets in order to see better.

The aerial view

Aircraft, on the other hand, are able to enjoy good visibility over the desert battlefield. This can be turned to great tactical advantage. In 1967 Israeli aircraft, with complete air superiority after the initial pre-emptive strikes against the Arab air forces, devastated Egyptian military traffic in the vital Sinai passes. Another example of the effectiveness of air power where ground forces are tied to a limited number of roads was the attack by just two Egyptian aircraft on Adan's division along the Macadam road on 11 October 1973. Sand dunes had prevented the dispersal of vehicles from the road and the Egyptians succeeded in setting Israeli ammunition trucks on fire, injuring more than 80 men and closing the road for over two hours. Similarly, although the motorised raiding parties of the Polisario guerrillas were able rapidly to cross vast distances of the western Sahara during their early campaigns against Moroccan and Mauritanian forces, they were vulnerable from the air. In 1976 one of their leaders, Ahmed el Wali, was killed when French aircraft wiped out a column as it returned from a raid on the Mauritanian capital.

But aircraft, too, are vulnerable in desert conditions, as the attempted rescue of the American hostages from Iran in April 1980 proved only too clearly. It was intended to fly in seven helicopters from American carriers in the Gulf of Oman in a six-hour flight over some 960km (600 miles) to a desert airstrip. The weather forecast was good, but severe dust storms forced down three helicopters while a fourth had hydraulic problems. With less than the minimum six regarded as essential, the operation was abandoned – but not before another helicopter had crashed into a C130 transport plane in the swirling dust kicked up by its own rotors. The mission was a fiasco, with eight men left dead after only three hours on the desert floor.

If the desert makes demands upon vehicles and aircraft it almost certainly makes more demands on

Above: Israeli armoured infantry in half-tracks move at speed through the desert as they practise rapid deployment manoeuvres.

the individual soldier and airman. The Sinai may serve as an example. The temperature is coolest and the sand firmest in early morning, but the sun is already blazing by 7 am and reaches a maximum between 11 am and 2 pm which, in summer, may be up to 54°C (130°F). The winds that invariably get up during the afternoons have no appreciable cooling effect and are a source of irritation through the sand and dust particles they carry. By contrast the nights are cold. In temperate climes an active man might require an average daily liquid intake of perhaps two to three litres (about four pints) but in deserts, where sweating is much increased and there is a need to evaporate that sweat from the skin through a substantially higher liquid intake, the average required climbs to 10 to 12 litres (17 to 20 pints) per day. The sensation of thirst may not keep pace with the actual amount of water required.

Those unfortunate enough to be cut off in desert

Curse of the desert

'You arrive at a desolate desert stretch. There is nothing at all that moves. You settle down in the silent landscape. Before you know where you are your enemies pounce upon you from somewhere or other in hundreds, thousands, and tens of thousands: The flies. Nobody can explain how they discovered you. Or what they had been living on until now before you arrive with your victuals. They swoop down upon you and make your day miserable.

'Desert flies are different from flies behind the lines. They have an unbelievable capacity for suffering and persistence. No waving of the hands is going to drive them away. They will enter your mouth and nose without hesitation, make a landing within the tin of conserves of your battle rations, and dive down into the spoonful of water allocated to you. They will not permit you to sleep even a moment in the noonday heat.

'At first you try to fight them. After several attempts resistance is weakened. You still engage in a number of actions while retreating, and finally surrender in despair. When a few days have passed you accept their existence and permit them to ramble at ease over your hands and face.

'One consolation is left. These flies fight by day. As soon as the sun sets they vanish as swiftly as they appear. Where do they go? Nobody has yet discovered the mysterious camps to which they fly as evening falls, and from which they emerge next day with the first ray of sunlight.'

Amnon Rubinstein, writing in the newspaper Ha'aretz, 20 June 1967.

Above: Israeli troops dig out a track which has been shed from their Centurion tank in the foreground. This incident occurred shortly before the tank was due to go into battle and emphasises the necessity of good back-up and logistics services if a modern army is to operate over such difficult terrain.

terrain can survive through moving at night, making use of sand to protect the body from sun during daylight and obtaining dew from desert vegetation in the mornings. One Israeli airman shot down near Bir Gifgafa in October 1956 walked for more than 30 hours on two successive nights to reach his own lines. A USAAF survey of desert survival during World War II recorded how a Wellington bomber crew covered 560km (350 miles) to reach safety.

Also associated with the desert are, of course, a wide range of heat-related complaints and diseases, ranging from sunburn to prickly heat, where clothing is too tight, to major heat exhaustion or the frequently fatal heat stroke. Given desert conditions the atmosphere inside a tank can well be imagined. In his account of the 1967 Sinai campaign, *Sabra*, Ted Berkman recorded how Israeli tank drivers suffered most: 'For him the pressure on eye and leg muscles, the nervous tension, the maddening racket of the engine never let up. His throat was constantly parched, his hands blistered. After a long run of driving, he had to be helped out of the cab, bent over like an aged arthritis victim into a crablike posture.'

There are also, of course, the insects and reptiles with which one has to contend – fleas, midges, snakes, scorpions, spiders and, above all, flies by day and mosquitoes by night. A standard Israeli joke in 1967 was that one fly was so large that when it landed at an Israeli airfield the ground crews were already servicing it when someone noticed there were no bomb racks! Ideally, a period of 8 to 10 days is required in order to become used to desert conditions, a factor which calls into question the likely effectiveness of the United States Rapid Deployment Joint Task Force, or any similar forces, should they be required to act urgently in the Middle East or Arabian Gulf. For fighting in desert conditions is one of the most difficult and specialised areas of modern military life. **Ian Beckett**

Key Weapons

The

A-4 SKYHAWK

part 2

Skyhawk in service

On 26 September 1956 the US Navy's Attack Squadron 72 received its first A4D-1 Skyhawk, an event marking the beginning of over a quarter of a century's operational use with seven countries. The length and geographical spread of the A-4's service made it almost inevitable that the aircraft would become involved in a shooting war. This has indeed occurred, the diminutive fighter-bomber having so far fought in the skies over Southeast Asia, the Middle East and, most recently, the South Atlantic.

As befits its American origins, the A-4 entered combat with the US Navy. Having participated in the Lebanon crisis of 1958 and the blockade of Cuba in 1962, the Skyhawk first fired its guns in anger over North Vietnam in 1964. On 2 August of that year, North Vietnamese naval vessels attacked the USS *Maddox* in what has become known as the Tonkin incident. The attack brought a swift response, and on the following day the carriers *Constellation* and *Ticonderoga*, cruising in the South China Sea, launched air strikes against North Vietnamese naval installations. Prominent among the aircraft used was the A-4, which rapidly became one of the most important weapons systems available to the US Navy in the Southeast Asian theatre.

Skyhawk strike operations over Vietnam settled into a pattern fairly rapidly. Sorties were divided between strategic strikes against targets in the North Vietnamese hinterland and close support missions over South Vietnam, Laos and Cambodia. To facili-

tate these operations, the American carriers adopted two operational zones, known respectively as Yankee and Dixie stations. Yankee station was situated in the Gulf of Tonkin and was the launch point for the raids on northern targets. Dixie, on the other hand, lay off the South Vietnamese coast and was used for the close support missions.

A-4 operations over the north fell into two distinct categories, namely 'Alpha' strikes and interdiction sorties against road and rail targets. The 'Alpha' strikes were full-blown carrier group operations involving all the available aircraft types and were aimed at strategic targets such as industrial plants, airfields, supply points and fuel dumps. The interdiction sorties were flown by pairs of a single type, usually the A-4 or Grumman's A-6 Intruder.

North Vietnam's air defences proved to be formidable and A-4 losses were heavy, especially during the early phases of the American bombing campaign. To begin with, A-4 sorties were flown at low level to avoid radar detection, a flight profile which left the Skyhawks vulnerable to even light automatic fire and with a far from satisfactory weapons delivery window. The structural integrity and strength of the A-4's airframe was proved many times as aircraft limped back to the carriers with sections of wings and fuselage blown away.

As losses mounted, the Skyhawk pilots switched to a fast high altitude approach with the actual target being attacked from a shallow dive. This mode of

Previous page: An Argentinian A-4Q is bombed-up in preparation for an air raid. Some 16 A-4Qs (converted USN A-4Bs) were delivered to Argentina in 1971. Above left: A line of A-4Es and A-4Fs stand on the flight deck of USS *Bon Homme Richard*. Above: A Skyhawk thunders off the deck of USS *Enterprise* on its way to carry out an attack mission over Vietnam.

Above: Skyhawks of USS *Forrestal* undergo preparation by ground crew. Top right: A TA-4J trainer about to land on its parent carrier. Above: Skyhawks wait to take-off from USS *Independence* while a Phantom is catapulted from the carrier.

operations took the A-4s out of range of all but the heaviest calibre anti-aircraft guns and allowed for much greater accuracy in weapons delivery. Even the deployment of the SA-2 missile did not pose too much of a problem as the Skyhawk proved to be nimble enough to out-manoeuvre the 'flying telegraph poles'. The type's manoeuvrability also proved a major asset in surviving interception attempts by MiG-17s and MiG-21s over North Vietnam.

South of the Demilitarised Zone dividing the two

Vietnams, the Dixie station aircraft were supported by Navy and Marine Corps Skyhawks operating from land bases such as Danang and Chu Lai. American A-4 units known to have operated in Southeast Asia include US Navy Attack Squadrons VA-22, VA-76, VA-93, VA-94, VA-106, VA-113, VA-114, VA-163, VA-164, VA-212 and US Marine Corps Attack Squadrons VMA-121, VMA-223 and VMA-311.

While the war dragged on in Southeast Asia, Israel began to receive its first Skyhawks. The Israeli Air

Force's first A-4 squadron, formed in 1968, was soon in action against PLO positions on the east bank of the Jordan. Although blooded, the A-4's real combat test in the Middle East came with the Yom Kippur War of 1973. At the start of hostilities, Israel had six operational squadrons flying a mixture of A-4Hs, ex-US A-4Es and A-4Ns. In the days that followed, these units flew as many attack sorties as all the other IAF aircraft combined. The intensity of operations was matched by the weight of losses. A total of 53 Skyhawks were destroyed, all but four of them falling to ground fire. Of the 49 aircraft lost in this manner, an estimated 36 were hit by SA-6 missiles.

The importance of the Skyhawk to the Israeli war effort was such that additional aircraft were requested from the Americans during the fighting in order to maintain front line strength. To this end, 30 of the Marine Corps' A-4Ms were rushed to the Middle East. The ending of the Yom Kippur War saw additional deliveries of A-4N aircraft so that, by the end of the decade, Israel was able to field a force of around 100 Skyhawks from a total of 279 single-seaters and 27 trainers procured.

The Israeli A-4s of the 1980s are perhaps the most sophisticated of the line in service anywhere in the world. Indeed, the Israelis see a place for the Skyhawk into the 1990s when it will be replaced by the indigenous Lavi strike fighter. The remaining A-4Es and Hs are being phased out of service and are currently being sold on the world's arms market, finding a purchaser in one of the protagonists in the Skyhawk's latest war, Argentina.

Below left: A Skyhawk of the Argentinian Air Force comes in to land on the aircraft carrier the *Vienticinco de Mayo*. Below: A flight of A-4H Skyhawks patrols the skies over Israel. While the Mirage acted primarily as an air superiority aircraft, the Skyhawk was highly successful in its ground-strike capacity.

Argentina received her first A-4 in 1966 and at the beginning of the Falklands War in 1982 had a reported front line strength of 46 A-4Ps and 12 A-4Qs. The A-4P aircraft were flown by the Argentinian Air Force's IV and V Brigadas Aerea from the bases at Rio Gallegos, San Julian and Rio Grande. The Argentinian Navy's A-4Qs operated from Rio Grande only.

Combat was joined on 1 May, when Argentinian air units, including 28 Skyhawks, mounted an inconclusive attack on the British Task Force which had made a provocative approach on the Falklands to test the enemy's reaction. For the next 20 days, Argentina despatched only 16 sorties of all types against the Royal Navy, lulling the Task Force into a false sense of security. By 21 May, British shipping was massed in Falkland Sound for the San Carlos landings. As daylight illuminated the scene, the Argentinian Air Force appeared in force. Over the next four days, 167 sorties were despatched from the mainland and 106 are reported to have attacked 'their assigned targets'. Skyhawks were in the forefront of this onslaught, which resulted in 10 British ships being either destroyed or damaged. The Argentinian attacks were mounted with considerable courage, the A-4s and Daggers flying at ultra low level and at the very limits of their operational range. By 25 May, the Task Force had claimed the destruction of 14 Skyhawks, the probable destruction of two more and hits on another two – a total of 18 aircraft. If these figures are correct then the loss rate among Skyhawks was almost 33 per cent.

After 25 May, air operations once more declined until 8 June when the British landings at Bluff Cove provoked a strong reaction. Thirty-seven Dagger/A-4 sorties were despatched which resulted in damage to HMS *Plymouth* and the carnage aboard the *Sir Galahad*. The Bluff Cove operation really marked the end of the air war over the Falklands, Argentinian units mounting only sporadic attacks during the remaining week or so of the fighting. There is dispute over the extent of Argentinian losses during the campaign. With regard to the A-4, the Argentinian authorities admit the loss of 20 such aircraft during the 14 weeks of fighting. The British, however, claim to have destroyed or damaged no less than 45. To make good the loss, Argentina has purchased 24 A-4E and H aircraft from Israel.

In combat, the Skyhawk has proved to be a most successful aircraft. The Vietnam and Middle East wars showed it to be resistant to combat damage and to be sufficiently manoeuvrable to hold its own against much higher performance interceptors. The Israeli

Bottom: A Skyhawk fires off rockets in its air support role in fighting over the Golan Heights during the Yom Kippur War of 1973. Aerial attacks by Israeli Skyhawks did much to blunt the advance of Syrian armour during the critical stages of the 1973 war.

Left: An Israeli C-97 Stratocruiser refuels two Skyhawks through the 'buddy' refuelling pods attached to the C-97's wings.

experience includes instances of Skyhawks receiving direct hits from heat-seeking missiles and still managing to regain their bases. In air-to-air combat, Israeli A-4s have evaded MiG-21 attacks even when fully 'bombed-up', and when 'clean' they have been able to out-turn even that ultimate Soviet dog-fighter, the MiG-17. Although never designed for air-to-air combat, the A-4 has on occasion notched-up 'MiG-kills'. A MiG-17 was destroyed over North Vietnam and Israeli pilots claim a number of victories, including a double 'kill' in May 1970 when an A-4H pilot bagged two Syrian MiG-17s over Lebanon, one with his cannon and the other with, of all things, an air-to-ground unguided rocket.

Right: Bombs are loaded onto the central ejector rack of an Israeli Skyhawk. Below: A pilot of the Argentinian Air Force prepares his Skyhawk for take-off. As with the Israelis, the combination of Mirages and Skyhawks acted as the spearhead of the Argentinian Air Force.

As an attack aircraft, the Skyhawk's ability to haul ever greater weights of munitions has proved to be one of its most useful assets. When first conceived, the A-4 was required to carry an offensive load of 908kg (2000lb). The first production model, the A4D-1, could lift a 2268kg (5000lb) war load, a figure which rose to 4100kg (9100lb) on the A-4M of 1974 – a 400 per cent increase over the original requirement.

This weight-lifting ability is enhanced by the range of weapons that the Skyhawk can accommodate. Starting life as a nuclear bomber, the A-4 was soon transformed into a close support platform which can use 'iron' bombs, unguided rockets, missiles such as the Bullpup, 'smart' munitions such as the Walleye and Shrike anti-radiation missiles which were used with considerable effect in Vietnam. When Ed Heinemann began work on the A-4 in the 1950s little did he imagine that it would remain a viable weapon a quarter of a century later, having become one of the most successful combat aircraft of the jet age.

Guns for sale

The world arms trade, 1945-55

It is undeniable that the availability of weapons is a major factor in modern warfare. Indeed, it is possible to show close parallels between the rising curve of arms sales to the Third World and the increase in warfare there. The shadowy hand of outside interference finds it easy to meddle by providing, or not providing, weapons; and many nations contain disaffected minorities that may be recipients of arms.

The decade after World War II saw the creation of a new international arms trade and the beginning of trends that were to assume great importance later. In the immediate postwar years, the Allies had huge stocks of surplus war material, and much of it was given away to the governments of countries where it happened to be when hostilities ended. For example, large amounts of British equipment were handed over to India and Burma when they became independent in 1947 and 1948.

The United States also started to give arms as a form of aid. In 1946 and 1947 $800 million worth of US arms were given to the Nationalist forces in China, and military assistance was also given to Greece and Turkey. As the Cold War took on a global aspect, the United States embarked on a programme of major arms transfers. In 1949 Congress passed the Mutual Defense Assistance Act, which established the milit-

Above: Samuel Cummings, the founder of Interarms, holds a Soviet 7.62mm SKS carbine. Upper right: The Interarms depot at Alexandria in Virginia, USA.

ary assistance programme. This enabled huge amounts of arms to be given away in aid as the United States set about rearming the Free World. By 1950, 14 countries were in receipt of arms under the programme and, in the 1952 fiscal year, transfers of grant-aided arms from the United States totalled $5 billion.

The United Kingdom was also divesting itself of surplus equipment, though far less of it was given away. The amounts were substantial. In the 10 years to 1955, £600 million worth of arms were sold to foreign governments and another £800 million worth of equipment was sold on the private market. Little information beyond the total values is available. The British government in 1955 refused to reveal details of government-to-government sales and confessed that details of private sales were destroyed after four years.

Investigation of the transfer of arms at an intergovernmental level presents relatively few problems. At the time, Britain and the US had a virtual monopoly and the arms trade at that level was part of the diplomatic and strategic design of the Western alliance. But the private arms trade was a different matter: it existed mainly because it could avoid the controls and regulations imposed by governments. With arms that were obsolete in some theatres being of vital importance in small, localised conflicts, the private arms trade threatened to boost regional arms races in many parts of the globe. The demand for obsolete weapons can be gauged by the fact that in the first Arab-Israeli War, 1948-49, the Israeli Air Force included 12 Messerschmitt 109s, three B-17s, two Mosquitoes, several Beaufighters, Mustangs and Harvard trainers. All of these were obtained on the private market.

In 1949, Britain, the United States and France established a Near Eastern Arms Coordinating Committee to control the flow of arms into the Arab-Israeli theatre and to prevent any party to the conflict achieving an overwhelming superiority. Britain's policy, when selling guns or tanks and armoured cars by auction, was to sell them as scrap or render them harmless by removal of the breech-block or turret.

Rifles and smallarms were sold only to dealers licensed under the Firearms Act. Even then, it was not possible to export any equipment without a licence obtained from the Board of Trade under the Import, Export and Customs Powers (Defence Act) of 1939. As the British government admitted at the time, however, assurances about ultimate destinations of arms from UK exporters, based on statements from foreign importers, did not afford an adequate safeguard.

Despite these international agreements and legal controls, 55 Sherman tanks out of a total of 109 exported under licence to France – supposedly to be converted into tractors – found their way to Israel. It is unclear in what condition the tanks arrived in Israel, but even if not in combat condition they could have been useful to supply spares for other Sherman tanks that Israel had purchased in 1948 and 1950. Similarly, 468 Valentine SPG platforms were exported under licence to Belgium, ostensibly to be sold as heavy duty construction equipment. One hundred were channelled to Egypt, where they were put into service as APCs.

Private dealership

It was the smallarms market that was the most difficult to control and which led to the creation of many of the major arms dealers in existence today. For example, a company called Western Arms Corporation, based in California, allegedly acted as an arms dealer for the US State Department and for the CIA in the first years of that organisation's existence. Western Arms' brief, so it is said, was to keep track of arms shipments, prevent them if possible from getting into the wrong hands, and to act as a covert source of weapons to groups acting in US interests. Employed by this company for a while was a man called Samuel Cummings, who in 1953 set up Interarms, the largest private arms firm in the world. Many of Cummings' more public deals shed light on the difficulties of controlling the destination of arms once they reach the second-hand market, and show just how long a life equipment can have.

Britain's policy was to sell only to licensed dealers, and licences were issued only to British citizens. Cummings knew that Britain wanted to sell a large number of MI Garands, and he also knew that he could sell them to the Guatemalan Army. But he could not obtain an export licence, or buy them as a registered dealer, and so he persuaded the sales director of Cogswell and Harrison, a British gun merchant, to bid for him as agent, obtain the export licence and ship them to the US, where Cummings took delivery. The rifles, which had originally been delivered to the UK from the United States under Lend-Lease, were eventually delivered to Guatemala. Although the deal took place in 1954, some of this batch of rifles were still being sold to Haiti and Indonesia in 1961.

Interarms rapidly became a dominant force in the private arms trade, so much so that it sometimes supplied arms to both sides in a conflict. In 1955 Costa Rican exiles, supported by General Anastasio Somoza of Nicaragua, invaded Costa Rica. The rebels, armed with Berettas and Madson machine guns supplied by Interarms, were repulsed by a Costa Rican army using MI Garands and 0.3in Browning machine guns also purchased from Interarms.

There is a constant supply of arms coming onto the second-hand market as governments need to replace

equipment with more up-to-date weapons. The second-hand market can help defray the cost of this modernisation. It can also help to dispose of weapons to destinations that some governments would not want to be seen supplying. It would have been difficult for the Swedish government to sell 26 Vampire jets to the Trujillo dictatorship in the Dominican Republic; but Interarms acted as the go-between, shipping them initially via New York. It is also said that the US State Department allowed the arms to be transferred through New York to preserve a rough military balance between the Dominican Republic and Venezuela, which had recently purchased 25 Vampires from Britain.

It would be wrong, however, to place too much emphasis on the private arms dealers. The largest component of the arms trade after World War II was that funded by the US Military Assistance Program. An idea of its size and impact can be gained by looking at the market for jet aircraft. The development of the jet engine transformed military aviation, causing the premature obsolescence of piston-engined aircraft. By 1948 the front-line squadrons of the leading military powers were being equipped with first generation jets. As the Cold War developed, arms research and development increased, and the need to re-arm and re-equip Nato forces led to an export boom not only in piston-engined aircraft but also in jets.

Only the British and American industries had the capacity to produce modern jet aircraft, and for some time they enjoyed a monopoly. The Gloster Meteor was the first jet fighter to be sold overseas. It was supplied to the air forces of Australia, Belgium, Denmark, France and the Netherlands as well as to many developing nations, a major order of 100 being supplied to Argentina.

With the Military Assistance Program paying for the purchase of British jets, a rough division of labour took shape. US aircraft like the F-80 went to Nato and the Far East, and British planes were supplied to the Middle East, Africa, South America and the Commonwealth. In the 10 years after 1945 a total of 911 British jets were supplied to the developing world. This period was a golden era for the British aircraft industry, with a total of 1150 Vampires being exported and licenced production of a further 500 taking place in France, Switzerland, India, Australia and Italy. The Canberra bomber also had significant overseas sales and saw service in most areas except the

Above: The rapid advances made by post-war aircraft designers (mainly in the development of the jet engine) and the scaling down of airforces after World War II meant that thousands of piston-engined aircraft became surplus equipment virtually overnight. Here rows and rows of US heavy bombers, although flyable, await the scrap heap.

Left: A De Havilland DH98 Mosquito of the Royal Norwegian Air Force. The Western European nations, whose armed forces had been destroyed early in World War II, relied on British and American material to re-equip.

Middle East and Central America.

The biggest programme of jet fighter exports, however, was that of the United States' F-86 Sabre. A total of 2800 of these aircraft were donated to foreign countries under the Military Aid Program, and a further 2200 were manufactured under licence in Italy, Japan, Canada and Australia. Most deliveries went to Nato, the Far East and other western European nations. In fact, the delivery of 375 Sabres to the RAF from Canada marked the beginning of the end of the duopoly between Britain and the US in the modern combat aircraft market.

The situation was somewhat different in terms of naval rearmament. By 1950 the European nations had resuscitated their ship-building capacity as Denmark, the Netherlands, France and Italy built up their own forces. Ex-Royal Navy carriers were delivered to both the Dutch and French navies in 1948, and the French fleet was buttressed with ex-German and Italian frigates and destroyers.

Between 1945 and 1955, a total of 91 warships were delivered to the developing world, 47 of them from the UK and 38 from the United States. Most deliveries were to Nato countries, or Greece, Turkey, Japan and Taiwan. The majority of the warships were from the reserves of the Royal Navy, or the United States and Royal Canadian navies. In the 10 years to 1955, only one per cent of warship transfers were of newly-built vessels.

In 1955 the world situation was to be transformed by the intervention of the other superpower on the world stage. During the late 1940s and early 1950s, the Soviet Union had equipped the armed forces of those eastern European countries over which it had control; it had allowed the communist Chinese forces to take over large quantities of Japanese equipment in Manchuria immediately after World War II, and the North Korean and Chinese forces that fought in the Korean War were largely equipped with Soviet armaments. By 1952, MiG-15s had seen service in Korea, as had Russian T34 tanks and other arms, which had also been supplied to communist China. But beyond countries under communist rule, major sales had not taken place. This changed dramatically in 1955 when a massive sale of arms took place via Czechoslovakia to Egypt. The Soviet Union, in this one deal, supplied 150 MiG-15s, 40 Il-28 bombers, several hundred tanks, two destroyers and three submarines. What had traditionally been a British market disappeared virtually overnight. This sale opened the floodgates, and within five years nine other countries were in receipt of Soviet arms. Straight competition between the superpowers for political influence in the Third World was now to be the order of the day.

Mike Rossiter

Below: In an attempt to both defray the cost of research and development and contain the spread of communism, the US sold weapons abroad under the Mutual Defense Assistance Act. The planes being unloaded here are for the Turkish Air Force and are being unloaded from the USS *Rendova*.

Sukarno rides the tiger
Revolt and repression in Indonesia

Left: Sukarno, the charismatic leader who dominated Indonesian politics for almost 20 years. Below: Indonesian government troops in M3 light tanks on operations against rebels led by dissident army officers in the mineral-rich island of Sumatra.

One man dominated Indonesian affairs from the late 1940s to the mid-1960s, a man whose revolutionary zeal continued even after he became president of the newly-formed Republic of Indonesia. Sukarno, who was to be the ruler of 100 million people, had been well suited to his earlier role of freedom fighter, a flamboyant man who eloquently exhorted his countrymen to throw off the shackles of Dutch colonial rule. After he formally became president in 1949, however, Sukarno found the problems of ruling an enormous, underdeveloped nation, riven by religious and political feuds, almost impossible to solve and his presidency was marked by constant outbreaks of violence and civil war.

In 1948, even before the final Dutch recognition of Indonesian independence, there had been disputes among the anti-Dutch forces, with the Indonesian Communist Party (PKI) heavily involved.

Tan Malaka, a veteran communist leader of the early 1920s, returned to Indonesia at this critical point and linked up with those who were dissatisfied with Sukarno's leadership. His efforts were rewarded when the PKI had 35 members elected to parliament. Another communist leader, Musso, arrived from Moscow in August 1948 and denounced Sukarno and his colleague Hatta, calling them traitors.

Although originally favouring negotiations with the Dutch, the PKI now openly opposed the government and made strenuous efforts to attract recruits from the army, which was then in the process of being reduced from 400,000 to 150,000 men. Demobilisation on this scale meant that there existed groups of discontented soldiers in various parts of the country which provided fertile ground for vigorous communist propaganda.

Musso toured the country, seeking to foment dissatisfaction and exploiting the grievances of units which were about to be disbanded. Although he realised it was far too soon to contemplate a national coup, the heady propaganda of revolution bore fruit more rapidly than he had expected – or wanted.

In eastern Java the Senopati Division took the law into its own hands at Madiun in September 1948 and occupied the government offices, declaring its own administration. Musso and other communist leaders had no choice but to endorse the action, which gave Sukarno and Hatta the opportunity to accuse the PKI of wanting to overthrow the government. The insurgents were driven out of Madiun and into the mountains of central Java, where they were dealt with ruthlessly by the army, Musso himself being killed in a skirmish.

Comparatively minor though it was, this communist revolt was to cast long shadows over Indonesian politics during the years that followed. The army leaders never forgave the PKI for stabbing them in the back at a time when the bulk of their forces were facing the Dutch. One man in particular, Colonel (later General) Abdul Nasution, chief of staff in central Java, became an implacable foe of the communists, and this deep-seated enmity lingered for years.

Following the final recognition of an independent Indonesia by the Dutch, Sukarno was installed as president in Djakarta in 1949. An era of parliamentary democracy followed until 1957, but from the start the omens were not favourable. Twenty political parties sought election, all gaining seats in parliament. Sukarno himself scorned 'ballot box democracy' as a product of the Western world that was unsuitable for Asia; instead he advocated a one-party system. The biggest party was the Masjumi, a Muslim party, but the PKI had enough elected representatives to form a political base. During the next three years, 7000 PKI cardholders attempted to build up national support by constitutional means, and only in isolated areas were occasional acts of terrorism carried out.

The PKI followed Stalinist policies until 1952, when three young men were elected to top posts within the party: Aidit (aged 30), Lukman (34) and Njoti (28). Under their vigorous leadership there was a concerted drive to organise a mass movement. At

Below: Student mobs in the streets of Djakarta. Crowd action, especially that sponsored by the PKI, always seemed to be an important weapon in Indonesia's fragile politics; but in the end, sheer force, in the shape of military intervention, was to prevail.

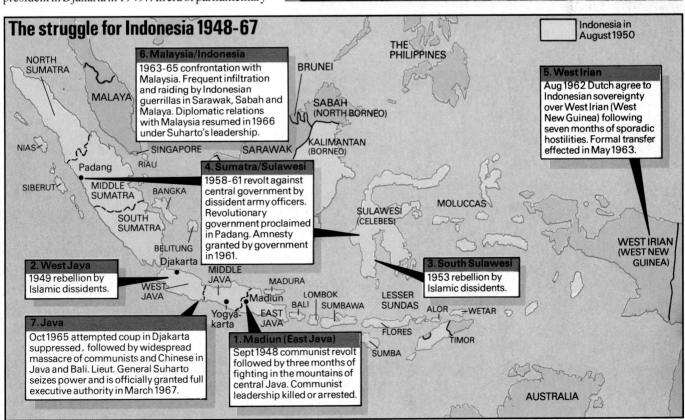

The struggle for Indonesia 1948-67

Indonesia in August 1950

6. Malaysia/Indonesia
1963-65 confrontation with Malaysia. Frequent infiltration and raiding by Indonesian guerrillas in Sarawak, Sabah and Malaya. Diplomatic relations with Malaysia resumed in 1966 under Suharto's leadership.

5. West Irian
Aug 1962 Dutch agree to Indonesian sovereignty over West Irian (West New Guinea) following seven months of sporadic hostilities. Formal transfer effected in May 1963.

4. Sumatra/Sulawesi
1958-61 revolt against central government by dissident army officers. Revolutionary government proclaimed in Padang. Amnesty granted by government in 1961.

3. South Sulawesi
1953 rebellion by Islamic dissidents.

2. West Java
1949 rebellion by Islamic dissidents.

7. Java
Oct 1965 attempted coup in Djakarta suppressed, followed by widespread massacre of communists and Chinese in Java and Bali. Lieut. General Suharto seizes power and is officially granted full executive authority in March 1967.

1. Madiun (East Java)
Sept 1948 communist revolt followed by three months of fighting in the mountains of central Java. Communist leadership killed or arrested.

the same time, Aidit publicly adopted a new line, proclaiming 'Long live Sukarno, Long live PKI', and the communists rapidly came to have considerable influence on government policy. Between 1952 and 1962 the PKI boosted membership to over 2 million; the communists were becoming a powerful force and the generals under Nasution were watching them with suspicion and apprehension.

The early 1950s were a period of jockeying for power between many forces. Problems of centralising the enormous group of islands that made up Indonesia connected religious or political grievances to regionalism; in the central government an uneasy seesaw of influence saw Sukarno and Hatta warily balancing each other. There were Islamic revolts in Java and in southern Sulawesi, while the two great institutionalised bodies in the country, the army and the communist party, were mutually antagonistic.

Sukarno attempted to straddle the three prevailing ideological forces – Islam, Marxism and nationalism – but even his charismatic leadership could not disguise the widening cracks in the political edifice. At times, Hatta seemed intent on establishing a dictatorship with himself as its head, while cabinet government proved ineffective and unstable.

The election of 1955 proved of no avail in breaking the political deadlock, and by 1957 Sukarno had evolved a concept of 'guided democracy', which in effect meant executive rule with consultation of representatives of major political parties and vested interests.

Far from stabilising the political scene, Sukarno's actions stirred up discontent and in various parts of Java mobs took over, incited by the PKI. The crisis was already acute when a motion in the UN General Assembly, calling on the Dutch to resume negotiations with Indonesia about the future of West Irian (Western New Guinea) which remained under Dutch control, failed to obtain the necessary two-thirds majority. This was to be the signal for outbreaks of violence throughout the country.

In 1957 and 1958, severe threats to the regime developed, especially in the islands of Sumatra and Sulawesi. Middle-ranking army officers (mainly colonels) led opposition to the Javanese central government that broke into open warfare, although on a limited scale, and from 1958 until a general agreement in 1961 there was, in effect, a state of civil war. The rebels in Sumatra and Sulawesi hoped for backing from the army as a whole, but this Nasution refused to countenance, and any immediate threat to the authorities in Java was soon dispelled; but the dissidents received some shadowy assistance (how much is not clear) from the USA.

Sukarno showed his skill in surviving politically – and escaping several assassination attempts. He continued to preach his personal philosophy, a mixture of nationalism, Islam and Marxism, and tried to keep all three forces under his control. Despite his eloquence, however, the separate parties never genuinely collaborated with each other. While Sukarno was still the single most important figure, by now the executive was dominated by the army. By the end of 1959, nearly a quarter of the posts were held by serving officers of the armed forces, General Nasution himself combining the posts of Chief of Staff of the Army and Minister of Security.

The economy was in ruins, caused initially by the sudden expulsion of Dutch experts which was fol-

lowed by a decree, issued in November 1959, that forbade foreigners to trade in many parts of Indonesia. By 'foreigners' was meant the Chinese, who had always dominated commercial life in the rural areas. Thousands of Chinese traders were expelled. As the nation floundered economically, the PKI continued to flourish by supporting the president and assiduously building up its following throughout the country.

In 1962 the dispute over West Irian was resolved when the Dutch ceded the territory to Indonesia, finding world opinion was against them. Sukarno had every right, during his National Day speech in August, to proclaim 1962 as 'the year of triumph'. Although his deputy, Dr Subandrio, claimed that West Irian had been won by diplomatic means, supported by groups of PKI volunteers, the army under Major-General Suharto had played a crucial role by persuading the Dutch not to resort to arms. At the height of his triumph, Sukarno felt sufficiently secure to be able to sack Nasution: he disliked being dependent on a 'king-maker', and the more pliable Major-General Yani took over the key post of army chief of staff.

The PKI claimed much of the credit for the West Irian crusade. At a huge rally Sukarno and Aidit openly embraced, and the party boasted that it was now the third largest movement in the communist world. The PKI was at the zenith of its power. Yet, however much he was attracted to Marxism, Sukarno never became a member of the PKI.

Towards the end of 1961 the Malayan prime minister announced plans to form a federation of Malaya and Singapore which would include the British terri-

In September 1965, the army took control in Djakarta (above); there followed the wholesale massacre of communists

in Java and Bali (below)
and detention camps
(right) soon became a part
of the regime of General
Suharto (top right).

grievances. Inevitably the PKI orchestrated the protest and, as a consequence, was frequently expelled from villages. Aidit and other leaders realised that the army's hostility could only be overcome by infiltrating the armed forces, and that propaganda should be directed at the younger officers. Aidit preached communism to junior officers and cadets of all three forces and, by 1965, the PKI had established strong links with the air force. Yet Aidit and his fellow leaders knew that without Sukarno's protection they could not take the last step to achieving power.

The day of reckoning came quicker than anyone expected. In August 1965, Sukarno became seriously ill and the various political groupings began plotting for the succession. PKI leader Aidit, for example, urged the politburo to support certain 'progressive officers' prepared to forestall an army coup. On 30 September 1965, soon to be called 'the Night of the Generals', six senior generals were either murdered in front of their families or taken away to be killed. The only one who escaped was General Nasution, but not before his five-year-old daughter had been killed. But while the conspirators vacillated next day, decisive steps were taken by General Suharto and the coup was crushed within a matter of hours.

PKI involvement, or indeed that of Sukarno, in the coup is impossible to estimate. What can be said is that the army at once used the opportunity to crush the communists. PKI headquarters was stormed and well-known communists were murdered. Sukarno was petitioned to ban the PKI, but he refused. The army thereupon took the law into its own hands and terror raged for weeks; in Middle Java alone, tens of thousands were killed, including Aidit himself. The carnage spread to East Java, Bali and other provinces and it is estimated that between 200,000 and 500,000 perished.

While Sukarno continued to rant and rave about 'crushing Malaysia', General Suharto initiated secret talks with the Malaysian government with a view to ending the costly war. Sukarno's influence dwindled, and once Subandrio had been condemned to death and the political power of the air force was smashed, Sukarno found himself isolated. Suharto was now effectively ruler of Indonesia, the president simply an embarrassment. The struggle to control one of the richest countries in the world had been resolved in favour of a military regime.   **E. D. Smith**

tories of Sarawak and North Borneo (Sabah). In Sukarno's eyes this was a hostile neo-colonial stratagem that threatened to encircle Indonesia. When the state of Malaysia was finally proclaimed in 1963, Sukarno said that his aim was to 'smash Malaysia'. This involved using armed forces stationed along the border between Kalimantan and the territories of Sarawak and Sabah. Initially, the campaign was waged by volunteers, trained and organised for the most part by the PKI, but in time the Indonesian Army took over, confronting elements of the British Army across the border and, eventually, clashing with them.

Unlike the West Irian campaign, Indonesia's opposition to Malaysia excited the hostility of world opinion. Even non-aligned countries showed little or no sympathy for Sukarno. Moreover, the campaign added to the economic problems which were crippling Indonesia and gave rise to a crescendo of

Castro's revolution

How the Rebel Army triumphed in Cuba

On 30 November 1956, while members of the 26th of July Movement fought against the police and the army in the streets of Santiago de Cuba in Cuba's eastern-most province, some leaders, located close to the harbour, anxiously scanned the sea. They knew that Fidel Castro, with 81 men, had sailed in the yacht *Granma* from Tuxpan, Mexico, five days earlier. Castro finally arrived on 2 December – but in the vicinity of another port, Niquero, far away from Santiago de Cuba.

Three days after landing, Castro's men suddenly ran into an Army unit. The combat was short, lasting less than half an hour. And casualties were low, four dead and one wounded. But the guerrilla novices were not only thoroughly defeated, they also panicked and dispersed. The official histories are silent on Castro's military performance in this, the first battle waged by the future Rebel Army, although Ernesto ('Che') Guevara later wrote, somewhat apologetically, that 'Fidel tried in vain to regroup the people in a nearby sugar plantation'.

Two weeks later, helped by reception squads, 22 survivors including Castro met in the Sierra Maestra. The Sierra Maestra is a mountain range that runs along the southern coast of Oriente province. It is about 250km (155 miles) in length and 45km (30 miles) at its widest. The highest elevation is the Pico Turquino which rises to 1960m (6430 feet). The ruggedness and wildness of the Sierra Maestra have been exaggerated – Regis Debray, who visited the Sierra after 1959 and later fought with Guevara in Bolivia, wrote that, compared with the rough Bolivian scene, the Sierra Maestra 'looked like a botanical garden' – but in the 1950s the Sierra Maestra was a very isolated and depopulated area. Most of its 50,000 inhabitants were

Above: A contemporary Cuban poster celebrating the 24th anniversary of Castro's forces shows two of the heroes of the revolution: Castro (right) and Cienfuegos (left).

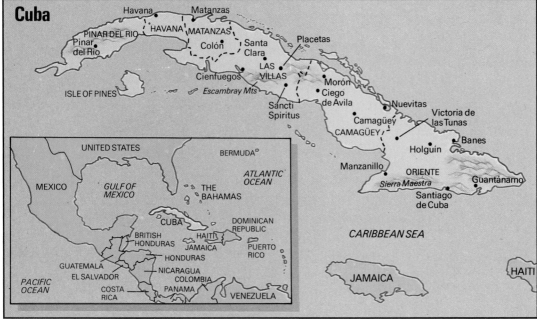

squatters, and there were also quite a number of outlaws. It was in the most inaccessible corner of this isolated region that the 22 survivors hid in the final days of 1956. They had hardly any food, few arms, and suspected every peasant to be an army informer, as Guevara recalled later. There is no conclusive proof that Castro left Mexico with the intention of starting a long guerrilla war. But now that both the uprising and the expedition had failed, the alternatives left were extremely limited. What we do know is that the rebels' next move was to send a representative to Havana to tell the world that Castro was alive – the international press had reported him dead – and to ask for help.

Between 1940 and 1952 Cuba had enjoyed a democratic regime. But on 10 March 1952, Fulgencio Batista overthrew the elected government and two years later secured his election as president – mainly by preventing the participation of any other candidate. Once the politicians had recovered from the shock, fragmented opposition began to emerge. The short, 12-year experience of democracy had not been long enough to make Cubans behave like Western democrats and, as in other Latin American countries, the consensus on the principles of political legitimacy was imperfect. Opposition groups followed a dual strategy: on the one hand they tried peaceful mobilisation of the people behind a campaign to restore democratic government, but on the other hand they engaged in more direct activities to get rid of Batista. On 26 July 1953, in the Moncada assault, Fidel Castro rose to the forefront of those committed to taking the path of violence.

Launched from a farm base near Siboney, against a garrison which had indulged in all-night celebrations, Castro's attack on the Moncada barracks – which housed 1000 government troops – comprised only 111 men. It was an act of open war. Armed with a variety of weapons, including three US army rifles, an old machine gun and six Winchester rifles, Castro's rebel force moved against the garrison at dawn. Yet despite careful planning, the assault force became divided. Loss of synchronisation meant that, while some objectives were achieved, the rebels were eventually forced to retreat under superior enemy fire, having sustained only three deaths and inflicted 19.

The post-assault atrocities inflicted on captured rebels by Batista's troops, and the fact that a band of rebels could launch an attack against the second biggest barracks in Cuba, was to have crucial consequences for the future. For they gave Fidel Castro a political credibility, in that he could justifiably be said to have led an effective attack on a tyrannous regime. Castro was imprisoned for a year, and in 1955 released under an amnesty; he left for Mexico in July, but not before he had laid the foundations for what became the 26th of July Movement (named in memory of the Moncada attack), the political grouping that was to become the basis of his successful military campaign.

Most of the early members of the 26th of July Movement were former members of another group, the Movimiento Nacional Revolucionario, and while Castro trained his small group of guerrillas in Mexico, the representatives in Cuba schemed and plotted. They maintained contact with groups such as the Directorio Revolucionario, and had some involvement with the Havana student riots of 1955 and the sugar workers' strike of December of that year.

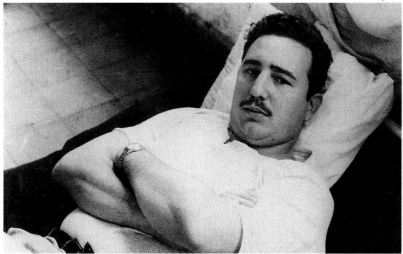

Top: Government troops inspect the pockmarked exterior of the Moncada barracks after the attack by Castro's rebels in July 1953. Above: Castro, without his famous beard, relaxes in detention after the failed Moncada attack.

Right: Cuban President Fulgencio Batista celebrating his victory after he overthrew the government of the day in 1952. His regime lasted for less than seven years.

Sudden encounter

After Fidel Castro and his rebels landed in Cuba, much of their weaponry was accumulated through attacks against Batista's soldiers. In this extract from his reminiscences, Che Guevara recalls an encounter with government troops.

'At dawn on the 22nd [January 1957] we heard a few isolated shots from the direction of the Palma Mocha River and this forced us to maintain even stricter discipline in our lines, to be more cautious and to await the imminent appearance of the enemy....

'At noon we saw a human figure in one of the *bohíos* [peasant huts].... it turned out to be an enemy soldier. Then about six others appeared; some of them left, and three remained in view. We saw that the soldier on guard looked around him, picked a few weeds, put them behind his ears in an attempt at camouflage,

and sat calmly in the shade, his face, clearly visible through the telescopic sight, showing no apprehension. Fidel's opening shot shattered him; he managed only to give a shout, something like "Ay, mi madre!" and fell over dead. The crossfire spread and the soldier's two companions also fell.

'Suddenly I noticed that in the closer *bohío* there was another soldier trying to hide from our fire. Only his legs were visible from my higher position, since the roof of the hut covered his body. I fired at him and missed; the second shot caught the man full in the chest and he fell, leaving his rifle stuck in the ground by the bayonet.

'Covered by Crespo, I reached the house where I saw the body, and I took his bullets, his rifle and a few other belongings. The bullet had struck him full in the chest, probably piercing his heart, and his death had been instantaneous; he already showed the first signs of *rigor mortis*.'

Early in 1956, talks between liberal politicians and an increasingly confident Batista broke down, and the violent revolutionaries benefited from new recruits. Some bombs were set off, and the 26th of July Movement was able to mount an impressive action to coincide with Castro's return in November 1956; two attacks on Santiago were very successful. Nevertheless, the early check to Castro's men after their landing was a profound disappointment.

The arrival of Castro's representative at Havana in 1956 reawakened revolutionary hopes. The highest priority of the activists was now to help the incipient Revolutionary Army of the 26th of July Movement. For this purpose, geographical factors made Santiago de Cuba a vital centre. Fortunately Frank País, who handled the Santiago attacks in November, was well qualified for the arduous and dangerous task of organising 'action groups' to channel supplies and new recruits to the men in the mountains.

Meanwhile, Castro did not stay quiet in the Sierra. On 23 January 1957 a small force of 23 men launched a successful attack against a military garrison. Victory, nevertheless, does not seem to have impressed the Sierra's people very much. Three weeks later the fighting force had been reduced to 18 men. Clearly, the guerrillas badly needed the support of the urban underground, *el llano* ('the rope') as it came to be

Above left: Fidel Castro and brother Raúl (wearing armband) soon after their arrival in the mountains. Above: The remote and overgrown terrain of the Sierra Maestra where Castro's small band of rebels began their campaign against Batista's regime.

Below, far left: Castro's 26th of July movement was not the only movement operating against Batista's regime. Here government troops inspect the bodies of members of Reynol García's rebel group, after their May 1956 attack against the military barracks at Matanzas. The attack was easily repulsed; Batista had trapped García into attacking the barracks by feeding him false information.

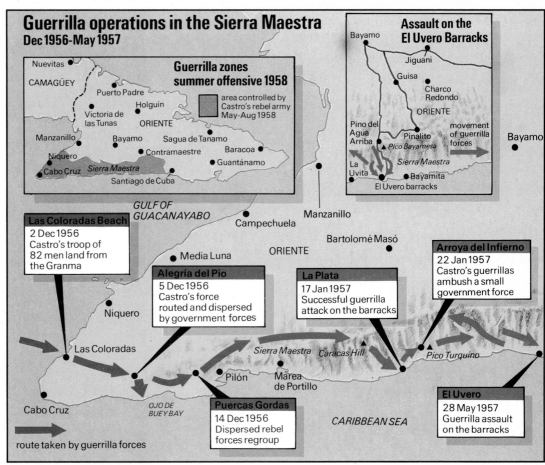

Guerrilla operations in the Sierra Maestra
Dec 1956-May 1957

Guerrilla zones summer offensive 1958

area controlled by Castro's rebel army May-Aug 1958

Assault on the El Uvero Barracks

movement of guerrilla forces

Las Coloradas Beach
2 Dec 1956
Castro's troop of 82 men land from the Granma

Alegría del Pío
5 Dec 1956
Castro's force routed and dispersed by government forces

La Plata
17 Jan 1957
Successful guerrilla attack on the barracks

Arroya del Infierno
22 Jan 1957
Castro's guerrillas ambush a small government force

Puercas Gordas
14 Dec 1956
Dispersed rebel forces regroup

El Uvero
28 May 1957
Guerrilla assault on the barracks

route taken by guerrilla forces

called by Guevara. The guerrillas were in such a desperate situation that the activity and daring of País became critical. He established clandestine lines of communication with the Sierra, sending money, food, clothes and arms; and by February 1957, 50 recruits from the underground were incorporated into the guerrilla force.

This was not the only help given by the underground to the guerrillas. In February 1957, Herbert Matthews was transported from Havana to the Sierra, where he held the interview that put the name of Castro on the front page of the *New York Times*. And, by the same means, Robert Taber arrived in April with the cameras that were to project the image of a Cuban Robin Hood on to the screens of the West. Finally, the

guerrilla dependence on the *llano* at this stage of the struggle is demonstrated by the numbers involved at El Uvero on 28 May 1957 – the battle said by Cuban official histories to be the coming of age of the Rebel Army. Eighty guerrillas took part in this action. Knowing as we do that 50 had arrived from the cities in February, it is obvious that local recruitment, after six months in the Sierra, continued to be minimal.

After El Uvero, the history of Cuba's guerrilla war can be divided into three periods: from El Uvero to the failure of the general strike (April 1958); from April 1958 to the defeat of the government's counter-offensive (May-August 1958); and the final months of 1958, when the two small columns that left the Sierra in August were able to open new fronts in the central

The spit-and-polish of these government police (left) who are guarding a polling station during the elections of 1958 (which were heavily rigged in favour of Batista's candidate) contrasts strongly with the uniforms worn by Castro's guerrillas (right).

provinces and to precipitate the demoralisation and final collapse of Batista's army.

Neither Castro nor the National Directorate of the 26th of July Movement – an imprecise body whose members have never been identified – initially had a clear strategy to defeat Batista. The guerrilla force increased very slowly in numbers and totalled fewer than 200 men by the end of 1957. Cuban revolutionary experience could hardly admit the possibility of a final victory by guerrilla war. The underground had lost its most important leader when País was killed in July 1957, and many fighters in the cities questioned the 'militaristic' style of Castro's leadership. Indeed, the 26th of July Movement had not even taken part in the most well-publicised attack on the Batista regime of 1957. This was the assault on the presidential palace on 13 March by members of the Directorio Revolucionario. The attack was a costly failure (35 rebels died) and in its aftermath the 26th of July Movement received many of the arms that their rivals had concealed. The failure also confirmed the dominance of the 26th of July Movement in the armed struggle.

By the end of 1957, although there were few rebels under arms in Oriente province, they were well established there. They moved at will over much of the countryside and had a good supply network. There

Above: Major Camilo Cienfuegos (centre) who commanded one of the two columns that destroyed Batista's army during late 1958, leads cavalry through the streets of Matanzas.

Below: Civilians scramble for cover in the streets as the rebels engage government troops in an open offensive following news of Batista's flight.

was continual sabotage and bombing in the cities; events were moving in the right direction for the insurgents.

In February 1958 a meeting of the leadership in the Sierra resolved to declare 'total war against tyranny' and called for a general strike. But *llano* leaders overestimated their forces. Repression and workers' apathy brought a bloody defeat. The defeat signalled the end of any influence exercised by the underground over Castro, the Sierra commander. The Revolutionary Army of the 26th of July Movement now came to be known as the Rebel Army. Castro had finally forged the kind of apparatus suited to his style of personal leadership.

Castro's cause was, meanwhile, being given its greatest asset in the gradual collapse into corrupt incompetence of the Cuban government and army. Batista, a former army sergeant, never became a military leader. His successes were due to political shrewdness, manipulative abilities, and corruption. Apparently, he was not at first particularly disturbed by the presence of the small guerrilla band in the Sierra. He personally knew Castro (the brother-in-law of one of his ministers) and, like every other Cuban politician who met Castro before 1959, Batista had not been impressed by him at all. Furthermore, the guerrillas presented a justification for the repressive policies he was implementing during his second term of office.

Unfortunately for the government, high-ranking-army officers also seem to have discovered ways to exploit the guerilla war for their own financial benefit. Supplementary salaries and rations, payola in the acquisition of supplies, and bribes from landowners for the illegal eviction of peasants in the expanded war areas – these were some of the rewards available to those officers who performed short periods of service at the front.

From early 1958, however, and particularly after the declaration of 'total war' by the Sierra leadership, both Batista and his henchmen began to have second thoughts about the result of their policies. There were now four combat fronts, instead of one. Raúl Castro (Fidel's brother) had moved to the north coast with a guerrilla column, while from February 1958, members of the Directorio Revolucionario were operating in the Escambray mountains. And in March 1958 the United States stopped the sale of military supplies. Realising the situation was getting out of hand, the

government decided to exploit the drop in revolutionary morale occasioned by the failure of the general strike and launched a large-scale offensive against the Sierra in May 1958. Thousands of soldiers were mobilised for the operation, 11,000 according to one authority, against Castro's 300 armed guerrillas. But in spite of such a remarkable difference in effectives, the army retreated after two months having suffered heavy casualties and leaving behind hundreds of prisoners.

There is no doubt that the guerrillas fought with distinction, but the endemic corruption in Batista's regime was a major cause of defeat. There is evidence, for example, that the military plans were in Castro's hands before the offensive even began. In this context, it is relevant that Castro issued orders for the organisation of the two small columns that later invaded the central provinces, even before the offensive was over.

The central battle of the campaign took place on 29th June when the 11th battalion, 1000 men strong, was attacked by just 300 guerrillas. The regulars proved unable to sustain the fight against an unseen foe, and their defeat spread panic to the rest of the army. Desertions increased; discipline and communication deteriorated; and even technological advantage was thrown away. At one point, government planes napalmed their own side.

The invasion of the central provinces completed the demoralisation of Batista's army. While officers were involved in conspiracy and corruption, soldiers surrendered without combat. Castro himself has left it on record that, at the end of the war, the Rebel Army had just 1500 men; but it would be wrong to define the revolutionary forces merely as the guerrillas under Castro's command. In the final months of 1958, at least in the three eastern provinces, 'guerrillerism' was a way of life, totally controlling the rural areas. In the other three western provinces, a similar process was developing very fast.

The imposition of the guerrilla regime upon the inhabitants was not always welcomed, but by the summer of 1958 it was certainly effective. Castro had his own newspaper, his own radio station. Eastern Cuba became unsafe for the government; sabotage was at such a pitch that railway timetables could hardly be relied on, while even US-owned sugar mills were often forced to pay a levy per sack to the insurgents.

Camilo Cienfuegos and Che Guevara commanded the two columns that moved onto the offensive in August. By mid-October they had arrived in Las Villas, where they established control over armed groups of communists (who, after staying aloof, were now joining the fight) and of the Directorio Revolucionario. The army was now thoroughly demoralised; at Guisa, for example, Guevara led 200 guerrillas against 5000 troops.

In December, Guevara suddenly struck in central Cuba, taking the communications centre of Placetas. Amid intrigues in Havana, Batista prepared to flee, and his decision was hastened by Guevara's successful assault on the provincial capital of Santa Clara on 28 December.

Batista flew into exile on 1 January, and his regime collapsed at once. Guevara's men arrived in Havana during the night of 1/2 January 1959, and on the 8th Castro himself arrived, having won an astonishing victory against seemingly impossible odds.

Above: Castro (centre) flanked by loyal supporters, prepares to make a victory address after his sudden success and the flight of Batista.

Right: Fidel Castro raises his arm in a victory salute as he acknowledges the praise of jubilant crowds in Santa Clara (where Che Guevara's forces fought one of the biggest actions of the whole campaign) in 1959. Overpage: A huge colour mural of Che Guevara bedecks the side of a building at a rally in Cuba in 1981.

Castro in control

Through strength of will and forceful leadership, Fidel Castro succeeded in overturning a corrupt regime and transforming Cuba into the first communist state in the Western Hemisphere. He was born on 13 August 1927 of middle-class parents and completed his education by graduating in law from the University of Havana in 1950. Castro was active in student politics and was involved in an attempt to overthrow Generalissimo R. L. Trujillo of the Dominican Republic in 1947. After graduating, Castro joined a reformist political group, intending to run for Congress. These hopes were dashed, however, when Fulgencio Batista overthrew the government three months prior to the election scheduled for June 1952.

Castro raised and armed a group of rebels and made an unsuccessful attack on the army garrison at Moncada on 26 July 1953. He was sentenced to 15 years in prison but, as a result of a political amnesty, he was released in 1954 and went to Mexico, where he met Che Guevara, and trained a band of Cuban exiles in guerrilla warfare. On 2 December 1956, with 81 followers, he landed in Cuba and began a campaign that led to victory on 1 January 1959.

The following month Castro formally assumed the presidency and set about introducing wide-ranging reforms. He established friendly relations with the Soviet Union and urged communist revolution throughout Latin America. He railed against American 'imperialism' and confiscated US property. The US replied by breaking off diplomatic links in January 1961 and sponsoring an abortive invasion of Cuba by CIA-trained exiles at the Bay of Pigs three months later. Castro was angered by the Soviet climbdown during the 1962 Cuban missile crisis but has continued to rely on Soviet aid.

With the aid of hindsight it is clear that Castro's victory opened a new stage in Latin-American history. A considerable body of literature is now available for the analysis of the Cuban experience, and there are, broadly, four main conclusions that one can draw. Firstly, it would be a mistake to see the Cuban guerrilla war as an instance of the so-called 'foco' theory – the idea that a small band of trained guerrillas, located in a favourable geographical area, can start a successful revolutionary war against any kind of regime. As has been seen, the guerrillas survived in Cuba because they were given help by the urban underground.

Secondly, the Cuban revolution was not a peasant revolution. With one or two exceptions, at most, the leaders were not peasants, nor had they any kind of peasant background. There is no satisfactory data concerning the followers, but it is persuasive to argue that they approximately reflected Cuban social stratification, with the exception of the upper classes.

Thirdly, the Cuban guerrillas were not explicitly anti-imperialist, or, even less, overtly socialist. From the beginning to the end, Castro made it clear that his political goal was the restoration of the 1940 constitution, and he promised to call elections after a short provisional government. Leaders like Guevara and Raúl Castro undoubtedly nurtured more radical intentions, but since they were under the military command of Fidel Castro, they, like the others, lacked the means to translate their intentions into political influence. There is no evidence that the communists, organised in Cuba under the name of the Socialist Popular Party, made any formal agreement with Castro before 1959. From the spring of 1958 the communists had adopted a dual strategy. One or two leaders went to the Sierra as political representatives, not fighters, while an unknown number of party members joined the guerrillas after the military offensive of 1958 had failed; but none of the fighting guerrilla commanders, as far as is known, was a member of the Socialist Popular Party.

Nevertheless, it does appear that in the final months of the struggle, both in the underground and among the guerrillas, there was a process of increasing radicalisation. Deepening involvement helped to renew revolutionary traditions, and some began to question whether the opportunity to grasp the nationalist and populist ideals cherished by José Martí and the revolutionary generation of the 1930s had not arrived.

Finally, the Cuban experience from 1953 to 1959 can be regarded as the first instance of 'popular revolutionary war' in the Americas – although the term was not used at the time. In the struggle against Batista, Castro applied every means – from negotiations with the church, businessmen, labour leaders, military officers, politicians both in government as well as opposition, and American officials, to terrorism and guerrilla war, including the use of 'front' organisations. But after the Moncada assault, every step taken was coordinated with the cardinal principle of Castro's strategy: to attack. Retreats and concessions were made when circumstances advised, but they were always subordinated to a single and ultimate purpose: to mobilise more resources for the next attack. This aggressive strategy, the most profound of Castro's military precepts, will always create problems for weak and incoherent Latin-American governments. **Andres Suarez**

Key Weapons

US NUCLEAR SUBMARINES

The origins of the nuclear submarine (sub-surface nuclear or SSN) can be traced back to 1939, when preliminary research began in the United States. Even though resources were later switched to development of a nuclear bomb, a small committee that had been given the task of looking at postwar uses for nuclear energy recommended that priority be given to marine propulsion.

Armed with this directive a US Navy team headed by Captain Hyman G. Rickover started work at Oak Ridge, Tennessee, on the development of a nuclear reactor capable of driving a submarine. Their reasoning was that a submarine would benefit most from nuclear propulsion; unlimited power could be generated without atmospheric oxygen, allowing a submarine to run fully submerged for long periods. Rickover used all his formidable powers of persuasion to get the Atomic Energy Commission to go ahead with a prototype reactor, and in August 1951 the US Navy was able to place an order for a hull. The USS *Nautilus* (SSN-571) was laid down at Groton, Connecticut, on 14 June 1952. Such was the drive and enthusiasm generated by Rickover that on 17 January 1955 it was possible to send the historic message, 'Underway on Nuclear Power'.

Apart from her revolutionary power plant, the USS *Nautilus* was very like previous American submarines in layout and equipment. Her reactor generated heat which, through the medium of a heat-exchanger, heated steam to drive a pair of steam turbines. The speed that resulted, 18 knots submerged, was not significantly greater than the German Type XXI U-boats of World War II, but it could be maintained indefinitely instead of in bursts of less than an hour, and there was no need to come to snorkel depth to recharge batteries. To show off her capabilities the *Nautilus* made a 'shakedown' cruise from New London to Puerto Rico, 2557km (1381 nautical miles) in

Previous page: One of the powerful Los Angeles-class submarines, the USS *New York City*, ploughs its way through the sea.
Above: The USS *Nautilus* represented an important advance in undersea weapons technology. Its two nuclear-powered turbines made speeds of 20 knots possible over an almost indefinite period.

Below: The most important part of the modern SSBN – the missile compartment. Here a crewman checks the Polaris missile tubes on the USS *John Adams*.

USS Nautilus

Type Long-range nuclear powered submarine
Complement 105 officers and men
Dimensions Length 98.7m (324ft); beam 8.4m (27ft 8in); draught 6.7m (22ft)
Displacement 3764/4040 tons (surfaced/submerged)

Engine Nuclear-powered twin-shaft steam turbine generating a maximum power output of 15,000shp
Nuclear reactor One S21 submarine thermal reactor

Speed 20/18 knots maximum (surfaced/submerged)

Armament Six 21in torpedo tubes in the bow with a provision for at least 18 torpedoes

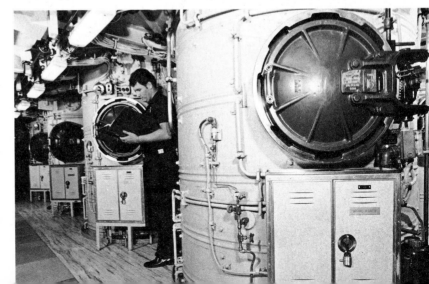

just 90 hours, or an average speed of 16 knots. It was the first time a submarine had maintained such a high submerged speed over a long period, as well as being the longest period spent underwater and the fastest long-distance run ever made by a submarine.

The *Nautilus* went on to establish further records, and to demonstrate the capabilities of nuclear submarines. But there were drawbacks in that the reactor needed constant cooling and the pumps proved very noisy. The next nuclear prototype, the USS *Seawolf* (SSN-575), was given an expensive and complex liquid sodium cooling system. It was never successful, however, and the problem of silencing nuclear submarine machinery remains unsolved even today. The first 'production' nuclear submarines were the four Skate-class vessels, basically improved *Nautilus* types launched in 1957-58.

These six nuclear submarines and the much larger *Triton*, launched in 1958, were modelled on conventional submarines, with a streamlined hull and twin propeller shafts. What was needed was a better hull form, and this was provided by the experimental diesel-electric boat *Albacore*, which began trials in 1959. She had a remarkable whale-shaped hull which proved not only fast but much more manoeuvrable than anything tried before. In fact the *Albacore's* underwater performance proved far better than her surface handling. Combining the pressurised water reactor of the *Nautilus* with the 'teardrop' shape of the *Albacore* produced submarines which could 'fly' underwater. The true submarine was a reality at last.

The first of the new generation were the six Skipjack-class, 3000-tonne boats which were only 76.8m (252 ft) long and yet could attain 30 knots on a single shaft. The Skipjack design also provided the first platform for the Polaris underwater-launched ballis-

Above: USS *Bluefish* is one of America's Sturgeon-class nuclear attack submarines, and is now used primarily in an anti-submarine role.
Left: A rear view of the Lafayette-class SSBN, USS *Simon Bolivar*, during trials in September 1965.

Below: USS *Whale* breaks through the ice pack and surfaces at the North Pole. Such feats illustrate the ability of the modern nuclear-powered submarine to cover vast distances through the world's oceans.

tic missile (SLBM), the hull being lengthened by inserting a section containing 16 launching tubes for the missiles. The five boats treated in this manner became the George Washington class. This amounted to a compromise, in order to get Polaris to sea by 1959, and the George Washingtons were followed by two classes of nuclear ballistic missile submarines (sub-surface ballistic nuclear or SSBNs) properly designed from the keel up, the Ethan Allen and Lafayette classes.

During the 1970s Lafayette-class submarines were fitted with the Poseidon C-3 CLBM, each missile armed with 10 40-kiloton warheads and possessing a range of 4020 km (2500 miles). Although this class was the most advanced of the SSBNs of the 1970s it became clear that it would be unable to house the new long-range Trident system and so the new Ohio-class SSBN was introduced. The first of these massive 18,700-tonne submarines, the *Ohio*, was laid down in April to be followed by the *Michigan* and a further

Opposite page: USS *Skipjack* (above) incorporated the new tear-drop hull, making increased speeds possible while submerged. However, this class is now at the end of its service days and can bear little comparison to the massive Trident-armed Ohio-class vessels like USS *Ohio* (below).

Below: An overhead view of the Los Angeles-class USS *Boston*, with officers carrying out a surface watch. Bottom: the USS *Birmingham* (also Los Angeles-class) thrusts itself from the ocean while on crash-surfacing trials.

eight vessels. The most powerful SSBN in the US Navy it is capable of being armed with the improved Trident II missile, which with a range of 9650 km (6000 miles) can allow Ohio-class submarines to operate from the relative safety of home waters.

Apart from the SSBNs and the six Skipjack-class boats, other non-standard nuclear submarines were constructed. The huge *Triton* (SSN-586) was a 6000-tonne boat driven by two reactors and designed to function as a radar picket vessel giving long-range warning of Soviet air attacks. The *Halibut* (SSGN-587) was intended to fire the Regulus cruise missile, while the *Tullibee* (SSN-597) was an attempt to build a much smaller 'hunter-killer' or anti-submarine submarine. The anti-submarine role was emerging as the most important role for the nuclear submarine (apart from the strategic role of the SSBN), for the SSN is an ideal sonar platform. Below the surface there is no wave-action to hamper the sonar, and thermal layers which 'bounce' sonar beams can simply be avoided by diving below them.

The early SSNs, although formidable craft, were not ideal. Their propulsion plants were very noisy and their diving depth was limited to that of much older diesel-electric types. As the Soviet Navy was building its own SSNs and SSBNs, the US Navy moved towards quieter and deeper-diving boats. Early in 1958 the first of a new type of SSN, the *Thresher* (SSN-593), was ordered. She used a special steel known as High Yield 80 (HY-80), capable of withstanding a pressure of 5625kg per square cm (80,000lbs per square in). This would allow her to dive to depths greater than 457m (1500ft) but improved sonar performance made her slower than the Skipjack class. Her 84.7m (278ft) hull was of larger diameter than those of the earlier vessels so as to enable the machinery to be isolated from the hull; the sound of gearing transmitted through the hull proved

to be the greatest source of noise in all the first-generation SSNs.

The Thresher class submarines were packed with electronics, notably the new BQQ-2 bow sonar, and the number of crew rose to 120, principally to provide maintenance for the electronics and weaponry. In addition to torpedoes, these vessels were armed with Subroc, a missile fired from the torpedo-tube which launched itself clear of the water and then flew a pre-set course. At the end of its trajectory Subroc would re-enter the water and become a nuclear depth-charge.

Up to this point the US Navy's nuclear submarine programme had been an outstanding success, but on 9 April 1963 the *Thresher* went out of control during a test dive and plunged far below her maximum diving depth. All 129 men on board were killed instantly when the 4000-tonne hull imploded. The exact cause of the disaster was never established, but the most likely theory is that a fault caused an automatic shutdown of the reactor, and the auxiliary electric motors could not be restarted in time to bring the submarine under control before she drifted down to her crush-depth. In May 1968 another 'nuke', the *Scorpion* (SSN-589), was lost off the Azores in equally mysterious circumstances. As a result of these two accidents a considerable amount of new design was incorporated in later SSNs.

By 1970 the US Navy had 86 SSNs, but the growing strength of the Soviet Navy in this type

forced the United States to take another step forward. American nuclear submarines were becoming slower because of their increasing size of boats while retaining the S5W reactor and so, to rectify this, the new Los Angeles class were introduced. They were to have a more powerful reactor, the S6G, developing 30,000 horsepower, double that of the S5W.

The lead-boat, the *Los Angeles* (SSN-688), was commissioned in November 1976, and since then a steady trickle have joined her. An eventual total of more than 40 are planned, but construction has been bedevilled by cost overruns and squabbles between the Department of Defense and the shipyards. At one stage the Electric Boat Division of General Dynamics stopped all work on the Los Angeles class until contractual disputes were settled.

The earlier SSNs and SSBNs are now obsolescent. The *Nautilus* herself, in memory of her unique contribution to history, has been laid up as a museum, but the others have been deactivated. Scrapping a nuclear submarine presents many headaches, and current proposals are to seal the reactor compartments and then scuttle the boats, sending them to the 'deep six' where their reactors will deteriorate sufficiently slowly to avoid an environmental hazard.

The Los Angeles class will form the main offensive strength of the US Navy's submarine forces until the end of the century. New weapons are coming forward to supplement the long-range wire-guided Mk 48 torpedo and the nuclear-tipped Mk 45 Astor. The Harpoon anti-ship missile has been adapted for underwater launching as Sub-Harpoon, and a similar method is used to launch Tomahawk cruise missiles. The missile is launched from the torpedo-tube in a canister which floats to the surface at a pre-set angle; the lid then blows off and allows the missile to fire and eject into the atmosphere, where it becomes a normal air-flight weapon.

There are no plans at present to follow the Los Angeles class, but advances in reactor design could result in smaller SSNs. Certainly spiralling costs have made them extremely expensive.

Top: The USS *Daniel Boone* sails seaward off the coast of Puerto Rico. One of the Lafayette class, this submarine illustrates the basic design shape of the modern nuclear submarine. Above: Inside the missile compartment – known as the 'forest' – of the *Daniel Boone*.

USS Los Angeles

Type Nuclear-powered attack submarine
Complement 122 officers and men
Dimensions Length 110m (360ft); beam 10.1m (33ft); draught 9.85m (32ft 4in)
Displacement 6000/6900 tons (surfaced/submerged)

Engine Two General Electric steam turbines on one geared shaft generating a maximum power output of 30,000shp
Nuclear reactor One S6G reactor
Speed 35/30 knots maximum (surfaced/submerged)

Armament Four 21in torpedo tubes amidships for MK48 torpedoes and nuclear-tipped Mk 45 torpedoes, Subroc and Sub-Harpoon missiles, Tomahawk cruise missiles

Cloak and dagger

Undercover operations in the Cold War

The Cold War was, at one level, a propaganda war in which ideology and public pronouncements of long-term aims were in the forefront; but at another level it was a ruthless undercover war in which secret agencies – the KGB and the CIA, for example – resorted to whatever methods were available to further spying and information-gathering, and the East and the West used all the means at their disposal to influence Third World governments.

Technically, perhaps, a positive state of Cold War – a state of tension and hostility short of actual war – did not occur until about 1947-48, when the Western alliance and the Soviet Union and their allies were openly distrustful of each other. But long before the end of World War II the infiltration of the USA and Canada by the Soviet Union had extended to some of the highest administrative positions in each nation. Sometimes this involved positive subversion and treachery, knowingly carried out, while at other

levels key ministers were manipulated into carrying through pro-Soviet policies.

This was, however, only a minor part of Soviet pressure, and only worked because the officials involved found Soviet arguments more persuasive than those of the British, of whom they were extremely wary. In any case, US governing circles rapidly changed their tune when Igor Gouzenko made his revelations about the Soviet spy rings in the West in 1945, and the nature of Soviet ambitions in Europe began to unfold.

The immediate response was to set up organisations to combat subversion, and to help anti-Soviet forces in the eastern European satellites. William Donovan, former director of the Office of Strategic Services (OSS), and Allen Dulles, his wartime subordinate in Europe, urged that the newly-created Central Intelligence Agency (CIA) should become more than a co-ordinator of intelligence from various

Fear of the extent of clandestine foreign power, especially US influence, expressed itself in public protest (top) and defiant political literature (above).

sections; it should also be an instrument to achieve American foreign policy aims by methods not open to diplomats. Thus the National Security Act of 1947 gave the CIA extensive powers, and in the early years of the Cold War proper – the late 1940s and 1950s – these were used to carry out a number of covert operations.

A crucial difference between Soviet undercover agencies and the CIA was that the Russians were able to conduct their Cold War in a relatively low key manner, whereas the brashness and lack of experience of the CIA frequently made it seem more crudely aggressive and thus exposed its errors.

Tom Braden, a former director of several CIA covert operations, declared that Josef Stalin's decision 'to attempt the conquest of western Europe by manipulation turned the CIA into a house of dirty tricks. It was absolutely necessary, but it lasted long after the necessity had gone.' To some extent there was a panic reaction to what seemed to be a threat by the USSR to overrun the whole of Europe. That threat seemed real enough, especially after the Russians blockaded West Berlin in 1948. So many covert operations were launched that it is doubtful whether the CIA was ever able adequately to monitor them.

Early on in the Cold War the CIA placed agents inside Soviet-controlled territory with the aim of inciting revolt, but it was quickly realised that this policy was not justified by results. The CIA found that far better intelligence could be gained, with fewer losses, by establishing contacts with emigré groups in western Europe and the USA.

Taking the fight to the enemy was an important part of CIA operations, and propaganda was an essential element. The Americans delivered huge quantities of printed propaganda by balloons. Old-fashioned as these tactics might seem, they angered the Russians and were loudly denounced.

Meanwhile the Russians were busy organising a concerted effort in western Europe to subvert key officials to their cause. To find the huge sums of money required, it had earlier been decided to search for German securities that could provide funds. A special Red Army intelligence unit was sent into the vaults of the Reichsbank after the fall of Berlin and, it is believed, removed German securities worth some £30 million. These were smuggled out of Berlin into East Germany and eventually sent to New York, almost certainly with the object of financing Cold War activities.

After the events of 1948-49 – the communist takeover in Czechoslovakia and the Berlin blockade – the CIA became even more active, subsidising labour unions and political parties in western Europe, especially in Germany. In these postwar years the CIA were greatly aided by the surrender to American military intelligence of extensive dossiers on the USSR collected by General Reinhard Gehlen, director of the Intelligence branch of the OKH in Nazi Germany. So valuable was this information that Gehlen was almost able to dictate his own terms for collaboration. Soon he was organising an intelligence agency for the CIA in West Germany for as much as $5 million a year. This operation continued until 1955 when Gehlen became Director of the newly constituted West German Federal Intelligence Service.

Agents undercover

At first Gehlen scored some astonishing successes, managing to infiltrate one of his own agents, Walter Gramasch, into the vital post of Director of the Department of Fleets and Harbours in East Germany. For seven years Gramasch sent Gehlen valuable top secret information. In the end, however, Gehlen overreached himself and, by trying to extend his organisation deep into Soviet territory, he was himself infiltrated.

Radio propaganda warfare was launched by the CIA in the early 1950s through the creation of Radio Free Europe, aimed at the Soviet satellites, and Radio Liberty, beamed at the USSR itself. Some of this broadcasting was a crude invitation to revolt, but it was considerably toned down after the failure of the Hungarian uprising of 1956, when the radio networks seemed to promise imminent help for the insurgents although none was forthcoming.

Of course, all the Western powers had their own undercover agencies able to launch offensive as well

Above: Ex-Nazi Reinhard Gehlen collaborated with the CIA against the USSR and led the West German intelligence service. Far right top: Soviet officials at a press conference complain about US 'spy' balloons which had been launched into USSR airspace. Right: The clandestine operation in which Commander Lionel Crabb, a British naval officer, disappeared made headline news in 1956.

Both East and West have continually struggled to gain footholds of influence in the Third World by providing such things as military aid and training, and Vietnam was an obvious theatre for such policies. Bottom right: US teams train South Vietnamese Rangers in the 1960s. Bottom left: A Soviet SAM-2 missile in North Vietnam.

as defensive operations. The British, however, had had an embarrassing experience during the visit of Soviet leaders Nikolai Bulganin and Nikita Khrushchev to Britain aboard the cruiser *Ordzonikidze* in 1956. Commander Lionel 'Buster' Crabb, one of the Royal Navy's most experienced divers, was sent on a secret mission in Portsmouth Harbour – believed to be an underwater inspection of the cruiser. He never returned and the Russians let it be known they knew all about the operation. A parliamentary storm resulted in the usual denials that Crabb had been operating on behalf of British intelligence, but shortly afterwards there occurred a major shake-up in Britain's security and intelligence services.

The undercover Cold War waged in Europe was soon to be dwarfed by the war waged in the newly independent nations of the Third World during the late 1950s and early 1960s. Here, the Soviet Union could hope to extend its influence by backing various nationalist groups and by extending military and civil

aid. In 1955, the first big delivery of Soviet arms to Egypt signalled a new broadening of Russian aims – they were now prepared to invest heavily in nationalist politics throughout the developing world.

With both Great Britain and France having vested interests in many former colonies, and with both Soviet and American influences at work, the instability of many regimes was magnified, while in others the background to politics became a complex web in which local ambitions were yoked to global concerns.

Vested interests

In Indonesia, for example, Sukarno was trying to establish a unitary state by juggling the power of the Communist Party, the Muslims, the nationalists and the army. Indonesia, one of the richest nations in the world in terms of mineral wealth, would have been a great prize for either East or West. Sukarno faced various secessionist or anti-governmental insurrections, the most notable being that led by army officers in Sumatra, the island most wealthy in mineral resources; there is evidence that this insurrection was backed by the CIA, which also seems to have kept close links with the army leadership as a whole. The Soviet Union and communist China were obviously anxious to extend their influence, and the Indonesian Communist Party carefully followed a Moscow line of cooperation with 'bourgeois nationalism'. In 1960, Indonesia received a large arms shipment from the USSR, and in 1965 Sukarno accepted 100,000 rifles from China that were intended to arm a 'Fifth Force' militia, which would have proved a counterweight to the army. These manoeuvres were, however, all overborne by the events of 1965-66, when the aftermath of what appears to have been a bungled coup led to the mass murder of communists all over Indonesia.

Attempts to destabilise regimes, to increase pressure or influence, to bring to power a government favourable to one of the superpowers – this occurred all over the world, and naturally led to inconsistency and compromise: to a democratic America claiming to uphold freedom while supporting brutal dictatorships, or to a supposedly socialist Soviet Union supporting small tyrannical elites. But the undercover Cold War, the fight for power and influence, was perhaps bound to lead to such hypocrisy.

Richard Deacon

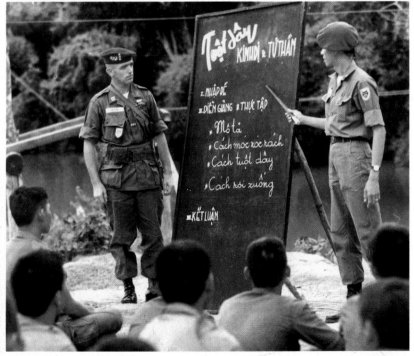

Spy fever

State secrets, espionage and treachery

As the world became ever more sharply divided between East and West from the late 1940s, so the need grew for each side to know what the other was doing militarily, scientifically and politically. The Soviet government invested enormous resources in expanding its foreign intelligence work and the Western powers soon followed suit.

The defection of Igor Gouzenko, a Soviet cypher clerk, in Ottawa in 1945 was the first major event to alert Western governments to the extent of Soviet espionage. Then the defection of Guy Burgess and Donald Maclean from the British foreign service in 1951 revealed how deeply Western institutions could be penetrated by enemy agents. But the Canadian spy network had been concerned primarily with atomic secrets, and Burgess and Maclean appeared to be special cases, the ideologically-motivated products of the political and economic crisis in Britain in the 1930s. In 1957, however, the world learnt of the first really professional Soviet spy when 'Martin Collins' was arrested in an eighth-floor room in a shabby hotel on 28th Street in New York.

'Martin Collins' was also known in Brooklyn as 'Emil Goldfus', an artist, but the name under which he was later tried was Rudolf Ivanovich Abel. He held the rank of colonel in the KGB, the Soviet security service. (It was learnt only much later that Abel had been born in the north of England and that his original name was William Fischer. He had emigrated with his father to Russia in 1921.)

Above: A Lockheed U-2 long range reconnaissance aircraft in flight. It was from such an aircraft that pilot Francis Gary Powers photographed Soviet installations while flying through USSR airspace in 1960. Right: Powers gives evidence during his trial for espionage in Moscow.

Abel was an 'illegal' Russian spy, as distinct from those operating 'legally' under cover of a diplomatic mission. He was in fact the 'resident' of the Russians' illegal network in the United States, responsible for planning and directing the work of numerous agents, for handling the finances, and for maintaining radio communication with Moscow. Abel was a spymaster and a master spy. When he was arrested by the FBI in June 1957 he had been operating undetected since 1948. He might have remained undetected to this day if Moscow had not sent him as assistant an utterly unsuitable and unstable Soviet-trained Finn, Reino Hayhanen, who defected to the Americans in Paris in 1957 and revealed Abel's identity.

It had taken many years to prepare Abel for his post

Right: The twisted wreckage of the American U-2, which crashed after it was hit by a missile while flying over a Soviet airbase. Soviet citizens flocked to see it displayed while Powers was on trial.

Below: Rudolf Abel, the Russian master-spy who operated a spy-ring from his Brooklyn attic for almost 10 years before he was discovered.

and to install him and his equipment in his attic room in New York. He had been recruited into the KGB in 1927 and, with his faultless English and German and fluent Russian, he was clearly cut out for work abroad. When the Russians started to plan the expansion of their spy network in the United States they chose Abel for the New York job. In 1947 he was provided with a new identity, and as 'Andrew Kayotis' he slipped into a displaced persons' camp in Germany. From there he emigrated to Canada, and in 1948 he crossed into the United States and settled down to live quietly as 'Martin Collins' and 'Emil Goldfus', owner of an art-photography studio in Brooklyn. He had a few friends and many acquaintances, all of whom spoke well of him. Nobody suspected what his real occupation was.

Abel admitted nothing after his arrest, but the contents of his flat gave him away. They included a powerful short-wave radio, a cypher pad for sending coded messages, microfilms hidden in hollow pencils, and large sums of money. Apart from that, Abel's behaviour under interrogation and in court amounted to an admission of guilt. He made no serious protest, politely rejecting an invitation to be 'turned', and gave nothing away. He was found guilty of spying and sentenced to 30 years in prison. But he served less than five years of his sentence: in February 1962 he was exchanged for the American U-2 pilot Francis Gary Powers and returned to an honourable retirement in Moscow.

The exchange of Abel for Powers was a very unequal deal.

Abel was undoubtedly a key man in Russia's spy network; Powers was a mere cog in the American intelligence-gathering machine. He was no spy in the usual sense, and he had no training in spying. He was simply a pilot, and his task was to fly one of the specially designed U-2 reconnaissance planes across the Soviet Union. All Powers was expected to do was to keep his plane on course and, at the right times, to switch on the battery of cameras fixed beneath the plane's fuselage. The U-2 programme applied modern technology to the business of spying.

The U-2 reconnaissance flights began in 1956 and continued for four years without a hitch. But on 1 May 1960, the automatic pilot mechanism on Powers' plane malfunctioned and Powers decided to fly it manually. Approaching Sverdlovsk, site of an air force base, he switched on the cameras. As he flew over the base the aircraft was hit by a missile. Unable to reach his destruct button, Powers bailed out, landing 32km (20 miles) from Sverdlovsk. He was soon captured. The aircraft crashed to the ground but did not burn up. Nor did Powers make use of the poison capsule with which he had been provided for use in the event of his being tortured. Powers was tried and sentenced to 10 years' detention, but he served less than two before being exchanged for Abel. The affair marked the end of the U-2 flights, which were soon superseded by flights of unmanned satellites carrying out round-the-clock photo-reconnaissance.

Reasons for treachery

The year 1961 was a very bad one for the British security services, still shaken by the flight of Burgess and Maclean to Moscow 10 years before. It saw the exposure of four major Soviet agents operating in Britain: Gordon Lonsdale, Peter Kroger and Harry Houghton (known as the 'Navy Spy Ring') and George Blake. Each spied for Russia in his own way; each had his own reason for treachery; each illustrated a different type of spy.

When George Blake was arrested in 1961 he had been working for the Russians for 10 years from within the British intelligence service. By then he had done immense damage, revealing to the Russians the identity of British agents working in Germany and east of the Iron Curtain, and the structure of the British service. He was exposed by another agent in Germany and by a leading Polish security officer who defected to the West in 1961.

Blake's motives were never clearly established. Prime Minister Harold Macmillan said after Blake's conviction: 'Blake received no money for his services. He was never at any time a member of the Communist Party or any of its affiliated organisations. What he did was done as the result of a conversion to a genuine belief in the communist system.' The 'conversion' appears to have taken place when Blake was a prisoner of the North Koreans in 1951.

Blake was an example of the most difficult type of spy to uncover – the man who has experienced an intellectual or emotional conversion for no apparent reason and with no external signs. He was sentenced to 42 years in prison. Just how valuable he was considered by his Russian masters was revealed in October 1966 when he escaped from Wormwood Scrubs prison and later reappeared in Moscow.

Gordon Lonsdale, whose real name is said to be Konon Molody, was a very different case. He was an

Above: Leading members of Congress are briefed about the U-2 affair in September 1960. Secretary of State Christian Herter (left) and the Director of the CIA, Allen Dulles (third from left) wait for proceedings to begin.

Left: Kim Philby, the third man in the Burgess-Maclean affair, disappeared from his flat in Beirut in January 1963 and turned up in Russia. For two decades he had been a Soviet agent.

Left: George Blake, the British traitor who was spirited away from Wormwood Scrubs by the Russians in 1966.

Right: Colonel Oleg Penkovsky (left) provided the West with valuable Soviet military information prior to his arrest in 1962. This photograph shows him in the dock of the Soviet Supreme Court during his trial for spying.

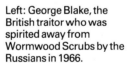

'illegal', like Rudolf Abel, for whom he worked briefly in the United States. According to his own account Lonsdale was born in Canada, returned to Europe in 1932, fought in the Polish and then the Russian resistance to the Germans, and settled in Moscow after the war, where he was trained as a military intelligence officer. In 1954, armed with a Canadian passport in the name of Gordon Arnold Lonsdale, he slipped across the border into the United States, from where he sailed to Britain and set himself up as a businessman in London where he operated unnoticed for five years.

New names and new identities

Lonsdale worked in collaboration with two other Soviet agents, Peter Kroger and his wife Helen, more correctly known as Morris and Lona Cohen, both of whom were convinced communists who had been forced to flee from the United States in 1950 when the Rosenberg atomic spy-ring was exposed. Kroger was the son of Russian-Jewish immigrants to the United States and made no secret of his commitment to communism. He and his wife appear to have been recruited into the Russian intelligence service in the 1940s. To re-establish themselves in Europe they had to acquire a new identity. In Paris they obtained false birth certificates and marriage lines and, as Peter and Helen Kroger, entered Britain and settled quietly in the suburbs of London.

As a cover for his espionage work Kroger set himself up as an antiquarian bookseller. At the same time he turned his suburban home into what the police described as 'the hub and the bank of the spy-ring'. A regular visitor to the Kroger home was Gordon Lonsdale, and it was he who led the police to the Krogers. Lonsdale was sentenced to 25 years in prison, while the Krogers were given 20 years each. But the Krogers were later exchanged for an English college teacher, Gerald Brooke, who had been arrested for distributing anti-communist literature in Russia – another very unequal exchange. Lonsdale also served only a few years of his sentence: he was exchanged for 'businessman' Greville Wynne in 1964.

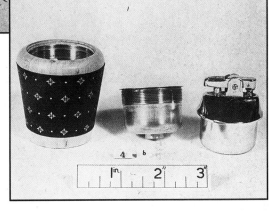

Above: This Soviet photograph claims to show an American diplomat collecting secret information in Moscow, purportedly left there by top Soviet official Colonel Oleg Penkovsky. Top right: Peter and Helen Kroger leave Heathrow for the Soviet Union, where they were exchanged for Briton Gerald Brooke. Right and far right: Two cigarette lighters, with secret recesses, used by Soviet agents.

Along with Lonsdale, the professional 'illegal', and the Krogers, committed amateurs, a very different kind of spy was sentenced: a British citizen, Harry Houghton. He was motivated by loyalty to no-one, and to no idea beyond his own personal gain. Houghton was a clerk in the British Navy who had exposed himself to blackmail while serving in the British embassy in Warsaw. After returning to England and obtaining a job in the Underwater Weapons Establishment at Portland naval base he was approached by agents of Polish intelligence and urged, with threats, to provide them with secret information about anti-submarine devices. In 1960 Houghton was transferred to Russian control and to Lonsdale, a move which led to the end of the spy-ring. Lonsdale was arrested along with Houghton and his girlfriend, Ethel Gee, as they were handing over information at Waterloo station in London. Houghton and Gee each received 15 years in prison.

The 'third man'

The experience of 1961 showed that the Russians found it relatively easy to infiltrate spies into Western countries. Western intelligence agencies had much less success in their efforts to penetrate the security-conscious communist world, however. But in 1962 there was arrested in Russia a man who was probably the highest ranking agent ever to operate within the Soviet system. He was Colonel Oleg Penkovsky who, from April 1961 to August 1962, provided Britain and the West with invaluable intelligence about Soviet military capacity and plans. Penkovsky was, like George Blake, a 'loner' who, despite his high rank, was disillusioned with the Soviet system and volunteered his services to the West (although it has since been suggested that he was in fact a double agent). He was tried by the Soviet Supreme Court in May 1963 and sentenced to death.

Whatever satisfaction the British security services could derive from the Penkovsky affair was offset by the report that on 23 January 1963 H.A.R. ('Kim') Philby, long suspected of having been the 'third man' in the Burgess-Maclean affair, had disappeared from his home in Beirut. Later in the year Russia announced that Philby had been granted asylum, and the British government confirmed that it knew Philby had long been a Soviet agent. The reverberations from those events on the British security services continue to this day.

David Floyd

Left: Iranian demonstrators burn an effigy of a CIA agent. Constant rumours of CIA intrigue in the politics of Iran made the agency an easy target for resentment.

CIA

The shadowy role of the US intelligence service

Every country that aspires to influence world events maintains an agency which gathers and assesses information on the military and economic potential and intentions of possible enemies. No other agency, though, has been so large and so visible as the US Central Intelligence Agency (CIA).

Henry L. Stimson, US Secretary of State from 1929 to 1933, once said about espionage, 'Gentlemen do not read each other's mail.' He would have been horrified at events 30 years later. In 1960 a U-2 spy plane was shot down over Soviet territory, causing the cancellation of a summit meeting between President Dwight D. Eisenhower and Nikita Khrushchev; and in 1961 John F. Kennedy, newly inaugurated, was acutely embarrassed over the abortive Bay of Pigs invasion in Cuba. Within a period of 12 months the US security service – an allegedly secret organisation – had publicly discomfited its own government in an unprecedented manner.

How had things come to such a pass? In many people's mind was the suspicion that at the heart of the US security apparatus was a rogue agency, at best temporarily out of control, at worst, beyond accountability. This explanation, however, was only partially true.

The CIA was set up under the National Security Act in 1947. Its origins, and those of many of its personnel, lay in the Office of Strategic Services (OSS) created in World War II. Modelled on Britain's Special Operations Executive (SOE) and largely created by William Joseph 'Wild Bill' Donovan, OSS had carried out the functions of spying behind enemy lines, aiding resistance movements and engaging in sabotage operations. Although OSS was wound down in 1945, there were pressures to maintain an intelligence apparatus, pressures which rapidly increased in the early stages of the Cold War. Many of the ex-OSS operatives were conscious of a new role for the US to play as the dominant world power. Many viewed the bombing of Pearl Harbor in 1941 as the result of intelligence failures and were determined that nothing similar should happen to the United States again.

The legislation of 1947 envisaged that the CIA would coordinate and evaluate intelligence. Its main function was to take material from the military intelligence organisations and other security agencies and evaluate it for the National Security Council, itself set up by the 1947 act.

Covert action was the responsibility of an organisation called the Office of Policy Coordination, headed by former OSS official, Frank Wisner. The Office of

Left: Two refugees from Czechoslovakia broadcast to their families behind the Iron Curtain using the Radio Free Europe network.

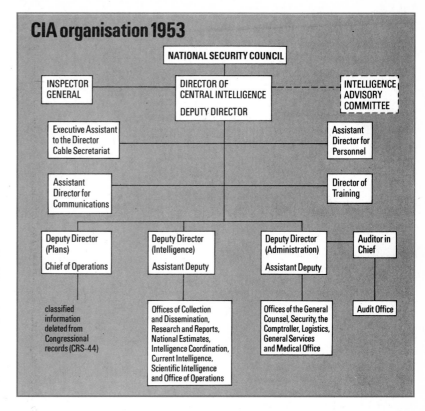

CIA organisation 1953

```
                        NATIONAL SECURITY COUNCIL

  INSPECTOR              DIRECTOR OF                      INTELLIGENCE
  GENERAL                CENTRAL INTELLIGENCE             ADVISORY
                         DEPUTY DIRECTOR                  COMMITTEE

            Executive Assistant                      Assistant
            to the Director                          Director for
            Cable Secretariat                        Personnel

            Assistant                                Director of
            Director for                             Training
            Communications

  Deputy Director    Deputy Director     Deputy Director      Auditor in
  (Plans)            (Intelligence)      (Administration)     Chief

  Chief of Operations Assistant Deputy   Assistant Deputy

  classified          Offices of Collection   Offices of the General   Audit Office
  information         and Dissemination,      Counsel, Security, the
  deleted from        Research and Reports,   Comptroller, Logistics,
  Congressional       National Estimates,     General Services
  records (CRS-44)    Intelligence Coordination, and Medical Office
                      Current Intelligence,
                      Scientific Intelligence
                      and Office of Operations
```

Policy Coordination was attached to the CIA, but Wisner reported directly to the Secretaries of State and Defense. A similar organisation, the Office of Special Operations, was charged with covert intelligence gathering and espionage. It did not take long for criticisms of the CIA to emerge, bringing pressure for change. The CIA did not, it was felt, deliver coordinated national intelligence estimates in the way it was supposed to. The surprise invasion of South Korea by the communist North in 1950 looked to some almost like another Pearl Harbor, and the intelligence community was reformed by General Bedell Smith, Eisenhower's chief of staff in World War II.

The two separate organisations, the Offices of Policy Coordination and Special Operations, were merged within the CIA to form the Directorate of Plans. This reorganisation then meant that intelligence assessment and analysis and covert action were carried out in the one agency. Yet the reorganisation solved nothing. Within the CIA there were now two virtually separate organisations, and the Directorate of Plans rapidly assumed the ascendancy, achieving an autonomy that was to lead to some highly questionable operations.

The reorganised CIA grew rapidly. In 1950 there

Below: Left-wing demonstrations on the Champs Elysées in Paris in 1948. The French Communist Party was supported by about 25 per cent of the electorate, and growing communist influence in Europe during the 1940s led the CIA to fund social democratic groups in an attempt to provide left-of-centre alternatives to communism.

were approximately 5000 employees; over the next five years this grew to 15,000, not including thousands of people who worked, sometimes unwittingly, for the agency in proprietary companies like Air America.

The Agency's budget also started to grow, with the covert operations being mainly responsible. It is estimated nowadays that about two thirds of the total budget and manpower of the CIA is earmarked for the Directorate of Plans and associated support operations. Only about 20 per cent of career employees, using less than 10 per cent of the budget, work on intelligence analysis and information processing.

Between 1947 and the reorganisation of 1951, the wide spectrum of activities engaged in by the CIA began to be established. The most important area of operations was Europe, and many assignments were carried out by former OSS staff. Some operations were disastrous, while others were more successful. The unsuccessful ones were, perhaps, those most heavily influenced by wartime operations. It seemed as though the running of agents and partisan organisations in enemy-occupied territory was too deep-rooted in many operatives, and they automatically applied it regardless of the situation. Such operations were to be tried against the Soviet Union, and subsequently China. The myth of enslaved populations, awaiting a signal to rise and free themselves, became a scenario that was applied uncritically around the globe, from the Balkans to the Caribbean.

In the late 1940s and early 1950s efforts were made to establish guerrilla operations in the Ukraine and Albania, a policy that British secret agencies had already initiated. Groups of exiles, many with links to the old pre-war right-wing regimes, were combed for volunteers. After a period of training they were sent secretly, either landing from submarines or parachuting into the countries concerned to establish resistance movements. In his memoirs, Kim Philby claims to have aided the interception of most of these spies by the communist authorities. Whether he did or not, they were never heard from again.

A similar operation was tried in Poland in the early 1950s and was even less successful, because by now the opposition had developed a more subtle response. Agents sent into Poland reported that prospects were good, and the CIA was encouraged to send other agents to aid what was claimed to be a growing movement of resistance. So more agents were deployed, as were the massive amounts of currency and gold that were also requested. In fact, these agents had been 'turned' and were working for the communists. The result was that large sums of money were transmitted by the CIA directly into the hands of the Polish counter-espionage service.

Operations in Europe were not confined to subverting the communist bloc, however. Perhaps the CIA's most successful operation involved bolstering social democratic movements in western Europe, isolating the communist-influenced popular organisations. Money was poured into non-communist political parties, notably in Italy and France, where communist parties possessed the electoral support needed to have a real chance of forming a government. Efforts were made to create social-democratic union confederations, in opposition to the Communist Party World Federation of Trade Unions. Youth organisations and student unions were given funding, and many of their leading members were encouraged to set up alternative organisations.

Monetary influence

Tom Braden, who was in charge of the CIA's International Organisations Division from 1950 to 1954, said: 'It was my idea to give the $15,000 to Irving Brown of the American Federation of Labor. He needed it to pay off his strong-arm squads in Mediterranean ports . . . . I went to Detroit one morning and gave Walter Reuther [the US labor leader] $50,000. The money was mostly spent in West Germany to bolster labor unions there.' In addition all sorts of cultural activities were also funded.

These activities should not be dismissed. They had a real and lasting impact on the politics of Europe, which survived their exposure in the late 1960s and 1970s. Many political parties and international organisations owe their existence to the Cold War operations of the CIA in the 1940s and 1950s.

Success in the traditional spying field eluded the organisation, however, and so far as is known, intelligence operations against the Soviet Union were of little value. Perhaps the greatest coup of the period was acquiring the transcript of Khrushchev's 'secret' speech at the Communist Party Congress of 1956 in which he roundly denounced Josef Stalin. The wide publicity that the speech achieved in the Western press had a considerable effect on communist parties outside Russia. Yet the long-term failure of traditional espionage can be gauged by the need to develop alternative forms of intelligence gathering, most notably the U-2 spy plane, followed by the SR-71. This programme of photographic reconnaissance, developed by the Science and Technology Directorate of the CIA, supplied more information about China, the Soviet Union and Cuba than was ever discovered by covert operations.

Yet covert operations blossomed, and the CIA was active around the globe. In 1953, in the Middle East, the Shah of Iran was installed by the CIA, using plans

prepared originally by the British MI6, when a military coup resulted in the overthrow of Prime Minister Mohammed Mossadegh. A successful coup was also managed in Guatemala in 1954.

In Asia, support operations were set up to enable Tibetan guerrillas to harass the communist Chinese. Air America planes were soon being used in Laos to bypass the provisions of the 1954 ceasefire agreement, which would eventually lead to the CIA's biggest operation, a clandestine war involving a secret army of 30,000 hill tribesmen, and would give Air America, the CIA's leading proprietary airline, the status of one of the largest airlines in the world.

By 1958 the CIA had embarked on a major operation to destabilise Sukarno's government in Indonesia. Headed by Frank Wisner, then Deputy Director of Plans, it involved supporting tens of thousands of rebels with air drops and beach landings, backed up by 15 B-26 bombers supplied by the US Air Force. (These same were later to be used at the Bay of Pigs.) Training bases were set up in the Philippines, and an old airfield was reopened on an island in the southwest Pacific. The Indonesian government constantly alleged US backing for the rebellion, but President Eisenhower responded at a press conference: 'Our policy is one of careful neutrality and

Top: Indonesian rebels on Sumatra with a US-supplied recoilless rifle. The CIA were intent on destabilising President Sukarno's regime. Right: Mohammed Mossadegh, Prime Minister of Iran, who was toppled by a coup backed by the CIA in 1953.

proper deportment all the way through, so as not to take sides where it is not our business.'

Three weeks later, an Air America pilot was shot down after strafing Ambon Island airstrip from a B-26. The pilot, Allen Pope, had concealed, against orders, enough documentation not only to link him to Air America, but also to the US Air Force, for which he had once flown and whose bases he constantly used. Immediately, the embarrassed US government felt compelled to lift an embargo on rice sales to Indonesia and a $1 million arms sale was allowed to go through. Pope was tried but kept on ice for the good behaviour of the US government. Wisner was fired.

The fragility of 'plausible deniability' – the idea that if an operation came unstuck the US government could deny all knowledge of it – was demonstrated again over the U-2 incident. The existence of the aircraft was a secret until one came down over Sverdlovsk in 1960. Richard Bissell, Director of Plans, gambled that the pilot would have been killed in the crash, and stuck to the story that the aircraft was a weather plane from Turkey that had strayed off course; and Eisenhower, too, lied. Unfortunately for the CIA, however, the pilot had survived and the truth came out. Yet Bissell remained in place, and went on to play a major role in the Bay of Pigs fiasco.

There was, perhaps, a lack of hard-headed realism in the intelligence community. Men like Wisner and Bissell in the covert services were just too plausible. They were also too security conscious to allow their plans and analyses to be scrutinised by people with other views and better judgement. But they were not out of control. All operations that the CIA launched and supported relied on the cooperation of the rest of the intelligence community, and of the armed services. Plans were approved regularly by the National Security Council and often by the president himself. And certainly, in the years preceding the Bay of Pigs, incidents had occurred which meant that no administration could be ignorant of the extent of covert operations. The image of an agency beyond responsibility, constructed after the Bay of Pigs, must be modified to recognise that the CIA was a creature of the various administrations it served; it was part of them and was used by them. It was, in fact, allowed to do almost anything – except get found out.

Mike Rossiter

Above: Demonstrators crowd a street in Iran in 1953 during the civil unrest surrounding the coup which greatly increased the power of the Shah. Right: An Air America transport aircraft in Vietnam. Air America was a proprietary company of the CIA and gave the agency a wide-ranging logistic capacity.

The Bay of Pigs

Fiasco and confusion in Cuba

'You have to make up your mind that you are going to have an intelligence agency and protect it as such, and shut your eyes some and take what is coming.' Thus Senator John Stennis, Chairman of the Joint Senate Committee for CIA Oversight, described the attitude of successive American administrations to their intelligence agency, and in particular the circumstances that led to the disastrously bungled attempt to overthrow the newly established revolutionary regime of Fidel Castro in Cuba – the Bay of Pigs operation.

The invasion at the Bay of Pigs was not the first time that the Central Intelligence Agency (CIA) had intervened in Latin America to overthrow a government. In 1954 the removal of Jacobo Arbenz Guzmán in Guatemala had been successfully engineered using covert methods. A propaganda operation had been established, using a broadcast transmitter based in Honduras. The CIA had supplied P-47 fighters to a mixed force of US mercenaries and Guatemalan exiles, and had created the impression that the insurgents were disaffected members of the Guatemalan armed forces. So successful was this ploy that the Guatemalan government was not prepared to trust its own air force, effectively grounding it. As a consequence, Colonel Carlos Castillo Armas and his insurgents were able to achieve power within a week of crossing into Guatemala.

It is not surprising then, that many of the people involved in that operation were also at a meeting in January 1960 to discuss the problem of Cuba, now ruled by left-wing revolutionaries. The meeting was held in the office of the Chief of the Western Hemisphere Division of the CIA in Washington and it was there that the first steps were taken that would lead to the Bay of Pigs invasion. In overall charge of the project was Richard Bissell, the Deputy Director of Plans, who was responsible for the agency's covert work. The day to day operations were to be run by Jake Engler, a former CIA Cuban desk officer and Station Chief in Guatemala.

The original plan was to set up a small guerrilla force with perhaps 30 Cubans being trained by the CIA, and to establish a covert broadcasting station for a 'government in exile'. The person put in charge of the radio station had organised the broadcasts from Honduras and Guatemala in 1954. Work was started straight away on acquiring a transmitter and locating it on a small island off Honduras.

There followed a meeting of the National Security Council (NSC), which directed the CIA to prepare a programme for the overthrow of Castro. This the CIA duly did, and at a meeting of the Special Group of the NSC presented the following plan: a Cuban government in exile was to be established; a powerful propaganda offensive would be launched and covert intelligence undertaken to create an active organisation inside Cuba; and a paramilitary force would be assembled outside Cuba for future guerrilla action. Also proposed was the acquisition of a small air-supply capability under deep commercial cover in another country. The time-scale for the operation was eight months.

Approval of the plan

At a cabinet meeting on 17 March 1960, the president approved the agency's plan. Perhaps the person most keen to see the operation succeed was Vice-President Richard Nixon. As a candidate for the presidency in November of that year, he had every reason for wishing to see Castro replaced in order to deflect the charge made by John F. Kennedy that the Republicans had neglected the security of the United States. It was not until August, however, that Eisenhower approved a $13 million budget for the programme, or that authority was granted to call on the armed forces for assistance – with the proviso that no US personnel were to be involved in the front line.

As the programme outlined by the CIA was implemented it began to assume major proportions. The size of the invasion force was repeatedly increased, a training ground was set up in Guatemala and an airstrip built. Pilots from the Alabama National Guard were recruited to train Cuban pilots in former US Air Force B-26 bombers. A site in Nicaragua was established both for this purpose and also to serve as a base for overflights of Cuba in order to drop ammunition and explosives to infiltrators who were expected to disrupt Cuban communications when the guerrillas landed. By the time the Kennedy administration took office in January 1961, the demands of the operation were beginning to cause serious doubts among senior officers in the armed forces.

The plan presented to the new National Security Council was that two days before the invasion, air strikes by the force of B-26s would immobilise Castro's air force. A landing would be made at Trinidad, a town near the Escambray mountains, and a beachhead would be established around the airstrip there. This would enable the guerrilla air force to carry out further operations from Cuban soil, maintaining the fiction that they were dissident members of Castro's forces.

Above: The *Houston* burns fiercely after receiving a direct hit from one of Castro's aircraft during the invasion at the Bay of Pigs.

Below: Cuban troops pack transport lorries to capacity. Castro's rapid deployment of his forces contributed much to their eventual victory.

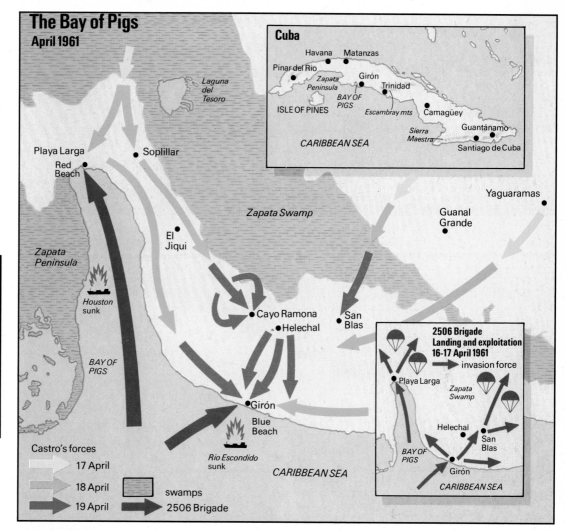

The Bay of Pigs
April 1961

Cuba

Havana Matanzas
Pinar del Rio
Zapata Girón
Peninsula Trinidad
ISLE OF PINES *BAY OF PIGS*
Escambray mts Camagüey
CARIBBEAN SEA
Sierra Maestra Guantánamo
Santiago de Cuba

Laguna del Tesoro

Playa Larga Soplillar
Red Beach

Zapata Swamp

Yaguaramas

El Jiqui

Guanal Grande

Zapata Peninsula

Houston sunk

Cayo Ramona
Helechal

San Blas

BAY OF PIGS

Girón
Blue Beach

Rio Escondido sunk

CARIBBEAN SEA

Castro's forces

17 April

18 April swamps

19 April 2506 Brigade

2506 Brigade
Landing and exploitation
16-17 April 1961 → invasion force

Playa Larga
Zapata Swamp
Helechal San Blas
BAY OF PIGS
Girón
CARIBBEAN SEA

Above: Richard Helms, Bissell's deputy in the CIA, opposed the Bay of Pigs plans and eventually headed the CIA after the abortive operation.

Partly as a result of criticisms, the NSC requested the Joint Chiefs of Staff to review the CIA's plans. The two officers detailed to do so found that there were few plans to review. Little had been committed to paper, and the logistics of the operation were hard to pin down. They were dubious of the outcome, but reported that the possibility of success was 'fair', and this depended on successful air strikes and a popular uprising. The CIA's own assessment was that an uprising was unlikely.

The Cuban operation had been totally isolated in the CIA, and had become the sole preserve of Bissell and the other agents in the Department of Plans. Richard Helms, Bissell's deputy, had decided early on to have nothing to do with the project. The Chief of the Western Hemisphere Division had also been isolated, as had the Deputy Director of Intelligence. As an attempt to achieve secrecy it was futile, for rumours and press leaks about the operation were extensive. All that the 'secrecy' served to do was to protect the plans from criticism inside the agency.

Further problems were also developing. President Kennedy was concerned that the operation should make as little 'noise' as possible – that is, he wanted US involvement to be totally deniable. He felt that Trinidad was too dangerous a target, and wanted the number of planes to be kept to a minimum. He was willing to provide an escort of five destroyers and the aircraft carrier *Essex* for the invasion fleet, but he stipulated that no US forces were to take any aggressive action whatsoever. To meet these objections, the

Above: Inspecting the wreckage of a US B-26 bomber forced down at Giron Beach near the Bay of Pigs.

Bay of Pigs was eventually chosen as the landing area, despite its military limitations, and the planned air support was much reduced.

Meetings of the NSC and other members of the cabinet continued during the run up to the invasion on 17 April. Senator J. William Fulbright, who knew all about the plans despite the supposed secrecy, presented a detailed memorandum to the president attacking the idea of intervention. His arguments rested on two points: first, that the US would be faced with the choice of letting the operation fail (because it would be isolated in Cuba), or of supporting it with greater military assistance; second, to follow the latter course would reveal the US as no better than the Soviet Union, and would commit the US to maintain security and stability in Cuba. Fulbright was allowed to put these criticisms to a cabinet meeting on 4 April. However, no-one was prepared to support Fulbright and demand answers from CIA personnel.

In the event, Fulbright's prognosis was correct. Two days before the invasion, President Kennedy required the aerial attack to be reduced further. Bissell complied, and just six B-26 bombers without defensive armament were assigned to remove the Cuban Air Force. They failed. The invasion forces had no effective air cover; along with the supply planes and freighters, they were subjected to devastating attack from the air. Unaccountably, no attempt was made to mobilise the network of agents in Cuba prior to the invasion. They were taken by surprise, rendering the months of infiltration and arms drops worthless.

Right: A poster celebrating the 15th anniversary of the Cuban victory at Giron shows Castro leaping from his command tank.

The invasion that failed

The landings at the Bay of Pigs took place in the early morning of 17 April 1961. After preliminary air strikes, which alerted Castro's government but did no effective damage to the small Cuban Air Force, about 1300 Cuban exiles ('Brigade 2506'), most of whom had received less than three months' training, went ashore, commanded by José Pérez San Román.

The advantage of the landing site was not that it was in an area ripe for revolt, but that swamps protected the beach-head and gave an invading force time to build up its strength. The failure of the initial air strikes meant that Castro's T-33s and Sea Furies were able to mount a series of attacks on the invaders and their supply vessels.

Castro acted swiftly and ruthlessly, arresting all suspects within Cuba and mobilising his troops against the small, beleaguered invading force.

Within a few hours of the invasion, the world was aware of what was happening, and Soviet Premier Nikita Khrushchev promised Castro 'every assistance'. On the night of 18/19 April, President John F. Kennedy was urged by the CIA to use the might of US air power to relieve the exiles. By the morning of the 19th it was too late, for Castro's numerically superior forces were pushing the invaders back. In all, 1180 were taken prisoner while almost 80 had died in the fighting and about 40 during the landings. Castro's forces sustained 3000–4000 casualties.

Inevitably, the invasion force of about 1300 men was isolated. Despite ferocious fighting, all were either killed or captured. No order was given for the intervention of the five destroyers and the *Essex*. The *Essex* despatched its Skyhawks on missions of harassment, but never fired at Castro's aircraft.

The political casualties were many. President Kennedy was seriously embarrassed, and the credibility of the US Ambassador to the United Nations, Adlai Stevenson, was gravely damaged. Stevenson had maintained what he believed was the truth, that the US had not been involved. Bissell was removed from his post and abandoned his ambition to head the CIA, a role which was to be achieved, ironically, by the very first critic of the venture, Richard Helms. Lyman Kirkpatrick, the CIA's inspector-general, conducted an inquiry into the disaster. His report remains secret, but he has gone on record seriously criticising the efficiency and judgement of everyone involved, from the CIA to the president himself.

Mike Rossiter

The exiles in action

'Cruz' was an officer in Brigade 2506 and his unit was one of the first in action during the invasion of Cuba. Here he describes an encounter with Castro's forces.

'I had two men about six hundred yards ahead to the front,' Cruz said, 'so they could observe the enemy. They came back about 2.30 pm and they told me that the enemy was advancing in a column. They were coming through the centre of the highway, straight on it, in a close formation. These people were crazy coming that way down the hill in the middle of the road. We were in a very good position at both sides of the road, camouflaged. Between the enemy and me there was a swamp and trees on both sides of the road. We were able to shoot well from this position....

'When they were about five hundred yards from us they stopped, and they started putting up their mortars and getting their weapons prepared. They didn't send any forward observers to see where we were. . . . When I gave the order to fire, you could see them flying up in the air. I threw everything at them with the three shells of the 75 I had left, with the 57, with the machine guns and all the weapons we had there. In 10 or 15 minutes there was a big mound of dead men all over the road.'

Key Weapons

The M48-60 SERIES
part 1

The M48 Medium Tank

The M48 Patton Medium Tank entered service with the United States Army in 1953. In December 1950 the Chrysler Corporation had received a contract to design and build a medium tank to replace the transitional T47, and one year later the prototype was ready. Production began in 1952, but the first years of the M48's service life were beset with problems. Reliability proved uncertain and mechanical breakdowns severely limited the tank's efficiency. The stereoscopic range finders also caused difficulties. These defects were, in time, remedied and a series of modifications have led to the present-day M48A5 version.

The original M48 had cupola fitting problems so that eventually a Sherman cupola with cradle mounted .50in M2 machine gun was installed. Turret and hull were of cast steel construction and the latter was divided into driving, fighting and engine compartments. Suspension was of torsion bar type and there were six road wheels each side with five track return rollers. A Continental AVDS-1790-7C 12-cylinder petrol engine powered the 47-tonne tank. In the original version range was limited and while the provision of additional fuel tanks provided a greater radius of action they also increased vulnerability. The M47's fire control equipment was retained in the M48.

The M48A1 mounted an improved cupola (the M1) with five periscopes and gunsight. Its .50in machine gun had a plus 60 degree elevation and minus 10

Previous page: The United States Army has been well served by the M48-60 series of tanks, which first came into service in 1953, and despite the introduction of the M1 Abrams MBT they continue to provide battle-front support for America's armoured divisions. Here two M60A1 tanks are on a live-fire exercise. Above: An Israeli M48A2 advances across the desert in the face of Egyptian anti-tank fire during the Six-Day War.

Right: The M48 was widely used during the Vietnam conflict and was considered a success by its crews – to the surprise of some tacticians who failed to realise the virtues of tanks in modern jungle warfare, despite problems of terrain and deployment. US Marine Corps tanks prepare for action (top and centre), and an M48A3 advances against enemy positions during Operation Sitting Duck in 1966 (bottom).

Above: The crew of an Israeli M48A2 emerge from their turret after an action during the Six-Day War. Alongside the Centurion the M48 was the major armoured success of the 1967 conflict.

degree depression, and thus had an anti-aircraft as well as a ground role. Main armament was the 90mm M41 gun with distinctive bore evacuator and blast deflector. The gun had automatic ejection and a vertically sliding breech, and the gunner occupied the front right-hand side of the turret in front of the commander, with the loader on the left. Sixty rounds of fixed case ammunition were available and types included HE, AP, HVAP and HEAT. A co-axial .30in M1919 machine gun was originally fitted as secondary armament but was later replaced by a 7.62mm M73. For battlefield illumination an 18in 2000 watt searchlight was carried, later to be replaced by a xenon infra red/white light type. A tensioning idler was installed in front of the rear drive sprocket to counteract the tendency to shed tracks, and on later

types two of the five track return rollers were removed. The AVDS-1790-7C petrol engine was retained, though fuel injection was introduced.

In the mid-1950s the M48A2 appeared. This had a larger M19 cupola with 360 degree traverse, and the engine compartment was completely redesigned and improvements were also made to the commander's override ability over the 90mm gun. Fuel capacity was increased and the transmission – which was still proving unreliable – received attention. The track compensating idler spindle was redesigned and the track tensioning idler of the M48A1 removed. Overheating problems attributable to the engine cooling fan resulted in improvements being made to the cooling system. Later versions carried the prototype turret for the M60 and had multi-fuel engines.

Armed with a 90mm main gun an M48A2 pauses for a mechanical inspection during the Israeli advance against Arab positions in 1967. A considerable weapon in its own right the M48's success, nonetheless, owed much to the tactical ability of the Israeli tank crews who consistently outfought their Arab opponents.

The Israelis fitted British 105mm L7 guns to their M48A2s which they received in the 1960s, and made a number of modifications including fitting diesel engines. Both the Israelis and the Jordanians used the tank in the 1967 war. The Israelis found it faster and more reliable than the Centurion although less well armoured, and by 1973 the M48 (and the new M60) had begun to replace the Centurion in Israeli front-line service.

In 1964 the M48A3 introduced Continental diesel engines into the M48 series with the AVDS-1790-2A. Fuel capacity was increased and range improved. The driver had three M27 periscopes, the middle one of which could be replaced by an M24 infra red scope. The commander's M1 cupola had five vision blocks and an M28C sight for the .50in machine gun. A coincidence rangefinder with x10 magnification and 4400m (4800yds) range was installed. The gunner

had both periscope and telescope with x8 magnification. No fire warning system was fitted, but a floor escape hatch enabled the crew to vacate the vehicle under its own cover. An M8 series dozer blade was available. In 1967 nearly 600 M48A1 tanks were brought up to M48A3 standard.

The M48A3 was the standard American tank in Vietnam and saw service there between 1965 and 1973. The complement of track return rollers was again made up to five, and cutting bars fitted to the tank's front enabled it to clear dense vegetation. Additional machine guns were mounted to improve firepower in close country. The tank's main armament proved particularly useful during combined infantry/armoured operations and the 90mm canister and beehive rounds were used to good effect. Some problems were understandably encountered with engine overheating and mud clogging the tracks, but the

Below left: An Israeli M48 prepares to pass its leader – whose tank has hit a mine – at one of the crucial actions of the Yom Kippur War on the west bank of the Suez Canal. Below: M48s were used by the Jordanians as well as the Israelis during the Six-Day War. Here a unit of Israeli Shermans pass a knocked-out Jordanian M48 near Kabatiya in Samaria. Bottom: An M48A2 races across the Sinai Desert in the Six-Day War, while in the background Egyptian armoured vehicles burn and explode.

Some of the differences in turret layout can be seen between an Israeli M48A3 (above) with a 105mm main armament and a US M48A2 (above right) with its less powerful 90mm gun. Right: An M48A3 supports infantry operations on a beach assault by men of the 7th US Marines.

Below: A US Marine M48A3 takes part in Operation Arcadio in 1966. The M48 proved popular with both the Marines and the army.

M48 was well liked by its users and despite adverse conditions the tank performed very well.

The M48A4 was essentially an M48A3 with the M60 turret and 105mm L51 gun. The old 90mm gun was deemed to be inadequate to counter the main armament of contemporary Soviet tanks and so the M48's fire power was updated. The M48A5 retained the 105mm gun and added a co-axial 7.62mm machine gun, while the loader received an additional machine gun. New tracks were fitted and a coincidence rangefinder installed.

In the M48 family were to be found the C series of mild-steel light-weight training tanks, AVLB scissors bridgelayers capable of crossing an 18.2m (60ft) gap, the M67 series of flamethrowing tanks, the M88 ARV and mine clearance variants.

The M48 was intended to equip the United States Army in the Korean War, though it arrived too late to see action in that conflict. It has since seen extensive service in a number of theatres of war, including the Indo-Pakistan war in 1965, where its Pakistani operators mishandled the tank and contrived to lose it in large numbers. Recipients have included West Germany (where at present the Bundeswehr operates 650 M48-series tanks rebuilt to house the 105mm L7 gun), Greece, Iran, Israel, Jordan, Morocco, Norway, Pakistan, South Korea, Spain, Taiwan, Thailand, Turkey and South Vietnam. Over 11,000 versions have been built, and in its up-gunned form the M48 remained a useful medium tank into the 1980s.

Modified Israeli M48s take part in exercises shortly after the end of the Six-Day War. A Centurion is just visible in the background behind the lead M48.

Right: An M48A1 climbs a steep gradient. Distinguishing features of this variant are the commander's cupola, the flat engine decks and the undercut rear hull plates. Below: The bridge-laying M48 AVLB sees serious action during fighting in South Vietnam in 1966.

M48A3 Medium Tank

Crew 4
Dimensions Length (gun included) 7.44m (24ft 5in); width 3.63m (11ft 11in); height (including cupola) 3.12m (10ft 3in)
Weight Combat loaded 47,173kg (104,000lb)
Ground Pressure 0.83kg/cm² (11.8lb/in²)
Engine Continental AVDS-1790-2A 12-cylinder air-cooled diesel engine developing 750bhp at 2400rpm

Performance Maximum road speed 48km/h (30mph); range (road) 463km (288 miles); vertical obstacle 0.92m (3ft); trench 2.59m (8ft 6in); Gradient 60 per cent; fording 1.22m (4ft), with kit 2.44m (8ft)

Armour Min-max 12.7mm-120mm (0.50-4.80in)
Armament One 90mm M41 gun; one 0.3in M1919A-4E1 machine gun co-axial with the main armament; one 0.5in machine gun in commander's cupola

Brother

against brother

The civil wars of the modern world

The world is divided into a number of 'states' – geographical entities containing people ruled by a recognised form of central authority which enjoys at least a degree of independent decision-making – and each contains within its boundaries the seeds of conflict. The population is unlikely to be completely homogeneous, particularly if the borders of the state reflect the arbitrary decisions of outside powers (as is the case with so many ex-colonial members of the Third World) or result from a history of expansion by conquest in the search for security.

This means that there will always be groups within the state who do not owe natural allegiance to the central authority, preferring the traditions and beliefs of their own ethnic, tribal or religious backgrounds, and this may lead to accusations of disloyalty as well as government-sponsored attempts to persuade or force them into conformity.

Similar divisions may result from an uneven spread of wealth or power within the state. Some areas may be starved of resources, growing resentful of the development of other, more favoured regions; others may hold a monopoly of a scarce resource and be loath to share their advantages with the rest of society unless they are given a corresponding monopoly of political power.

Overpage: Two of the most intractable civil wars in modern times have been fought in the Lebanon and Angola. Top: Palestinians rush for cover during street fighting in Beirut in 1975. The mass influx of PLO guerrillas into Lebanon after their expulsion from Jordan complicated enormously Lebanon's problems. Bottom: A Cuban instructor trains an MPLA recruit in the use of a mortar in Angola.

Below: A Christian Phalangist in Lebanon lines up women and children who have claimed neutrality.

In some states these divisions may be controlled by a strong central government which exercises its power by means of accepted forms of democracy or effective totalitarian repression, but even then the potential for internal conflict remains. In extreme cases it may be manifested in the creation of an entirely new state through the secession of the disaffected areas – in 1971, for example, Bangladesh (East Pakistan) seceded from West Pakistan, with Indian aid, after years of being treated as a 'poor relation' by the central authorities in Islamabad – but the more common result is civil war.

Defined as 'war between belligerent factions seeking by organised violence to acquire a monopoly of force and political power in a state', civil war is a type of conflict feared by most countries. It is by definition divisive and by its nature requires the channelling of energies and resources inwards, to the detriment of trade, state development and international relations. It is extremely destructive, not just in the physical sense but more importantly in the moral, creating deep divisions within society which may take generations to repair. It invariably creates a political vacuum as rival centres of authority emerge, and this invites foreign interference which may be difficult to shake off once the war is over. In short, civil war threatens the independence of the state and tears its fabric apart.

Such wars have affected many states, but they have increased in both frequency and importance since 1945. In part this is due to the simple fact that since that date the number of independent states in existence, and therefore susceptible to civil war, has more than tripled in the aftermath of European decolonisation, but there is more to it than that. The division of major parts of the world into two rival ideological camps has pitted communism against capitalism in even the most sophisticated states, deepening already-existing political divides, sometimes to the point of violence. Improved communications have shown people that other groups have attained a level of economic or political development that contrasts sharply to their own, leading to a questioning of government policies and a drift towards conflict. Such groups may, of course, be exploited by outside powers but whatever the background, civil war has developed with ever-increasing frequency.

Many of the more intractable and long-lasting of the conflicts that have taken place since 1945 bear the hallmarks of civil war, even though they are not normally described as such. The Vietnam War, for example, was fought mainly by members of the same Vietnamese culture, and until the intervention of US and North Vietnamese forces the combatants came from within the same state. In Northern Ireland, too, the 'troubles' of the 1970s often seemed a species of civil war, with the British Army almost an outside force.

Communism and capitalism

Looking in more detail at the specific causes of civil wars since 1945, it is obvious that the ideological clash between communism and capitalism has had a dramatic impact. In direct terms it has produced two of the most significant civil wars of the period, albeit with different results. In China the offensive launched by the communists under Mao Tse-tung in 1946 was designed to destroy the Western-orientated government of Chiang Kai-shek. Although the resultant war had its origins in the political chaos which had beset China since the overthrow of the Manchu dynasty in 1911, the fighting of 1946-49 was firmly based upon opposing political views. In the end, the communists prevailed. A similar clash of ideologies fuelled the civil war in Greece between 1945 and 1949, with the communist-led Democratic Army fighting the Nationalist government, but in this case it was the Nationalists who won, not least because of Western commitment to their cause.

The fact that events in Greece almost led to a more general confrontation between the rival camps of East and West undoubtedly muted the degree of direct support offered by the superpowers to factions in subsequent civil wars. But this does not mean that ideology has ceased to play an important role, merely that the superpowers have become more circumspect, preferring subversion to open battle and using proxies to provide the necessary aid. Events in Angola in 1975 illustrate the point, with the communist MPLA receiving arms, advisers and equipment from the Cubans rather than the Russians in their struggle to defeat the South African-backed and CIA-funded forces of the FNLA and UNITA. Of course, the ideologies in question do not need to be those of East and West – the civil war in North Yemen (1962-67)

saw a clash between monarchism and republicanism that was just as bitter.

In many cases, however, it is still local issues which cause civil wars, centred upon purely internal differences. In Nigeria, for example, the civil war of 1967-70 had its origins among the Ibo tribe of the eastern provinces, who felt that the federal government in Lagos was actively discriminating against them. At first the Ibos used the technique of the military coup (January 1966), but after this had been nullified by a counter-coup six months later, they attempted to secede from the federation by creating the new state of Biafra (July 1967). As the federal authorities fought to prevent the disintegration of Nigeria, the war devolved into one of the most destructive yet to affect the Third World.

A similar pattern of events occurred in Chad after 1968, when the tribes of the northern and eastern provinces, convinced that their rivals from the south and west were enjoying a monopoly of political power, revolted under the banner of Frolinat (the National Liberation Front of Chad) and initiated a civil war which has yet to be completely resolved. It was made more bitter by the fact that Frolinat was a Muslim organisation opposed to the Christian central authority, for religion can make a potent contribution to internal strife. In Sudan a civil war took place from the moment of independence in 1956 until a partial reconciliation in 1972 between the Christian/animist inhabitants of the south and the Muslim-dominated government in Khartoum, while the Lebanese Civil War of 1975-76 had its roots in the inevitable clash between the Maronite Christians of the governing elite and the dissatisfied Muslim majority. In all these cases the disaffected factions undoubtedly used their spiritual beliefs as convenient rallying-points, particularly in the quest for outside support.

Outside influence

If the causes of civil wars are many and varied, the results are often predictable. Although the superpowers may be deterred from offering direct support, it is one of the characteristics of the post-1945 period that few civil wars have remained self-contained. In an interdependent world, beset by problems of ideological and resource rivalry, too much is at stake to prevent outside interference and this can often be decisive in terms of the outcome or longevity of internal squabbles. The civil war in North Yemen was sustained by the fact that Egypt supported the republicans while Saudi Arabia backed the monarchists; in

Lebanon the rivalries of 1975-76 have been fuelled by Syrian and Israeli intervention; in Chad it was the French and Libyans who offered aid.

In each of these cases, intervening states stood to make substantial gains from the victory of their chosen allies – in Chad, for example, the French committed troops to protect their valuable stake in the mineral resources of the country – and this makes a peaceful or lasting solution extremely difficult to achieve. Local issues disappear beneath more global pressures, the degree of violence increases as more sophisticated weapons and even troops are made available, and the fighting drags on, achieving either stalemate (as in North Yemen and Sudan) or eventual victory for the faction which enjoys the most effective outside support (as in Greece, Nigeria and Angola). It is a sad pattern which shows no signs of being broken in the civil wars that will inevitably occur in the future.   **John Pimlott**

Above left: Outside intervention (often of a clandestine nature) and the intensity of feeling common in civil war makes the position of prisoners very difficult. Here a Cuban, captured by Unita forces in Angola, is about to be displayed to the world's press. Inevitably civilians also suffer in internal conflicts. Above: The most tragic case of civilian involvement was in Biafra, Nigeria, where millions died of famine. Here a federal soldier guards Biafran refugees. Below: Civilians move from a bombed-out area in Lebanon.

Crisis in Chad

Unending conflict in the heart of Africa

On 28 November 1958 the French territory of Chad, an area of 1.28 million square km (495,700 square miles) with a population of just over 2.5 million, was given its independence. It was known from then on as the Republic of Chad. Soon, however, it became evident that the shaking off of the colonial yoke was a mixed blessing. Almost from the day the Tricolor ceased to fly over the capital Fort Lamy, renamed N'Djamena, and the first president, François Tombalbaye, had been sworn in, active rebellion broke out.

Small as is Chad's population compared with its vast land mass, it is multi-racial, multi-lingual and deeply divided by religious differences. Power had passed into the hands of the black Africans, Christian or animist, while the northern tribes were mainly Arab-speaking and Muslim. Two of Chad's most powerful neighbours, Libya and Sudan, were actively seeking greater unity within the Islamic world while a third, Nigeria, was also largely Muslim, if not so fanatical. In the early days of Chad's independence, Libya was ruled by the comparatively moderate King Idris. On 1 September 1969, the king was ousted by Colonel Muammar Gaddafi, who was to prove himself one of the world's leading trouble-makers. One of his first moves was to step up aid to the rebellious Chad tribes of the long, inaccessible, northeast frontier.

To begin with Tombalbaye endeavoured to make his parliament genuinely representative, but by the mid-1960s he had become so exasperated by opposition within his cabinet that he expelled all the Arab-speaking ministers, including Abba Siddick, Minister of Education. Siddick fled to Libya, condemned the N'Djamena regime, founded the Front de Libération Nationale de Tchad (the National Liberation Front of Chad, or Frolinat) and raised the standard of revolt in the northern province of Tibesti.

By 1969 with Frolinat bands dominating the north and threatening N'Djamena itself, General Malloum, the army chief of staff, persuaded the president to invoke the Franco-Chadian Treaty, which provided for mutual aid in times of crisis. There were many in France who objected to bolstering the shaky regime of a former colony. Nevertheless, basing its argument on the fact that Frolinat was being exploited as an instrument of Soviet expansion in Africa, the French government duly authorised the despatch of five companies of the 2nd Foreign Legion Parachute Regiment and a *compagnie de marche*, made up of volunteers and men of the 2nd Foreign Legion Infantry Regiment, commanded by Colonel Lacaze, who later became chief of staff of France's armed forces.

On arrival in Chad, the French were formed into two mobile, motorised commands. This manner of deployment – the men mounted in half-tracks, protected by armoured cars, and with helicopter air cover – proved highly successful against the Frolinat bands which, though well supplied with modern (mostly Russian) weaponry, lacked the training to be able to tackle such highly professional soldiers as the Legion paras with any hope of victory. There were frequent skirmishes, but no major engagements on the Algerian scale. Most of the clashes took place in the

Top: Frolinat rebels, armed with 7.62mm AK assault rifles, engaging government troops in northern Chad. Above: Tombalbaye, the first president of Chad, who, exasperated by the internal pressures caused by the civil war, invoked the Franco-Chadian Treaty in the hope that French military aid might help crush the rebels.

north. Frolinat bands were first isolated, then destroyed piecemeal. In the less fanatical south, a mere show of force was usually enough to persuade the half-hearted dissidents to return to their homes. 'I am convinced,' wrote one Legion officer, 'that the population of the straw-hutted villages is really only interested in pursuing its traditional way of life and remaining on the good terms enjoyed with French troops over the last hundred years.'

By 1971 only isolated pockets of resistance remained in the north. But these were 'sheltered in caves', wrote a French officer, 'situated high up in the walls of bare and precipitous mountain slopes which served both as observation posts and citadels'. Casualties began to mount as, abandoning their trucks, the troops became engaged in operations more suited to mountain troops. Nevertheless, by the autumn most of the gangs had been mopped up and in December President Tombalbaye declared the crisis over. The French departed, having lost 8 killed and 90 wounded of the 980 involved.

The withdrawal, however, was to prove only temporary. After a brief honeymoon between Tombalbaye and Gaddafi when the former broke off diplomatic relations with Israel in November 1972, the situation within Chad deteriorated rapidly. Tombalbaye was having to deal not only with rebels backed by Libya and Sudan , but with serious contention within his own party. Internal dissension mounted until, on 13 April 1975, a coup took place in which Tombalbaye was killed. A military junta led by General Malloum took over, but immediately had to face increasing threats from Frolinat, now dominated by Goukouni Oueddei, son of a tribal chieftain from the Tibesti, and Hissène Habré, who had studied in Paris and held a law degree.

In early 1978 Hissène Habré, who had been secretly in contact with Malloum, decided to throw in his lot with the government in return for his appointment as prime minister. But the rebellion, still led by Goukouni and even more actively supported by Libya, was creating such chaos that once again an appeal for French assistance was made. President Valerie Giscard d'Estaing had inherited de Gaulle's dream of France remaining a powerful influence behind the scenes in black Africa, and he responded by sending a second and larger expeditionary force to

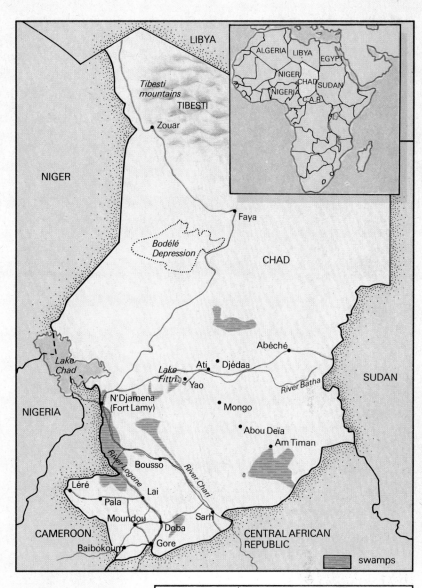

While Frolinat were usually well-armed (below), the dying tribesman (shown inset) was armed only with a spear when he attacked the French troops who have just shot him.

Above: Leader of the rebels, and later president of Chad (though eventually deposed), Goukouni Oueddei, the son of a Tibesti chief. Left: Government troops resting between battles, stand guard over their 75mm recoilless cannon mounted on a jeep.

Chad. It consisted of the 2nd Foreign Legion Parachute Regiment, a squadron of the 1st Legion Cavalry Regiment's light tanks, two companies from the 2nd Foreign Legion Infantry Regiment, and a company of Marines popularly known as the 'Marsouins'.

The French were surprised by the large area controlled by Frolinat, and also by the fact that the rebels were armed with the very latest smallarms. Clearly the situation had changed dramatically since 1971, enemy groups no longer operating on a purely territorial basis. Many of the units active in the south were identified as members of the Toubou tribe, the most warlike of those of the northern frontier. But the presence of French professional troops soon began to take effect.

Sending in the paras
A typical operation of the early stages of the campaign was that which ended with the relief of the small town of Ati. At about 2200 hours on 3 April 1978 Colonel Lhopitalier of the Legion paras received a radio message at his headquarters in Mongo that Ati had been overrun and that the gendarme detachment, besieged in its barracks, was having difficulty hanging on. Though he had only a limited force at his disposal – two companies of the Chad Army led by Legion paras, the 'Marsouin' company, and a platoon of 81mm mortars – he decided to move immediately. By 1045 next day he had reached the banks of the Batha River, 2km (1¼ miles) from Ati, the walls and fortress of which were clearly visible.

Crossing the river, the force proceeded until they were within 200m (220 yards) of the walls. They were then met by enemy fire from ultra-modern Russian weapons, including anti-tank rockets, 106mm recoilless guns and heavy machine guns. At the same time, from about 2km (1¼ miles) beyond the town, mortar batteries opened up. For 20 minutes the rebel fire pinned them down. Then Lhopitalier called for an air strike by missile-carrying Alouette helicopters and Jaguars, which effectively destroyed the Frolinat positions. By the time a detachment of light tanks arrived, the assault on the town was able to be resumed, the streets cleared and the hard-pressed gendarmes relieved.

By 1300 the Frolinat survivors were in full retreat. They left 80 dead and most of their equipment, including a 120mm mortar, an 81mm mortar, a recoilless 75mm gun and six machine guns; government losses amounted to three killed and nine wounded. Five days later the 150 Frolinat, nearly all Toubous, who had escaped from Ati were surrounded in the Djédaa palm forest and wiped out. It had been a hard pursuit in temperatures that exceeded 49°C (120°F).

During this period a Spanish journalist, Xavier Nart, travelled with the Frolinat forces. He believed that the government would be unable to repress the rebellious elements because the entire Arab-speaking, Muslim population would never be reconciled to it. To emphasise his point, he drew attention to the fact that many of the rebel fighters were a young as 12, and that their ranks included teenage girls. He portrayed them as 'dour nomads capable of lying up three days on end in ambush in the hollow of a rock'.

It was not long before the French forces found themselves more involved in governmental squabbles than in fighting the Frolinat, for in 1980 Goukouni ousted Hissène Habré, who fled to Algeria. Wrote one Legionnaire: 'It became increasingly

Above: A Frolinat trooper, armed with a Canadian-made rifle. Below: While the Chad governments's call for aid was answered by the arrival of the French Foreign Legion in 1969, 1978 and 1983, the rebels' appeal for aid was answered by Colonel Gaddafi's Libya with supplies of arms and ammunition (right).

difficult to distinguish between yesterday's friend and today's foe when our HQ was transferred to N'Djamena itself and we found ourselves engaged in protecting French personnel and property and acting as a buffer between rival local factions.' Nevertheless, much to the relief of every French soldier, the government was confident that the crisis was over and that outside aid could be dispensed with.

In fact, however, this was far from the case. War against the Frolinat dragged on and internal strife mounted. Hissène Habré had put himself at the head of a movement called Forces Armées du Nord, and on 7 June 1982 he staged a successful attack on the capital, forcing Goukouni to flee for his life, and had himself sworn in as president the following day. Goukouni made his way to the ever-rebellious north to raise a Libyan-backed army and carry on the civil war.

Further trouble arose in April 1983 when Nigeria accused Chad of driving 3000 Nigerian fishermen from their villages on the disputed shore of Lake Chad. Nigerian warplanes and artillery bombarded and shelled Chadian villages in retaliation. Civilian casualties are thought to have been heavy, at least 90 being killed in a single raid.

On 8 June, the anniversary of his accession, Hissène Habré announced he was willing to negotiate with Nigeria to seek a peaceful solution to the dispute. He also launched a vitriolic attack on Libya, describing the Gaddafi regime as 'terrorist and bloody' and accusing the Libyans of being 'worse than the colonisers, dyed-in-the-wool slavers and barbarians'. Goukouni, for his part, marked the anniversary by announcing the capture of the town of Faya in the Northeast.

And so Chad's troubles persisted into the 1980s. What had begun as a civil war bid fair to become an international conflict as Libyan troops arrived in force and as Zaire and France sent in help to the Chadian government while the USA looked on anxiously from the wings, ready to intervene should Libyan aid to the rebels prove decisive.

Patrick Turnbull

The civil war in Chad was originally fought along quite clear racial and religious lines, with Arab/Muslim rebels (above left) attacking an army representing the black African/Christian government (above).

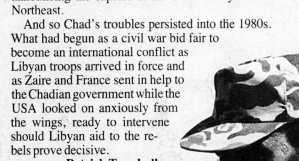

The Third World

New nations and new wars

Undeniably the most important political relationship in the years since 1945 has been that between East and West: the relationship between the Soviet bloc of states, led by the USSR, and the Atlantic alliance led by the USA. From the late 1940s these mutually hostile groups faced each other in Cold War confrontation. Perhaps equally crucial, if less dramatic, however, has been the relationship between North and South, between the economically developed and predominantly white states of North America, Europe and the Soviet bloc and the economically underdeveloped states of Asia, Africa and Latin America. These countries of the South have come to be known collectively as the Third World.

The emergence of a common Third World voice may be regarded as a protest by the emergent states against Northern, and particularly Western, domination. The independent states of the South – the Latin American republics plus a handful of African and Asian countries – exerted little influence in world affairs immediately after World War II. Moreover, most of South and Southeast Asia, together with virtually the whole of Africa, remained the domain of Western colonial powers.

During the following two decades, however, this picture changed dramatically. Nationalist movements within the colonies became increasingly powerful, and the demand for independence became seemingly irresistible. As the costs of empire rose – in economic, military, political and moral terms – the colonial powers gradually relinquished control.

The consequences of decolonisation were profound. In 1945 there were some 70 sovereign states in the world. By 1983 there were nearly 170; of the 100 or so new states, over 90 were ex-colonial or ex-dependent territories.

The repercussions of the colonial revolution were not simply arithmetical, however. The emergence of the new states transformed the very substance of international politics. Throughout the 1950s the world had been dominated by two armed camps, East and West, facing each other. Gradually, however, a more complex situation developed with the rise of independent power centres, such as the Chinese People's Republic, and the emergence of the South, notably the Afro-Asian states, as a distinct and collective entity.

The newly emergent states refused to adhere unconditionally to either major power bloc which, they felt, would undermine their newly gained sovereignty. Nevertheless, some Third World states, such as those of South America, associated themselves loosely with the West, while others, notably Marxist regimes like Cuba (from 1959), associated with the Soviet Union. But in general the states of the Third World, including those with eastern or western links, formed their own distinct organisations and institutions. These bodies were concerned not so much with the global Cold War as with harnessing the collective power of the Third World in pursuit of specific

Below: Eritrean guerrillas display their devotion to the cause that is at the heart of one of the Third World's most difficult problems. Far right top: Biafrans demonstrate against the aid given to the Nigerian federal government by East and West.

common interests: economic development, the eradication of colonialism and the promotion of regional and international solidarity.

Such cooperation was reflected in the proliferation of regional bodies. An early example was the Organisation of American States (OAS), established in 1947/48 to foster closer relations in Central and South America, although the inclusion of the USA gave rise to the charge that the OAS was not a truly Third World body.

Movement towards unity

Two other regional bodies, however, consisted entirely of Third World members. The League of Arab States – also known as the Arab League – was formed in 1945 and consisted initially of seven members. By 1982 the League had grown to 21 members and included every Arab state except Egypt, which had been suspended in 1979 for signing a peace treaty with Israel. Even larger is the Organisation of African Unity (OAU), formed in 1963 by 32 African states with the aim of furthering African unity, coordinating policies and eliminating colonialism and white minority rule from the continent. By 1983 membership had grown to 51 states. Other regional bodies formed by Third World countries include the Association of Southeast Asian Nations (ASEAN), established by five Southeast Asian countries in 1967 to promote economic development, and the Caribbean Community (CARICOM), a West Indian common market formed in 1973.

Third World countries also formed the non-aligned movement, which first emerged as a coherent force at the Bandung and Belgrade conferences in 1955 and 1961 respectively. Its founders were President Gamal Abdel Nasser of Egypt, Jawaharlal Nehru of India and Marshal Tito of Yugoslavia. Their aim was to create a new force in international affairs dedicated to the principles of neutrality, non-alignment, peaceful coexistence and national self-determination. Bandung and Belgrade set the pattern for further summit conferences held at Lusaka (1970), Algiers (1973), Colombo (1976) and Havana (1979). At these conferences, members sought detente between East and West, nuclear disarmament and the eradication of colonialism, racism and imperialism. They also pressed for a new international economic order, more to the advantage of the Third World. By 1981 the non-aligned movement had 93 full members, most of which were African and Asian.

The same demands were also advanced by Third World countries in the United Nations, which was transformed by the entry of the new states. When the UN began life in 1945 it was essentially a Western body. With the influx of African and Asian states, however, the UN underwent a marked change. The resolutions of the General Assembly began to reflect the demands of the Afro-Asian nations, although these countries were unable to make the same impact in the limited-member Security Council, still dominated by the major powers.

If the emergence of the Third World has been marked by regional and international cooperation it has also been marked by conflict. Many Third World states, including Algeria, Angola, Vietnam and Mozambique, gained independence only after prolonged armed struggle. But even after independence, the incidence of conflict in the Third World has remained high.

Important Third World leaders were Nasser (above addressing the Bandung conference), Tito and Nehru (left, centre and left), and Castro (below).

Third World states may have important common interests, but they undoubtedly are diverse in terms of culture, language, religion, race, political systems and ideologies. These differences have sometimes made a mockery of attempts to present a united front in regional and international bodies – and have at times erupted in war. In a number of cases the cause of conflict has been ideological. The war between North and South Korea (1950-53) was essentially ideological as was the protracted conflict between North and South Vietnam (1959-75). Both these conflicts drew in outside powers.

Territorial disputes have also been a common cause of conflict between Third World states. In 1977-78, Ethiopia and Somalia waged war over the disputed territory of the Ogaden, a Somali-inhabited region of Ethiopia. Indonesia's confrontation with Malaysia from 1963 to 1966 was also motivated by territorial claims. In other cases territorial disputes have merely exacerbated more deep-seated differences between countries. The three Indo-Pakistan Wars (1948-49, 1965 and 1971) can only partly be attributed to territorial differences. Perhaps the underlying cause lay in mutual antipathy – political, religious, cultural and otherwise – between these neighbours. The same

is perhaps true of the war between Iran and Iraq which began in 1980.

If the incidence of conflict *between* Third World states has been high, the incidence of conflict *within* Third World states has been even higher. The reasons for this are many. One of the major causes is that many Third World states inherited boundaries drawn up by colonial powers that did not accord with older tribal or ethnic frontiers. National solidarity, therefore, has not been easy to forge.

On occasions, the fighting between tribes or communities has gone further than a mere struggle for ascendancy. Tribal or national groups have sometimes attempted to break away and set up their own states but have been resisted by the central government. Thus Nigeria was the scene of a fierce war between 1967 and 1970 when the Ibo people tried to secede and set up an independent state of Biafra. Earlier, the Belgian Congo (subsequently called Zaire) had been torn apart immediately after independence in June 1960 by rebellions and secessionist movements, notably in the province of Katanga. A successful war of secession occurred in 1971 when the territory formerly known as East Pakistan broke away from West Pakistan to form the separate state of

Superpower competition for influence in the Third World took various forms; from the Soviet Union supplying the Cubans with equipment to fight in Angola (right), to the United States intervening directly in Latin America. The most notable US intervention was in the Dominican Republic in 1965 (below) which involved US troops in monitoring civilian movements.

Third World states often had to fight colonial powers for their independence (above: Portuguese operations in Mozambique), but once independent might then in turn face separatist threats (below: A Polisario guerrilla, fighting against Morocco and Mauritania).

Bangladesh. This was achieved with the assistance of India.

Given that few Third World countries possess the economic stability, political traditions or national cohesion necessary for Western-style democracy, changes of government have often come about by force. Coups, rebellions and insurgencies have been commonplace, particularly in Africa and Latin America. Left-wing guerrillas fought successful campaigns against right-wing regimes in Cuba (1956-59) and Nicaragua (1970-79), although they were unsuccessful in Argentina, Brazil and Uruguay and were crushed decisively in Bolivia in 1967. The conflict in El Salvador, begun in 1980, remains undecided. Guerrilla campaigns have not, however, been waged solely by the left. Two Marxist regimes in southern Africa, namely Angola and Mozambique, have been embattled by guerrilla attacks since they became independent in 1975.

These conflicts within and between Third World countries have tended to involve outside powers. Neither America nor the Soviet Union, nor for that matter, other powers like Britain, France and China have been willing or able to ignore Third World conflicts. On the contrary, outside powers have often felt compelled to intervene – on ideological, economic, strategic and other grounds.

Strategic intervention

States located nearby Third World countries, for example, have often intervened in local conflicts. The United States sent troops into the Dominican Republic in 1965 to secure a friendly regime there, and the Soviet Union, on a much larger scale, invaded Afghanistan in 1979. Israel and South Africa, the political whipping-boys of Third World states, have both intervened in neighbouring countries. Israel launched a limited invasion of Lebanon in 1978 and returned with much stronger forces in 1982. The main objective on both occasions was to secure the northern border of Israel, although the most recent incursion involved political objectives as well.

Military involvement has sometimes been a legacy of the imperial past. France has continued to assist friendly regimes in Africa, and Britain's retreat from empire often involved her in defending former colonies, as occurred during Malaysia's conflict with Indonesia in the 1960s.

Britain's role in defeating communist insurgents in the 1950s can be also regarded as part of a general Western effort, waged principally by the United States, to contain communist advances in the Third World. The US has granted economic and military assistance to numerous Third World countries for this purpose and has also intervened militarily to contain communism in Korea and Vietnam. The Soviet Union, on the other hand, has rarely employed its own troops in Third World conflicts but has offered military aid and used proxy forces such as Cubans.

For both East and West, therefore, the Third World has been contested territory. With East-West hostility stalemated in the North by conventional and nuclear deterrence, both camps have turned their attention to the South in order to increase their influence and power. The conflicts of Third World countries have not always been caused by East or West, but interventions by East and West have undoubtedly compounded the problems. The Third World has thus been rendered a zone of war.   **Francis Toase**

War on the Nile

The internal strife in the Sudan

The Sudan is an enormous country, the largest in Africa, some 2,505,813 square km (967,494 square miles) in extent – about 10 times the size of the United Kingdom – and its population by the mid-1960s was a mere 16 million. Like so many former colonies, however, it contains within its borders a diversity of racial and religious groups, reinforced by a clear geographical divide.

In the northern desert region, where the Nile is the source of all wealth, live Arab-speaking Muslims who make up about 40 per cent of the total population and have traditionally dominated the administration of the country. In a central band of savannah and grassland, the population is again largely Muslim; but in the south it is very different. The south has always been one of the most remote corners of the world and was one of the last areas to be claimed during the 'scramble' for Africa. This region is dominated by the great swamps of the Sudd region; its inhabitants are animist or Christian, not Muslim.

For much of the 19th century, northern Sudan was ruled by Egypt. In the 1880s, the revolt of the Mahdi established an independent theocracy until British forces conquered the country in the 1890s, after which it was administered under a joint Anglo-Egyptian condominium. After World War II, the inevitability of British withdrawal led to intense debate about the future of the country. Egypt wanted to retain some control but the Sudanese rejected this and the relationship between north and south was never equitably formalised. The British had always treated the south as a separate region, but it was too backward financially and educationally, and too divided within itself between tribes such as the Dinka and the Azande, to promote independence for itself or autonomy within a federation. What happened instead was that resentment steadily increased.

Violence broke out in the summer of 1955, during the preparations for independence in the New Year, when there was rioting in the south by workers who had been dismissed from industrial concerns. The administration in Khartoum, in the north of the country, faced a dilemma: whether to try and restore order by using the locally raised Equatoria Corps, largely made up of southerners but officered by northerners,

Above: The British Commissioner of Equatoria Province takes the salute for the last time as Britain withdraws from the Sudan. Right: The emerging force for independence for southern Sudan. Anya-Nya scouts flank a rebel armed with a sub-machine gun, purchased from defeated Congolese Simbas. Below: Scenes reminiscent of General Gordon's murder in the 19th century as crowds storm the Ministry of the Interior in Khartoum in the late 1950s.

or whether to fly in more reliable troops from the north. In the event, northern troops were flown in, and the Equatoria Corps was ordered to prepare to be posted to the north. Within the corps there were persistent rumours of disarmament and disbandment and it soon became clear that the soldiers were not willing to obey the order. Indeed, on 18 August 1955 the troops rebelled and attacked their officers. Weapons were stolen from garrison armouries as the mutiny spread to other units and the rebels went on the rampage. The government declared a State of Emergency and 8000 government troops were air-lifted southwards to quell the revolt.

It was the intervention of the British Governor-General, Sir Knox Helm, that eventually defused the situation and by 27 August all resistance had ceased. The subsequent meeting arranged between rebel and government leaders to discuss the grievances and surrender of the rebels never in fact materialised because, fearful of retribution, many rebels disappeared into the forests taking their weapons with them. These fears were subsequently proven well founded when, after the British withdrawal from Sudan in late 1955, 300 rebels were executed.

Within the National Assembly the south was poorly represented, and southern requests for federal

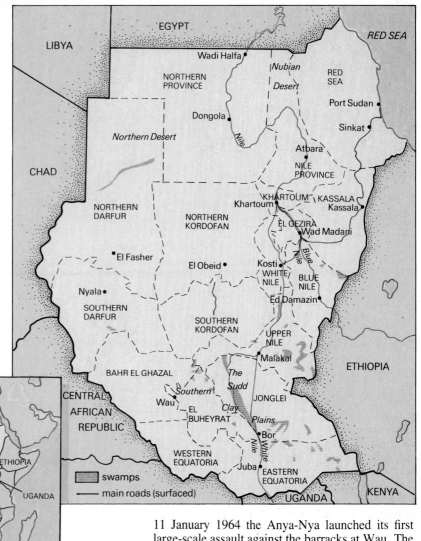

status were repeatedly ignored. In December 1957 their proposals were rejected outright. During 1958 events began to move quickly; opposition to the premier, Abdullah Khalil, was openly voiced, the cotton crop – Sudan's biggest export – failed, and rumours from the south were that the rebels of 1955 were about to re-emerge. Outside powers, notably Egypt, were also taking advantage of the prevailing instability. On 17 November 1958 there was a bloodless military coup and General Ibrahim Abboud, commander-in-chief of the army, ended the brief period of quasi-democratic rule.

Throughout the early years of Abboud's administration, despite harsh repressive measures against the southern population, the rebels of 1955 maintained base camps in the forest and although poorly armed, continued to frustrate, harass and ambush government troops. In 1961, this small army was increased in size when 800 veterans of the Equatoria Corps mutiny were released from jail and immediately joined up with the rebels. Hostilities became more pronounced, and in September 1963 the insurgent force began to assume a more definite shape and took the name Land Freedom Army. Popularly known as the Anya-Nya, the military wing of the exiled Sudan National African Union, it united various groups of rebels under Major-General Emilio Tafeng. On

Above left: President Khalil who mishandled the situation in southern Sudan. Below: An Anya-Nya rebel manning a 12.7mm heavy machine gun of Soviet origin. Such weapons were a rare acquisition for the rebels and this one was almost certainly captured from government troops.

11 January 1964 the Anya-Nya launched its first large-scale assault against the barracks at Wau. The attack failed and 60 guerrillas were captured but the remainder had time and space to re-group.

By the end of 1964 the Anya-Nya numbered some 2000 troops, and although weapons were in short supply, morale was rising. After the attack at Wau, increased government activity in the south, in the form of political arrests and military saturation of urban areas, had encouraged southern-born officials to join the guerrilla movement, leaving a Muslim Sudanese army, approximately 20,000 strong, supporting a dominant northern administration bent on extending Muslim influence in the southern provinces. As the government cracked down, foreign Christian missionaries were expelled and public order

Above: President Nimeiri, whose agreement with rebel leaders brought a halt to 16 years of bloody war.

Below: Mobile and lightly armed, the Anya-Nya rebel proved to be an elusive enemy. Inset: Sudanese rebels in camouflage during battle training at their forest hideout.

deteriorated. Anya-Nya forces were crossing the unmarked borders at will, and Zaire was accused by the government in Khartoum of aiding the rebels.

On 8 May 1964, Sudanese troops crossed into Zaire in order to move against a guerrilla training camp. Government raids also extended into Ethiopia and Uganda in search of rebel units. Similarly, the Anya-Nya increased its attacks.

The activities of the Anya-Nya and the administration's failure to defeat them forced public opinion in the north to push for a change in government. The consequent upheavals, civil unrest in Khartoum, the shooting of demonstrators and total political chaos led to the resignation of Abboud and the purging of army factions in the government on 15 November 1964.

By then Anya-Nya strength had risen to some 5000 men, although only about 10 per cent were using modern weapons. Some equipment, including 600 automatic weapons, was obtained from the Congolese Simbas, who had suffered heavy defeats in the Congo. Although Abboud's military regime had fallen, and the possibility of renewed talks with the new government seemed likely, Premier Muhammed Ahmad Mahjub was no less enchanted by a policy of repression than his predecessor. By 1966, however, the administrative system in the south had completely collapsed. Furthermore, famine and epidemics of sleeping sickness and other diseases placed enormous strains on the internal structure of the country, and during this time it is estimated that 1.5 million people, almost 10 per cent of the total population, died.

In military terms, these conditions were perfect for sustaining a guerrilla war. With the political and civil systems disintegrating, much effort was distracted from suppressing the rebels. The vast expanses of desolate land allowed the guerrillas to operate from isolated bases deep in the countryside. Despite their lack of weapons, the guerrillas managed to ambush government troops efficiently, often replenishing their armouries with the spoils of a successful assault.

Military stalemate

The continued success of the Anya-Nya was such that in 1967 it proclaimed the establishment of the Southern Sudan Provisional Government in Equatoria province, which it now almost completely controlled. Only the towns were held by the Khartoum government's troops, 18,000 of whom were deployed in the south by the mid-1960s. Although these troops were superior in both weapons and numbers, their strength was only of significance if they could actually engage a rebel unit – which, generally speaking, was not the case. For most of the time the Anya-Nya attacked static targets and occasionally, as in 1968, occupied entire districts such as Wau. The inability of the government to pin down the guerrillas had created an effective military stalemate.

It was the rule of Colonel Gaafar Nimeiri, after a successful coup in May 1969, that heralded the end of this stalemate. But not until February 1972 were 16 years of bloody civil war finally brought to an end by an agreement reached between leaders of the administration and leaders of the Anya-Nya. Henceforth the south was to be ruled directly by an autonomous regional council, and indirectly by the central government which would supervise legislation, trade, and economic and social planning.

Despite repeated attempts to remove Nimeiri from power, the agreement was ratified and the south gained far more than they believed possible a year earlier. Although the majority of Anya-Nya leaders accepted the proposals, some veteran southern politicians could not entertain the concept of anything other than complete independence for the south. One such was Gordon Mortat who, from his position in exile, agitated and recruited extensively for continued fighting in the south in order ultimately to achieve independence. The efforts of Mortat and others similarly inclined have prevented the complete pacification of the south, and guerrilla conflict was still continuing into the early 1980s.

Alexander McNair-Wilson

Key Weapons

The M48-60 SERIES

part 2

The M60 Main Battle Tank

The M60 was a development of the M48-series tank and was intended to replace medium and heavy classes of tank in US Army service with a main battle tank. The Chrysler Corporation initially received the production contract in 1959 for 180 examples. The first tanks were built in 1960 and entered service with the United States Army in November that year. The combination of gun and chassis proved successful and an order was placed for a further 770 M60s.

The year 1962 saw the introduction of the M60A1 variant. This improved an already sound design and featured an enlarged and pointed cast-armour turret with M19 cupola providing eight periscopes, as well as hull design changes to improve protection. The M60A1 was built with a cast hull, and was provided with torsion bar suspension with six road wheels. The drive sprocket was positioned at the rear, the idler at the front, and three return rollers were fitted. The Continental AVDS-1790-2A diesel engine developed 750bhp at 2400rpm. An NBC system was made available, with full infra-red/white-light equipment standard. The driver's optics were similar to those in the M48, but a passive night-vision sight replaced the M24.

The well proven 105mm gun with power-assisted elevation had 60 rounds available in the M60 and a further three in the M60A1. Its eccentric fume extractor mounted towards the rear of the barrel provided a recognition feature to distinguish the M60 from the M48. A rate of fire of between six and eight rounds per minute was attainable. The gun can be elevated to plus 20 degrees and depressed to minus 10 degrees and a 7.62mm M73 machine gun is co-axially mounted. The commander's M19 cupola has an electrically operated .50in Browning M85 machine gun which,

Previous page: A US M60A3 main battle tank takes part in a combined-nations tank competition in Germany, 1980. Above: While observing the effects of gunfire the commander of an Israeli M60 ensures that his tank is well sited in a hull-down position.

Right: An M60A1 of the US Army. Despite the attempt at camouflage the high turret silhouette of the M60 is only too apparent, a fault accentuated by the commander's cupola.

Right: Armed with a 105mm M68 gun an M60A1 blasts away on the firing range. Some 63 rounds of main armament ammunition can be carried within the tank.

Above and inset: The M60A2 incorporated a 152mm gun/launcher system, capable of firing a number of conventional ammunition types as well as the Shillelagh missile. The M60A2 entered service in 1966 but due to a succession of teething problems did not become operational until 1974.

with elevation of plus 60 degrees, has a dual role. For the .50in machine gun, 900 rounds are available, and for the 7.62mm 5500. The M17C coincidence rangefinder provides a high level of accuracy up to 4400m (4800yds) and an electronic ballistic computer increases the chances of a first-time hit.

The M60A2 was developed in the mid-1960s and introduced a new concept in tank gunnery. The idea was to mount, in a redesigned turret, a 152mm weapon capable of either launching a Shillelagh missile or firing conventional rounds with combusti-

ble cases. When firing the weapon in the missile mode the gunner acquires his target with infra red, then launches the Shillelagh which flies towards the target steered by command guidance. The disadvantage is that the M60A2 can only fire the missile – of which 13 are carried – from the halt; and stabilisation problems with the turret and tracking systems have caused severe difficulties. The complicated nature of a breech designed to accept a missile or a round, and the problems caused by incomplete combustion of the case, ensured a long delay in introducing the M60A2

Left: The M60A1 was the major production model in the M60. Below left: The crew of an M60A1 take a rest while on an armoured exercise in central Norway. This M60 is fitted with a dozer blade.

Below: A column of Israeli M60s ploughs through the sands of the Sinai Desert. Bottom: A derivative of the M60A1, the M728 Combat Engineer Vehicle was armed with a 165mm demolition gun and, in addition, was equipped with a dozer blade, an A-frame boom with an eight-foot lift and a winch with an 11-tonne pull.

into front-line service. In 1971, however, these problems were largely solved and during the 1970s a total of 526 Shillelagh-armed tanks entered US Army service.

Production continued with an up-rated M60A1, with hydraulic gun stabilisation and an improved air cleaner which led to the M60A3 in 1978. This version has an AN/VVG-2 laser rangefinder and XM21 ballistic computer which, linked to the all-weather capability AN/VGS-2 tank thermal sight in conjunction with a new APFSDS M735A1 Stabiloy round, provides a high degree of accuracy up to a range of 3000m (3300 yds). A laser fire-control system and muzzle reference system for the gunner ensure a good first-time hit probability rate. Many other improvements to optics, suspension and electrical systems have been made and further ones are planned to help keep the M60 abreast of contemporary developments.

The M60A3 arrived in Europe in mid-1979 and there were plans to build over 2500 of them. Israel and

Jordan have both placed orders for this variant, and the US Marines operate it too. By early 1975 over 3000 M60 or M60A1 main battle tanks had entered US Army service, over 100 were with the Marines, and over 900 had been exported. By the time production was run down in 1982 more than 13,000 tanks had been built.

The M60 has proved to be a reliable vehicle in service and, while production of the advanced M1 Abrams tank is under way, the series will continue to provide armoured support in Europe well into the 1990s. During the war in Vietnam the M728 Combat Engineer Vehicle and AVLB versions saw extensive action; and the Middle East War of 1973 gave the M60 an opportunity to be tested in battle, where it performed creditably. An undoubted export success, it has been sold to many countries including Austria, Ethiopia, Iran, Israel, Italy, Jordan, North Yemen, Saudi Arabia, Singapore, Somalia, South Korea, Sudan and Turkey.

M60 MBT

Dimensions Length (gun included) 9.31m (30ft 6in); width 3.63m (11ft 11in); height 3.26m (10ft 8in)
Weight Combat loaded 48,987kg (108,000lb)
Ground Pressure 0.79kg/cm² (11.241lb/in²)
Engine Continental AVDS-1790-2A 12-cylinder diesel engine developing 750bhp at 2400rpm

Performance Maximum road speed 48km/h (30mph); range (road) 500km (310 miles); vertical obstacle 0.91m (3ft); trench 2.59m (8ft 6in); gradient 60 per cent; fording 1.22m (4ft), with kit 2.44m (8ft)

Armour Min-max 12.7mm-120mm (0.50-4.80in)
Armament One 105mm M68 gun; one 7.62mm machine gun co-axial with main armament; one 0.5in machine gun in commander's cupola

(The M60A2 mounts a 152mm gun/launcher capable of firing a Shillelagh anti-tank missile)

Top: A unit of Israeli M60s halts while on a desert patrol in the Sinai. Above right: An M60A1 of the US 2nd Armoured Division fords a river on an exercise in America.

Right: An M60A2 lies in wait by a road during manoeuvres in Germany. The redesigned turret – capable of housing the 152mm gun/launcher – is clearly visible.

FLN triumph

The road to Algerian independence

At the beginning of the 1960s it was still not easy to imagine that the Front de Libération Nationale (National Liberation Front or FLN) would secure its war aims in Algeria. Military victory appeared to be within the grasp of the French and, even if that victory were not total, the Fifth Republic inaugurated by General Charles de Gaulle seemed politically strong enough to sustain a low-intensity struggle indefinitely. Added to this was the knowledge that France's interest in holding Algeria had been increased by the discovery of oil and gas reserves in the Sahara. It was a gloomy time for the FLN, which had failed to attract powerful political backing from either the communist bloc or the West because of its determinedly non-aligned stance. No-one could have guessed that de Gaulle would have risked losing the loyalty of his army, and even of starting a civil war, in order to rid his country of the Algerian problem.

President de Gaulle's own disillusionment with the idea of a French Algeria was a gradual process. Before the events of May 1958 brought him to power, his main emotion seems to have been a profound loathing of the politicians of the Fourth Republic coupled with a pessimism about their ability to hold Algeria – which he regarded then as desirable. However he had told a journalist in April 1958 'Certainly Algeria will be independent', and he was guarded in his statements when he visited Algeria in the wake of his return to power. Just once his emotions overcame him, and in Mostaganem on 6 June he assured an attentive crowd that France was in Algeria forever and cried: *'Vive l'Algérie française!'* He later explained that the words had just 'escaped' him and were not to be counted on. His real feelings at this time were probably most accurately reflected in a reply he made in November 1958 to Paul Delouvrier, his Delegate-General to Algeria, when Delouvrier had assured him that Algeria would be independent: 'In 25 years, Delouvrier, in 25 years,' he said.

There is no doubt that de Gaulle was bitterly disappointed that the FLN refused to negotiate a ceasefire as soon as his first visit to Algeria had proved his popularity with Muslims as well as *colons* (the European settlers). In default of this he ordered General Maurice Challe to crush the FLN in Algeria militarily so that he could force it to the negotiating table. By the summer of 1960 Challe's offensive had been so successful that de Gaulle secretly met the only representative of the ALN (Armée de Libération Nationale – the military wing of the

Overpage above: Although the celebrations of Algerian independence were considered by most of the indigenous population to be celebrations of the victory of the ALN (overpage below, one of the first ALN soldiers to enter Algiers), in reality the outcome of the war was in many ways contrary to the military decision within Algeria, which had been a very successful campaign for the French Army.

The Generals intervene

Senior officers of the French Army made two major attempts to intervene in politics as a result of the Algerian War. The first was successful; the second a failure.

In May 1958, during yet another political crisis in the Fourth Republic, General Raoul Salan, commander-in-chief in Algeria, sent an ultimatum to Paris demanding that any new government proclaim its unequivocal backing for *Algérie française*. This was accompanied by riots in Algiers, and Generals Salan and Jacques Massu joined a Committee of Public Safety set up in the city. The generals threatened to make incursions into France itself if their choice of prime minister, General Charles de Gaulle, was not returned to power. On 2 June de Gaulle formed a government, and order was re-established.

Having asserted themselves once, the upper ranks of the army were soon prepared to repeat their actions. There was bitterness and unrest as de

Gaulle's policy developed into one of acceding to the demands of the FLN. Salan retired prematurely in 1960, while Maurice Challe resigned in 1961.

On 21 April 1961, Generals Challe, André Zeller and Edmond Jouhaud set up a command HQ at Zéralda, base of the 1st REP, which was prepared to act as the striking force of the revolt and, during the night of 21/22 April, took over Algiers without a shot being fired. At the same time, Oran fell into the hands of rebel troops under General Gardy and Colonel Argoud, while Salan flew in to join the putsch.

On 22 and 23 April, Challe tried, unsuccessfully, to rally the army to the revolt. On the afternoon of the 25th, after four tense days, Challe announced that he would surrender to the authorities; Zeller was arrested on 6 May, while Salan and Jouhaud went underground into the OAS. Government representatives moved back into control of Algiers, and the 1st REP was formally disbanded.

FLN) that he was to speak to directly in the war.

This was Si Salah (real name Mohamed Zamoun), chief of Wilaya 4, who offered to accept a ceasefire and bring his men in from the *djebel* (mountain areas) in return for de Gaulle's vague promise of self-determination for Algeria. Although Si Salah offered to use his considerable influence to persuade other ALN commanders within Algeria to follow his lead, de Gaulle rejected his offer. It seemed to the president that he needed agreement with the FLN in Tunisia.

Although de Gaulle turned down Si Salah's overtures he was probably not above letting the Provisional Government know that the internal revolt was crumbling, in order to lever its members towards negotiation. This almost certainly cost Si Salah his life at the hands of agents of the Provisional Government. Whatever the truth behind these murky dealings the initial result was exactly what de Gaulle wished for: on 25 June 1960 a mission arrived in France from the Provisional Government to negotiate a peace settlement. By this time de Gaulle had already advanced a certain way down the road to offering the Algerians independence, but the negotiations that took place in Melun in great secrecy were brief and unfruitful. The French wanted a ceasefire to precede negotiations while the FLN demanded that a ceasefire should only be part of an overall settlement. Within four days of its arrival the FLN delegation left France, the Provisional President, Ferhat Abbas, declaring 'Independence is not offered, it is seized'.

Meanwhile, the French government was finding that its freedom of action was restricted not only by the normal problems of democratic politicians – impending elections, for example – but also by the intensity of feeling within Algeria and the army. In January 1960, General Massu gave an interview openly criticising de Gaulle's policy. He was recalled to Paris and sacked. *Algérie française* activists called for demonstrations and on the 24th crowds in Algiers clashed with gendarmes. Barricades went up, and Challe, commander-in-chief in Algeria, ordered paratroops into the city. During the 'week of barricades' that followed, the troops openly fraternised with the rebels while negotiations took place. The barricades came down peacefully after de Gaulle made conciliatory statements, but the episode had revealed a dangerous unreliability among France's crack troops. There was especial unrest in the Legion, notably in the 1er Régiment Etrangère Parachutiste (1st REP).

De Gaulle had a keen sense that it was his destiny to

Left: *Algérie française* activist Lagaillarde appeals to crowds at the end of the 'week of barricades'. During the week, French troops, initially sent in to control the *colons*, began to fraternise with the civilians. Left below: A legionnaire on lookout in the Algerian mountains. The Legion's historic ties with Algeria made its troops increasingly restive as de Gaulle pressed ahead with his plans for French disengagement.

revive and modernise France. He felt that the Algerian imbroglio was holding up his historic plans and that, due to his age (70), time was short. He also had little sympathy with France's Algerian connections: he valued the Saharan gas reserves and the naval base at Mers-el Kébir but he cared little for the turbulent *colons* and appeared to feel no debt of loyalty to the Algerian Muslim *harkas* (scouts) who served France at such danger to themselves and their families.

On 4 November 1960 de Gaulle took matters a stage further by referring in a broadcast to Algerian emancipation and to an Algerian Republic of the future. He may well have been trying to prepare French public opinion for the inevitable, but his fateful words stirred up a hornet's nest among those committed to a French Algeria. In January 1961 he won 75 per cent of the vote in a referendum which gave him authority to organise Algerian self-determination, but many abstained and the *colons* voted heavily against the proposal. De Gaulle had to weather the attempted putsch of French generals in

April 1961 before his concession had its reward and the FLN again agreed to talk – at Evian in May.

To warm the atmosphere at Evian, de Gaulle had imposed on French forces in Algeria what amounted to a unilateral truce and released many FLN prisoners as a gesture of goodwill. The FLN, however, were not to be wooed and simply took advantage of this weakness so that the number of violent 'incidents' increased by 50 per cent and most of the released prisoners rejoined the fighting ranks of the revolutionaries. In addition to this the FLN delegates fiercely rejected the French conditions to the offer of independence. These conditions involved maintaining French possession of the Sahara and extending guarantees of dual citizenship and property rights to the *colons*. De Gaulle very nearly despaired as the talks reached an impasse by 28 July, but he had already broadcast on the 12th that France was prepared to accept 'an entirely independent' Algerian state. The French position was crumbling even as the FLN maintained its hard line.

Searching for a settlement

By the autumn de Gaulle's determination to be finished with the whole crisis was hardened by yet another attempt on his life. In September he revealed that France must relinquish any claim to the Sahara and by the New Year he pressed the point that disengagement was of paramount importance. Strangely enough the FLN were equally worried that he might be assassinated, for a French military government would prove a formidable obstacle to them.

These fears brought both sides together again. They met at a secret retreat in the Jura mountains in February 1962 with de Gaulle so utterly determined to reach agreement that he repeatedly urged his delegates to give in on details just so long as they secured a ceasefire. Under this pressure an agreement was reached but, when it came to be drawn up at Evian in March, the FLN adopted an even harder line.

The final 93-page settlement was signed on 18 March 1962 and it was, in every respect, a victory for the FLN. All claims to the Sahara or a French connection had been abandoned, and even the slight protection afforded the *colons* during the transition period was rendered valueless by an agreement that French forces would not intervene if the Algerians infringed the treaty terms. Besides this the settlement had been made between France and the unconstitutional body of the Provisional Government of Algeria – any real future government could repudiate it.

For de Gaulle, at least, it was enough. He agreed that the application of the agreements would be capricious but said: 'As for France now it is for her to interest herself in something else.' For him it was an honourable end, but for hundreds of thousands of others it was a disaster. There were occasional massacres as the ALN troops took over, but most of the *colons* fled to France. Only a few of the 60,000 *harkas* managed even to become penniless refugees and treatment of them was merciless: a common form of execution was preceded by the individual being forced to dig his own grave and swallow his medals. Even for the long-suffering people of Algeria peace did not come immediately. Factional fighting and disorder were widespread until Houari Boumédienne came to power in June 1965. It was then that this savage war was truly ended and the independence won in 1962 finally realised.   **P.J. Banyard**

Above: De Gaulle visits Algiers in 1960. Left: Ben Bella, on his return from imprisonment in France, addresses a crowd following Algerian independence. Below: Police move into action against a crowd in Algiers.

O.A.S

Terror tactics from a secret army

The Organisation Armée Secrète (OAS) had its origins in the bitter feelings of resentment against President Charles de Gaulle's policy of self-determination for Algeria, announced in his speech of 16 September 1959. Not only did the majority of the European settlers in Algeria, the *colons*, find this unacceptable, but a substantial group within the army blamed the president for betraying a cause which had already cost so much French blood.

The abortive generals' coup of April 1961 was one symptom of the army's anger. But the OAS had come into being at an earlier point. In January 1961 a young *colon*, a lawyer who had made the mistake of supporting de Gaulle's policy, was murdered by two ex-soldiers. A fortnight later in Madrid, two leading *colons* hit upon the name Organisation Armée Secrète for the title of their underground group. By March, OAS posters were a common sight in Algiers and during that month the organisation mounted its first, and rather unsuccessful, attacks on prominent politicians. The OAS added immensely to the atmosphere of political instability that surrounded the Fifth Republic during the period of negotiations for an independent Algeria.

After the failure of the generals' coup in April, the OAS was strengthened by the addition of many of the officers involved in the plot and it soon assumed a structure familiar to those who had read the works of the theorists of *guerre révolutionnaire*. France and Algeria were divided into zones, with sectors, sub-sectors, districts and cells. General Raoul Salan was in overall command, with his headquarters in Algiers; General Paul Gardy controlled the Algiers-Sahara area and General Edmond Jouhaud the zone around Oran. Captain Pierre Sergent, formerly of the crack 1st Legion Parachute Battalion (BEP) organized the OAS in metropolitan France, and Colonel Yves Godard – for some years one of the army's leading counter-insurgency specialists – was responsible for propaganda and psychological warfare. Special teams collected funds, carried on the propaganda war, used plastic explosive (*plastique*) to create terror, and assassinated leading adversaries.

In many respects the OAS resembled the Front de Libération Nationale (FLN), against which so many of its members had fought. There was, though, far less centralisation than is the case with many underground groups. This fact, on the one hand, made it difficult for government agents to penetrate the OAS, but, on the other, led to tactical errors that often had counter-productive results.

The OAS achieved some early successes. In May and June 1961 it carried out spectacular *plastique* attacks to mark the negotiations being conducted at Evian, and on 31 May its agents murdered Commissaire Gavoury, head of the police anti-OAS section. On 5 August the group achieved a considerable propaganda victory when it blew up television cables and broadcast a tape of General Gardy calling for a revolt against de Gaulle.

Throughout the summer of 1961 the OAS carried on its campaign of terror with sub-machine gun, grenade, knife and *plastique*. The OAS hit-squads, known as Delta Commandos, were led by a former Foreign Legion lieutenant, Roger Degueldre, who had deserted in December 1960. Although a ruthless disciplinarian, Degueldre was unable to exercise effective control over all the OAS attack groups. Salan himself became somewhat disenchanted after the garage opposite his refuge was blown up twice, showering him with glass.

Despite the growing number of outrages committed by the OAS, several serving officers remained well-disposed towards it while a much larger number were reluctant to fight against it. Nevertheless, the government scored some successes, notably because of the work of Commissaire Louis Grassien, who built up a detailed picture of the OAS similar to that which Godard had constructed of the FLN during the battle of Algiers.

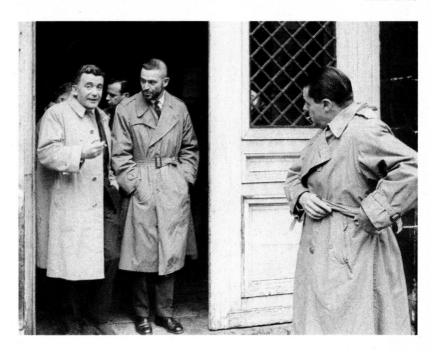

Right: Colonel Godard (left) during the court proceedings after the 'week of barricades' in January 1960. Godard went on to become a leading member of the OAS and, ironically, it was the system of organisational analysis he had developed to combat the FLN in Algiers that the French police, under Commissaire Louis Grassien, used against the OAS.
Bottom: One of the early meetings of the white *colons'* organisation from whose military wing the OAS emerged.

As the campaign went on, the leadership of the OAS became increasingly divided. Salan and his supporters in Algiers believed that OAS activities within Algeria would force de Gaulle to reconsider self-determination, while the Madrid group, which included Colonels Antoine Argoud and Charles Lacheroy, were in favour of applying vigorous pressure in France as well.

There was also disagreement over tactics. When, on 9 September 1961, OAS agents narrowly missed killing de Gaulle at Pont-sur-Seine, Salan publicly disavowed their actions in a letter to *Le Monde*. In France, Sergent was reluctant to embark upon attacks which might kill women or children, and the disfiguring of four-year-old Delphine Renard in February 1962 provoked an outburst of popular fury against the OAS. Matters were made worse when the police over-reacted in their attempt to control a left-wing protest against the outrage: eight people were killed and over 200 injured.

The tragedies of February were followed, a month later, by the Evian agreement, under whose terms Algeria was eventually to become independent. The OAS carried out a wave of attacks in an effort to disrupt the referendum on Algerian independence. Meanwhile, the government was increasingly effec-

tive in tracking down the OAS leaders: Jouhaud was captured in March and Salan in April. At his lengthy trial, distinguished by the brilliance of his defence lawyers, Salan acknowledged his 'total responsibility' for the OAS, although he was eventually sentenced to life imprisonment rather than to death.

With the capture of Salan, the OAS fell into the hands of the colonels, and the struggle went on. In June, however, a ceasefire was negotiated in Algiers. Nevertheless some diehards fought on until late July, shortly before the Algerian independence which they had so resolutely opposed became an established fact.

There can be no denying the fact that the OAS failed in its aim of keeping Algeria French and had pursued a bloody campaign of terror. Like so many other similar organisations, it attracted its fair share of misfits and criminals, but it also contained a large number of men who embarked upon terrorism with heavy hearts, and who believed that only by taking up arms against their own government could they preserve their personal honour. Many of them knew that they were ruining fine careers by supporting the OAS. If the OAS ultimately merits censure as a terrorist organisation, some of its members deserve to be acknowledged as men wrestling with intractable moral problems.

Richard Holmes

The OAS was backed by elements from both the *colons* and the army. After the abortive generals' coup in 1961 led by Jouhaud, Salan and Challe (top, left to right) many officers went underground. Captain Sergent, ex-Foreign Legion (above) led the movement in France and Lieutenant Roger Degueldre, also ex-Foreign Legion (left) led the OAS hit-squads.

War without honour?

The French Army and counter-insurgency

The outbreak of hostilities with the Viet Minh in December 1946 confronted the French Army with a situation which, superficially at least, was not unfamiliar. During the 19th century France had been a major colonising power and, in the course of acquiring a huge colonial empire in Africa and Indochina, French soldiers had gained vast experience of operations in inhospitable terrain against determined enemies. Although France had, in 1946, no comprehensive corpus of counter-insurgency doctrine which could compare with that which was to evolve as a result of the fighting in Indochina, there was at least a general agreement on the way in which colonial campaigns should be conducted. But the war in Indochina not only illustrated the weaknesses of existing doctrine: it also contributed to the development of *guerre révolutionnaire,* which was later to dominate the French response to insurgency in Algeria.

The doctrine of pacification formed the basis of French strategy against the Viet Minh. This was a concept, developed to a fine pitch in the 19th and early 20th centuries, which emphasised the social and civilising role of the army. The insurgent forces were to be defeated and peaceful conditions re-established, conditions in which the population would receive military assistance with a wide variety of public works projects. This emphasis on combined military and political action was crucial. Indeed, as Marshal Joseph Galliéni had written from Madagascar in 1898: 'It is by the combined use of politics and force that the pacification of a country and its future organisation will be achieved. Political action is by far the most important.'

The doctrine of pacification had, however, several important deficiencies when combating communist-inspired insurgency. Its successes had been achieved against an opposition which was tribal or even semi-piratical. It had rarely faced a cogent nationalist movement, and it lacked the vigorous appeal and moral certainty of the communist revolutionary process. Furthermore, the political situation in Indochina was totally unlike that in any other French theatre of operations. Political uncertainties within France meant that French soldiers and administrators in Indochina no longer had a clear sense of mission, and even by 1946 the problem in Indochina had become internationalised, making it unlikely that any solution could be found by France alone. And while pacification had worked well enough in a 19th century context, it was ill-suited to meet the aims and aspirations of colonial populations in the post-1945 era.

Even when operating within the framework of pacification, French forces had traditionally employed counter-insurgency tactics based upon the inter-related characteristics of mobility and firepower. In the fighting in Algeria in the 1830s and 1840s the French had developed the flying column, a light, all-arms formation usually of weak brigade strength. These columns operated from solidly-held strongpoints, and the desert fort, manned by Foreign Legion infantry in white *képis* and blue *capotes*, became the popular image of the French Army in North Africa.

Defensive positions

French operational doctrine in Indochina was characterised by the same combination of positional defence and tactical mobility. French reliance upon defensive positions was always somewhat questionable, however. These positions, either large ones like Cao Bang, Na San or Dien Bien Phu, or small ones, like the hundreds of tiny *postes* – 1200 by the end of 1951 – which made up the de Lattre Line, were always vulnerable to defeat in detail. In October 1950 the Viet Minh overran the French positions on the Cao Bang ridge in north Tonkin, causing heavy casualties and capturing enough arms and equipment for an entire Viet Minh division.

The French often reacted too slowly to threats to their defensive positions. Sometimes, when they did react, their riposte had been predicted by the Viet Minh and the relieving force was itself ambushed. The parachute battalion dropped to support the withdrawal from the Cao Bang ridge suffered over 80 per cent casualties. Moreover, even when positions held firm, their achievement was of limited relevance to the real war. The demands of a large network of garrisons worsened manpower difficulties; all too often French garrisons spent the hours of darkness secure behind their defences while outside the Viet Minh controlled both countryside and population. Yet the record of defensive positions was not uniformly sterile: in late 1952 Giap lost some 6000 men in fruitless attacks by his 308th Division on Na San, and the successful defence of Mao Khe in March the previous year had also caused severe losses.

The record of mobile operations in Indochina was equally mixed. French mobility was limited by the fact that the helicopter, the principal source of tactical mobility in Algeria, was still in its infancy. For most of the war the French never had more than 10 helicopters available, whereas no less than 600 were in use in Algeria by the time of the ceasefire in 1962. Airborne forces in Indochina had far less flexibility than heli-

borne forces in Algeria. Not only was the terrain often unsuited for airborne operations, but a parachute force could only be extracted with difficulty.

Given these severe limitations on air mobility, the French were forced to rely upon mobility on the ground – which generally meant movement by road. This confinement to roads enabled the Viet Minh to screen a column; they could ambush it if they chose to do so, or elude it altogether. In October-November 1952, for example, the French mounted Operation Lorraine, a deep thrust into the Viet Minh communication and supply system along the Red River (now known as the Hong). The force totalled 30,000 men. Progress was painfully slow as columns moved along roads damaged by the Viet Minh. Logistic support for the operation consumed much of the available air transport, and although some large Viet Minh weapons dumps were found, the French force only encountered the Viet Minh in strength once it had begun its withdrawal. On 17 November an ambush at Chan Muong cost the French one tank and six half-tracks, together with 314 casualties. Operations on the scale of Lorraine were simply too ponderous, and reflected a concern with conventional warfare on the European pattern rather than the realities of guerrilla war in Southeast Asia.

Yet even while the fighting was still in progress in Indochina it became apparent to some officers that the French had failed to grasp the true nature of communist insurgency. The strategy of pacification, and tactics based upon fortified positions and road-bound columns, were no answer to a revolutionary process involving protracted war and a struggle for the loyalty of the population.

Recognition that the population was a key element in the struggle encouraged some attempts at resettlement. Although this was not tried in Vietnam, a pilot scheme achieved some success in the Cambodian frontier province of Svay Rieng in 1946 and, on a larger scale, in the province of Kompong Chau in 1951. Several relocation points were established, each with its own defences, and the population was encouraged to move there. The Viet Minh, deprived of food and recruits from the local population, were forced to fall back on their bases, leaving the security forces in control of the previously infiltrated areas. This policy was to be used on a vastly increased scale in Algeria, where the Special Administrative Sections (SAS) took responsibility for the administra-

Marshal Galliéni (above) developed techniques of pacification that proved very successful in the early 20th century, but were overtaken by the strength of communist-inspired insurgency in the 1950s in Indochina, where the French Army suffered a severe defeat. The shattering experience of this defeat – and its aftermath of capture for many officers (above left) – led to new methods of counter-insurgency that were applied in Algeria, most notably by the 10th Parachute Division of General Massu (below left) in 1957.

tion, education and political mobilisation of these new villages.

Commando groups were another potentially useful innovation. Called Groupements de Commandos Mixtes Aéroportés (GCMA) until December 1953 and Groupements Mixtes d'Intervention (GMI) thereafter, these were guerrilla forces, each group based around a core up to 400 strong with a few French officers and NCOs leading locally-recruited tribesmen. By mid-1954 there were 15,000 men in the GMI. Opinions varied as to their usefulness. Some officers believed that they consumed specialist manpower and scarce air transport to little purpose, while others suggested that they caused considerable damage in areas which French conventional forces could seldom reach. In October 1953, for example, a commando group, reinforced by a parachute platoon, raided Coc Leu, deep in Viet Minh territory, destroying storage depots and killing 150 Viet Minh. The lessons of the GMI were not forgotten: in Algeria the French made good use of locally-recruited auxiliaries (the *harkas*) and long-range penetration forces, the *commandos de chasse*.

The experience of Indochina did more than point the way towards new tactical methods. It formed the catalyst for the evolution of a new doctrine of counter-insurgency, the concept of *guerre révolutionnaire*. The apostles of this creed had all served in Indochina, and some of them, after their capture at Dien Bien Phu, had learned, first-hand, the power of communist ideology. In the period immediately after the Indochina war several French officers wrote books or articles assessing the nature of communist revolution. The works of Colonel Roger Trinquier and Colonel Charles Lacheroy were among the most important: it was no accident that both these officers were to play key roles in the struggle for Algeria.

The theorists of *guerre révolutionnaire* constructed

models of the revolutionary process in which the insurgents combined guerrilla warfare with psychological warfare to secure eventual control of the state. They divided the process into a number of phases, starting with the infiltration of the population and the creation of a guerrilla infrastructure, passing through a phase in which the insurgents established secure base areas in which they formed the *de facto* government, and ending with an all-out coordinated offensive against the government and its supporters.

This assessment of the nature of revolution inspired a comprehensive doctrine of counter-revolution. Firstly, the guerrillas were to be cut off from foreign assistance, for the French were well aware of the immense value to the Viet Minh of sanctuary in and assistance from China. Accordingly, fortified barriers (*barrages*) were constructed along the Tunisian and Moroccan borders, and by early 1958 they had effectively cut off the Algerian insurgents from their supporters in Tunisia and Morocco. Secondly, internal support for the guerrillas was to be reduced by the large-scale removal of the civilian population from certain areas – 300,000 around Constantine alone – which became, in effect, free-fire zones. The population shifted from these areas was re-housed in 'model villages', where intelligence teams operated.

Deployment of manpower

Hand in hand with this process of isolation went attempts to defeat the insurgent forces in the field. Large numbers of troops – 300,000 by 1959 – were deployed in *quadrillage*, a chequerboard of small garrisons across the face of Algeria. Large offensives were carried out by the Réserve Générale, consisting of some 30,000 men, mainly from elite units such as the paras, marines and the Foreign Legion. The *quadrillage* units helped control the countryside, protect the population and furnish intelligence, while the Réserve Générale carried out increasingly sophisticated operations for which its tough and well-motivated soldiers were ideally suited.

These largely military attempts to cut off the insurgents from foreign and internal support, and to smash their armed power within Algeria, were accompanied by a determined psychological warfare campaign. In 1956 a Psychological Action and Information Service was set up under Colonel Lacheroy, and in the following year psychological warfare departments – the 5th bureaux – were inserted into the headquarters of combat formations and regional commands. The bureaux had as their goal not only the destruction of enemy morale by propaganda, but also the bolstering of French morale by the dissemination of a wide variety of publications, ranging from the mass-circulation *Bled* to the high-quality *Revue de Défense Nationale*.

Inevitably, the duties of the 5th bureaux took them onto dangerous ground. Their activities in the re-education of captured enemy personnel attracted hostile comment and, particularly in the period 1959 to 1960, the 5th bureaux assumed a role that was little short of political. They were abolished early in 1960, after it had become clear that they had been involved in the manipulation of anti-government demonstrations by the settlers.

The issue of the 5th bureaux highlights the strains endemic within the doctrine of *guerre révolutionnaire*. On the one hand it was a clear-sighted and comprehensive response to the insurgent threat, but

on the other it brought the army squarely into the political sphere. In the words of Lieutenant-Colonel J. Rousset, writing in the *Revue de Défense Nationale* in 1960: 'To recognise that war has become total is to recognise that the army can no longer handle more than a part of the war.' The combination of military and political action had long been a feature of French counter-insurgency, but the development of *guerre révolutionnaire* took the army well outside its own realm of competence, posing a serious challenge to French politicians and, ultimately, helping to discredit the army as a whole. **Richard Holmes**

Left, above: Restricting the movement of rebels in remote areas was helped by constant identity checks. Left, below: French paras move through the casbah in Algiers. Above: Colonel Godard briefing officers prior to a counter-insurgency operation. Below: Colonel Bigeard (seated), the man who defeated the FLN in Algiers.

Military coups are usually associated with unstable countries in Latin America and Africa. Great Britain, for example, has not experienced military government since the 17th century, when Oliver Cromwell ruled England through his major-generals and the New Model Army. Following the restoration of the monarchy in 1660 the British were determined to prevent the army from exercising such power again, and so the military were successfully subordinated to civil authority.

But the British tradition is not experienced by many other countries. Military intervention in politics has frequently been a normal event and military governments rule many countries today. The widespread occurrence of military intervention results from a number of causes. Armed forces are often the largest, most organised and best disciplined group within a country, as well as being extremely nationalistic and patriotic. They also, of course, are able to deploy substantial military force. In periods of political crisis, civil strife and war, the power of the armed forces is enhanced and, either because of political chaos or the absence of any sovereign authority, they are in a position to take over the functions of government.

Although armed forces are hierarchical, disciplined, uniformed and in theory obedient, military coups are rarely the consequence of all the military conspiring and acting together. They are most often led by a small group of activists based either in elite units or in headquarters, and drawn from middle-ranking officers. The activists are at the major and colonel level, and sometimes the generals are initially less than enthusiastic.

One of the main elements leading to military intervention is political and economic instability. This is why military intervention in politics is widespread in Third World countries, which have faced the upheavals of 'wars of liberation', decolonisation and almost insurmountable political and economic problems. And yet, since 1945, military intervention in politics has occurred in several European countries, too. France faced military coups in 1958 and 1961; Turkey in 1960, 1971 and 1980; Greece in 1967 and 1973; Cyprus in 1974; Portugal in 1974 and Spain in 1981.

National characteristics

Particular national characteristics are important in explaining military coups in Europe since 1945. The circumstances varied from one country to another, and differences existed in the organisation and attitudes of the individual armies.

The French military coups of 1958 and 1961 were a product of the experiences of World War II and subsequent colonial defeats. They were organised and led by minorities within the army whose objective was not a military government but a more sympathetic civilian one. The French Army has generally supported the primacy of constitutional authority. Nevertheless, although France could not be classed as politically or economically backward, a tradition did exist of military intervention in domestic politics at moments of crisis. The most traumatic experience for the military was the rout of 1940 and four years of German occupation. The loyalty of the French Army was divided, the majority obeying what appeared to be the legitimate authority of the Vichy regime while only a few supported Charles de Gaulle in exile.

After the successful Allied breakout from the Normandy beach-head in the late summer of 1944, the task of rebuilding the French Army fell to de Gaulle and his supporters. Most of de Gaulle's army was built on the colonial garrisons outside Vichy's control, and the divisions of occupation had scarcely healed before France was involved in two colonial wars. French involvement in Indochina (1946-54) was unpopular with a large section of the public within France and after the defeat at Dien Bien Phu and subsequent withdrawal, the veterans blamed not only political corruption at home but the incompetence and conservatism of senior officers who had served only in the metropolitan army.

In Algeria (1954-62) the regular and colonial veterans were determined to defeat the insurgents – even if it involved a change of government in France. When the resolve of the government appeared to weaken in 1958, the French military in Algeria effectively forced its resignation and supported the recall of de Gaulle. Ironically, de Gaulle came to favour the granting of independence to Algeria just when the army believed it was winning. When the colonial and para element in Algeria attempted a military coup

nt of

erals

s in Europe

Military coups are normally associated with the imposition of authoritarian, right wing rule – as was the Turkish coup of 1980 (led by the officers shown above) and as intended by the Spanish conspirators in 1981 (below left). But in Portugal, the regime of General Spinola (left) led to a more open political situation that resulted in street violence (far left) and mass demonstration (overpage).

against de Gaulle in 1961 it failed because the conscripts in Algeria refused to participate, and the metropolitan army remained loyal.

The Turkish Army, intensely patriotic, regards itself as the creator of modern Turkey and the guardian of the constitution. Military intervention in politics has been on the initiative of senior officers who, in 1961, were happy to return to barracks, in 1971 exerted sufficient pressure on the civil authority without having to use force, but since 1980 have been unable to resolve Turkey's political instability and have remained in power.

The Greek Army has a long history of political intrigue and military intervention in politics. The majority of officers after 1945 were fiercely nationalistic and anti-communist. The traditional feud with Turkey was exacerbated by Cyprus, to which each laid claim, and the military coup of 1967 was organised and led by a small group of middle-ranking officers. Their attempt to run the government as civilians was a failure, and extreme nationalism and traditional dislike of Turkey led to their fall in 1974, after the Turks had invaded and occupied the predominantly Greek island of Cyprus.

The traditional power-holders in Portuguese society have been the church, financial groups and the army. The Portuguese Army has a long tradition of attempted coups and helped bring Antonio de Oliveira Salazar to power in 1932. From 1932 until 1974 Portugal had an authoritarian government under Salazar and then his successor, Marcello Caetano.

Throughout this period there were 12 military revolts and attempted coups. The greatest strain on the loyalty of the Portuguese armed forces, however, came with the loss of the Indian colony of Goa in 1961, which was seen as a national and military humiliation, and the impact of the colonial wars from 1961 to 1974 in Africa. Many officers became critical of these campaigns and, in turn, of the political dictatorship at home. In April 1974 a group calling itself the Movement of the Armed Forces overthrew the government and there followed two years of political turmoil and military involvement in politics.

The abortive military coup by elements of the Spanish armed forces in 1981 was an attempt to put the clock back. It was a reaction against the constitutional reforms of King Juan Carlos by a hard core of right-wing officers who believed he was betraying the legacy of Francisco Franco. The Spanish Army had a long history of political involvement and its officers supported right-wing, authoritarian and anti-communist views. Following Franco's death in 1975 and the gradual move towards a democracy under the guidance of the king, many of the 'old guard' officers of Franco's army reacted negatively. The military coup of 1981 failed because of the king's opposition and the refusal by the majority of the armed forces to support it.

In geographical terms, these coups were concentrated exclusively in southern Europe. In addition, with the exception of France, all the countries concerned had a relatively poor economy in comparison with most of western Europe. But economic prosperity is not necessarily the main criteria for judging whether a country is prone to coups. The Italian

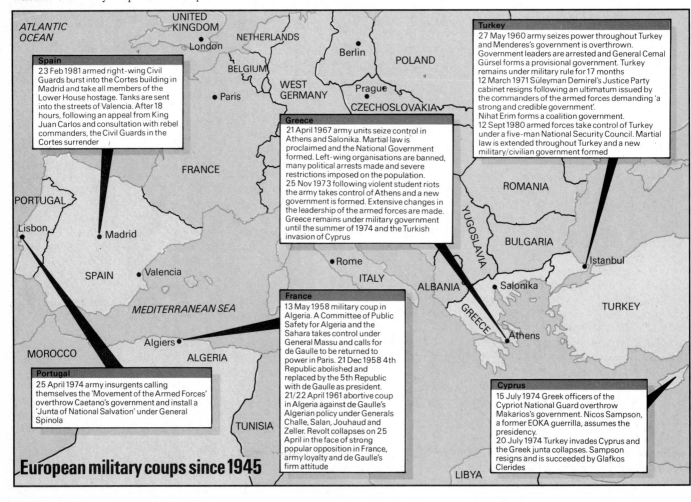

Spain
23 Feb 1981 armed right-wing Civil Guards burst into the Cortes building in Madrid and take all members of the Lower House hostage. Tanks are sent into the streets of Valencia. After 18 hours, following an appeal from King Juan Carlos and consultation with rebel commanders, the Civil Guards in the Cortes surrender

Turkey
27 May 1960 army seizes power throughout Turkey and Menderes's government is overthrown. Government leaders are arrested and General Cemal Gürsel forms a provisional government. Turkey remains under military rule for 17 months
12 March 1971 Süleyman Demirel's Justice Party cabinet resigns following an ultimatum issued by the commanders of the armed forces demanding 'a strong and credible government'. Nihat Erim forms a coalition government.
12 Sept 1980 armed forces take control of Turkey under a five-man National Security Council. Martial law is extended throughout Turkey and a new military/civilian government formed

Greece
21 April 1967 army units seize control in Athens and Salonika. Martial law is proclaimed and the National Government formed. Left-wing organisations are banned, many political arrests made and severe restrictions imposed on the population.
25 Nov 1973 following violent student riots the army takes control of Athens and a new government is formed. Extensive changes in the leadership of the armed forces are made. Greece remains under military government until the summer of 1974 and the Turkish invasion of Cyprus

France
13 May 1958 military coup in Algeria. A Committee of Public Safety for Algeria and the Sahara takes control under General Massu and calls for de Gaulle to be returned to power in Paris. 21 Dec 1958 4th Republic abolished and replaced by the 5th Republic with de Gaulle as president. 21/22 April 1961 abortive coup in Algeria against de Gaulle's Algerian policy under Generals Challe, Salan, Jouhaud and Zeller. Revolt collapses on 25 April in the face of strong popular opposition in France, army loyalty and de Gaulle's firm attitude

Portugal
25 April 1974 army insurgents calling themselves the 'Movement of the Armed Forces' overthrow Caetano's government and install a 'Junta of National Salvation' under General Spínola

Cyprus
15 July 1974 Greek officers of the Cypriot National Guard overthrow Makarios's government. Nicos Sampson, a former EOKA guerrilla, assumes the presidency.
20 July 1974 Turkey invades Cyprus and the Greek junta collapses. Sampson resigns and is succeeded by Glafkos Clerides

European military coups since 1945

Above: Andreas Papandreou; although imprisoned by the military junta (top) in 1967, he became Prime Minister of Greece in 1982 and formed a socialist government.

economy and political system have been in a parlous state since 1945, and yet Italy has not suffered from a military coup since the overthrow of Benito Mussolini in 1943.

Political attitudes

The political attitude of army officers is always crucial. In every European military coup since 1945 the military have claimed to be acting in the national interest, protecting the state and the people against politicians who have betrayed their trust. The Turkish Army sees itself as the guarantor of the constitution with the legitimate right and duty to intervene in politics if the constitution appears to be in danger.

Those soldiers taking part in military coups have usually held right-wing political views and been virulently anti-communist. The activists among the Greek Army officers who seized power in 1967 had been influenced by their experience of the civil war in the 1940s and were convinced that a communist plot existed to subvert the state. The French military conspirators were also convinced anti-communists and believed that the war in Algeria was part of a wider communist plot. However, Portuguese officers had a broad range of political views and included traditional conservatives as well as socialists and communists.

When considering the prevalence of military coups in southern Europe since 1945 it is necessary to explain their absence from other European countries. In northwest Europe the majority of countries maintain effective armed forces; but they have no recent history of military intervention in politics and are well-established democracies with effective governments and a long tradition of military obedience to the

Night of the colonels

In the early hours of Friday 21 April 1967 a bloodless coup toppled the civilian government of Greece and ushered in seven years of military rule.

From 1965, there had been political deadlock in Greece. King Constantine II had urged the leaders of the two main parties, Premier Panayotis Canellopoulos of the conservative National Radical Union and George Papandreou of the Centre Union, to sink their differences in the national interest should parliamentary deadlock result after the elections scheduled for 27 May 1967. But the spirit of amity was broken when Papandreou declared that the appointment of Canellopoulos as premier had amounted to a royal coup. He called for demonstrations in Salonika on 23 April. Up to 500,000 were expected to attend, and military leaders drew up contingency plans should violence occur.

Others, however, wanted to go further, and a conspiracy was planned by four officers. They were Colonel George Papadopoulos, deputy director of the operations branch of the General Staff; Colonel Nikolaos Makarezos of the intelligence service, KYP; Brigadier Stylianos Pattakos, commander of the armed forces in Athens; and Lieutenant-Colonel Michael Roufogalis, deputy director of KYP. Their wish was to set Greece on a new course; they despised the politicians and were guided by an egalitarian – but strongly anti-communist – ethos.

A meeting of the Supreme Military Council in Athens on the night of 20 April provided them with their chance to neutralise the armed forces leadership. At midnight on 20/21 April a company of paras set out for the milit-

ary HQ building, nicknamed 'the Pentagon', where the council was meeting. Within the hour the building had been captured and 50 M47 and 25 M48 tanks were stationed across main highways and outside government offices and key installations throughout the capital. Everyone had been taken by surprise.

The king, when told that tanks were roaming the city, ordered loyal units to march on Athens, but the chief of staff had removed the army from royal control and linked the name of the king with his own instructions. Political leaders were then arrested. Papandreou, 'the Old Fox', when roused from sleep, looked at the young officer standing over him and said: 'You know, son, you are nervous because this is the first time you've done this. But for me it is the fifth.'

By dawn it was clear that the coup had succeeded. That day the king grudgingly acquiesced but insisted on choosing a civilian prime minister. In December a countercoup by the king was hopelessly bungled and he fled with his family to Italy. And in June 1973 the Greek monarchy was formally abolished.

civil authority. It is true that in Germany, historically a major military power, there had been military intervention in politics but, after the total defeat of 1945 and the division of the country, that activity was firmly stamped upon. In Norway and Denmark there is a strong tradition of pacifism and neutralism, and armed forces are regarded as an 'evil necessity'. In both countries, as in Belgium and Holland, the military do not occupy a position of importance and exert little influence on politics. In the neutral countries of Sweden and Switzerland, effective political control and civilian participation in the defence effort prevent any tendency towards military independence.

Both Holland and Britain faced the difficulties of colonial wars after 1945. Although the Dutch fought a bitter war in the East Indies and were forced to withdraw in 1949, the military accepted the political decision. The British had the longest and most extensive experience of colonial wars after 1945 but, like the Dutch, the British military accepted the political decisions.

The most powerful military presence in the West since 1945 has been the United States. The Americans have had an ambivalent attitude towards their armed forces. Until World War II, apart from the civil war of the 1860s and World War I, the USA maintained a small, neglected army which was politically irrelevant. Until the Korean War, the USA had decisively won every war it had fought and its armed forces had only experienced temporary reverses. The Vietnam War, however, marked a shattering defeat for the USA and its armed forces and provoked passionate debate concerning strategy, tactics, morality and the extent of political control over the military. Although American civil-military relations were shaken by the experience, the historical tradition of civil supremacy was maintained.

Historically, the armed forces in eastern Europe have played an important role in politics, but since 1945 the countries of eastern Europe have been dominated by the Soviet Union. Ever since the 1917 Revolution the Soviet armed forces have been strictly controlled by the Communist Party, which demands unquestioning political obedience. This is achieved by close scrutiny, the activities of political paramilitary organisations and by continuous political education. In eastern Europe the Russians promote a similar system of civil-military relations to maintain in power the national communist parties and ensure that the parties and their national armed forces remain loyal to the Soviet Union.

Effectively there have been no military coups within eastern Europe, although on occasions, as in Hungary in 1956, the national army has participated in a national uprising against Soviet control. Authoritarian rule, political vigilance and the careful selection and promotion of local party members loyal to the Soviet Union have largely succeeded in preventing military coups. The fact that Poland now has a military government does not disprove the case. It was because Communist Party rule had led to economic chaos and social turmoil that the Soviet Union was prepared to allow party members who controlled the Polish armed forces and who had proven their loyalty to Moscow to step in and maintain the status quo. **Keith Simpson**

Above: Colonel George Papadopoulos who became prime minister of Greece after the successful coup of 1967. Below and bottom: The immediate aftermath of a coup usually involves restrictions on the civilian population. Here roadblocks and sweep and search operations in Turkey prevent civilian opposition to the 1980 coup from gathering momentum.

Key Weapons
The
F-14 TOMCAT

Grumman's F-14 Tomcat had its origins in the disastrous attempt to make a naval fighter out of the USAF's F-111, a scheme initiated by Secretary of Defense Robert McNamara. One of the 'bright young men' brought into government by President John F. Kennedy, McNamara was horrified by the waste, duplication of effort and sheer cost inherent in the existing arms procurement policy. He believed, based on his industrial experience, that it was perfectly possible to combine various needs into a single system with all the savings such a solution afforded. Thus the policy of 'commonality' was born, and the Navy was informed that its standing requirement for a long-range, missile-armed fleet defence fighter would be met by a version of the F-111.

The US Navy was opposed to such a plan, believing that the F-111 could never meet their specification. Grumman, whose long experience in building carrier aircraft won it the position of chief contractor, rapidly came to the same conclusion as the company struggled to make the type into a naval fighter. The end result, the F-111B, amply fulfilled the worst prophecies. Not only did it have very little in common with the airframe used for the land-based versions, but its weight and landing speed made it totally unsuitable for operations from all but the biggest American carriers.

The F-111B was cancelled, much to everyone's relief. This left the navy still without its fighter but gave Grumman the opportunity to submit its own design. The new aeroplane owed much to the company's experience with the F-111B, not least in the retention of the type's fire control system and missiles and in the use of a variable-geometry wing design. More subtly, the design was large for a fighter, Grumman realising that while the F-111B was just too big and heavy, the navy's requirement could only be

Previous page: A Grumman F-14 Tomcat prepares to land on a US aircraft carrier. Above: A Tomcat banks over to starboard to reveal its impressive weapons-load of six AIM-54 Phoenix air-to-air missiles. Capable of ranges up to 160km (100 miles) the Phoenix is a formidable weapon and when allied to a sophisticated weapons-control system it provides the F-14 with the ability to engage six targets simultaneously.

Right: With wings in the 'unswept' position and arrester hook down, a Tomcat pilot makes his descent onto the carrier deck. Below: The Super Tomcat – an F-14D equipped with uprated F-101DFE engines.

met by a substantial airframe capable of lifting the fuel, missiles and advanced avionics stipulated in the specification.

Of the five submissions received by the navy, the Grumman Model 303 was judged to be the most suitable and so the company was instructed to proceed with development on 15 January 1969. Work, on what was now known as the Grumman F-14, progressed quickly and the prototype made its maiden flight on 21 December 1970.

The new aeroplane was an impressive looking machine. The variable-geometry wings were set high on the sides of an 18.89m (61ft 11in) fuselage, making an almost delta shape when they were fully swept back and blended with the tail planes. Equally distinctive were the twin fins, which were slightly canted outwards. Less noticeable was the all-up weight of around 26,000kg (57,320lb), which was considerably in excess of the figure incorporated in the original specification.

In its production form, the Tomcat is primarily intended for the intercept and escort fighter roles but possesses a secondary ground attack capability. The advantage of the F-14's variable geometry or 'swing' wings stems from the fact that a wing shape designed solely for high speed flight does not function well at low speeds, and vice-versa. Equally, all aircraft have to operate at both ends of the speed spectrum, which results in the wing design being a compromise with inherent problems at one or other end of the scale. The ability to change wing shape in flight therefore confers tremendous advantages.

On the Tomcat, the wings have 20 degrees of leading edge sweep when fully extended, for landing and take off, increasing to 68 degrees when fully swept back. The flexibility of the system is improved by being computer controlled so that the wings automatically adjust in concert with the speed and altitude at which the aeroplane is flying. At speeds above sound, small foreplanes are deployed ahead of the wings to relieve the shock waves which build up over a wing moving supersonically. At the other end of the scale, wing loading and lift are enhanced by manoeuvring slats and flaps which operate when the wings are fully extended.

At the heart of the F-14's ability as an interceptor is the combination of the Hughes AN/AWG-9 weapons control system and the AIM-54 Phoenix missile. AN/AWG-9 allows a Tomcat's flight officer to track no less than 24 targets and simultaneously attack six of them, all flying at different speeds and altitudes, at ranges of up to 160km (100 miles). The Phoenix, six of which can be carried, can be used against a wide range of targets, from sea-skimming missiles to high-speed aircraft such as the MiG-25 capable of flying at altitudes in excess of 23,000m (75,000ft). Equally important is the fact that the AIM-54 is a 'fire and forget' weapon which has its own terminal guidance system. Most current, non-infra-red missile systems require the launch aircraft's radar to 'illuminate' the target until the moment of impact. The Phoenix's self-contained system does away with this need and allows the parent aircraft to engage other targets with the minimum time loss.

Impressive as the AIM-54 is, it forms only a part of the Tomcat's armoury. Four underfuselage stations and two wing racks allow the carriage of combinations of missiles drawn from the six AIM-54s, six AIM-7 Sparrows and four AIM-9L Sidewinders. For the secondary ground attack role, these stations can also carry bombs, and the F-14 can lift a total weight of 6577kg (14,500lb) of external stores. This weaponry is complemented by an internal 20mm M61A-1 Vulcan cannon mounted in the port forward fuselage.

To date, three versions of the F-14 have appeared and a further two models are expected to enter service during the latter part of the 1980s. The F-14A was deployed during October 1972 and joined operational squadrons (VF-1 and VF-2) in September 1974. As originally envisaged, the TF30-PW-414-powered F-14A was to have been quickly superseded by the more powerful B model with Pratt & Whitney F401 engines. The first two F-14Bs were flown during 1973, but escalating production costs and major problems with the TF30 conspired to all but end the entire Tomcat programme. In the event, the F-14B was cancelled, the number of F-14As on order for the navy was reduced and those machines destined for the Marine Corps were cancelled.

The problems with the TF30 engine accounted for the two-year delay between the Tomcat's deployment and its introduction to operational squadron service. Continuous work by both Grumman and the engine's

A newly-landed Tomcat awaits the attention of the carrier's ground grew. The ability to get an aircraft airborne again in the quickest possible time is of the most vital importance in combat conditions.

Above: The Tomcat forms the most important single element in the modern US aircraft carrier's armoury. Here an F-14 is parked on the flight deck. Opposite page: An F-14 lets loose its powerful Phoenix missile. Inset above: A rear view of one of the few F-14s sold to Iran before the fall of the Shah in 1979. Inset below: An F-14 claws its way skyward shortly after leaving its parent carrier.

Below: Following take-off an F-14 refuels from a KA-6D Intruder in order to compensate for the large quantity of fuel consumed by the afterburners on take-off.

manufacturer has greatly increased the TF30's reliability, but the F-14A is still considered by many authorities to be slightly underpowered for its size. At the present time, the Tomcat programme seems once more to be moving forward with the navy now expected to receive a total of 521 F-14s. In 1984-85 it is proposed to introduce the F-14C, which is to be powered by General Electric F101 engines and equipped with more advanced electronics and a television identification system. This feature is being developed by Northrop and has been retro-fitted to a number of F-14As. It is hoped to follow the C with the F-14D during 1987-88, the new model featuring a digital radar and avionics systems, an improved computer, stores management and inertial navigation systems and a lengthened fuselage housing additional fuel.

In addition to these four models, 49 F-14As have been modified to accept the Tactical Air Reconnaissance Pod System (TARPS) first developed for the A-7. TARPS comprises an underfuselage fairing housing a KS-87B frame camera, a KA-99A panoramic camera and an AN/AAD-5 infra-red reconnaissance system. TARPS Tomcats were introduced into service during 1980-81 and aircraft so equipped are attached in threes to a number of standard F-14 fighter squadrons. TARPS aircraft can be rapidly converted back to interceptors.

Apart from the US Navy, the only other user of the F-14 to date is the Iranian Air Force. During the mid-1970s, the Shah of Iran ordered 80 Tomcats which differed from the F-14A only in having modified electronic countermeasures equipment. The sale of such a sophisticated weapons system to a country already showing major signs of instability created considerable alarm in America. Despite these misgivings, the Carter administration sanctioned the sale and the first three F-14s arrived in Iran during January 1976. The downfall of the Shah and the creation of a fundamentalist, revolutionary, anti-American Islamic Iran three years later, confirmed the worst fears of those who cautioned against the original sale. The fate of the Iranian F-14s and their AIM-54 missiles is unknown. The general consensus is that they are grounded for lack of spares and experienced personnel.

Despite a somewhat chequered development history, the F-14 has proved to be an extremely capable combat aircraft during its 11-year service life. Ample proof of its potential was provided in 1981 when the Tomcat first fired its missiles in anger. During August of that year, the USS *Nimitz* was exercising off the coast of Libya. The exercise area took in the Gulf of Sidra, which the Libyans claim as part of their territorial waters. This claim is not recognised by America and, in consequence, there was considerable Libyan air activity near the carrier. On the 19th, two F-14s flown by Commander Kleemann and Lieutenant Muczynski were launched to provide the carrier with a combat air patrol. Some time into the sortie, two Libyan Su-22 aircraft appeared, one of which fired a missile at Kleemann. US Navy standing orders state that any aircraft fired on may retaliate, and so, within seconds, both pilots fired AIM-9L Sidewinders which destroyed the aggressor aircraft.

F-14A Tomcat

Type Two-seat, carrier-borne multi-role combat aircraft

Dimensions Span minimum sweep 19.54m (64ft 1½in), maximum sweep 11.65m (38ft 2½in); length 19.1m (62ft 8in); height 4.88m (16ft)

Weight Empty 17,659kg (38, 930lb); maximum take off 33,724kg (74,348lb)

Powerplant Two 9480kg (20,900lb) Pratt & Whitney TF30-PW-414 afterburning turbofans

Performance Maximum speed at 12,190m (40,000ft) Mach 2.34 or 2517km/h (1564mph); maximum speed at sea level Mach 1.2 or 1300km/h (807mph)

Range Tactical radius approximately 3200km (2000 miles)

Ceiling Over 15,240m (50,000ft)

Armament One 20mm M61A-1 Vulcan rotary cannon (675 rounds); four AIM-7 Sparrow missiles on lower edges of inlet ducts or four AIM-54 Phoenix missiles on belly pallets; two underwing pylons each carrying either one Phoenix or one Sparrow and one AIM-9 Sidewinder, or two Sidewinder missiles. In the attack mode up to 6577kg (14,500lb) of assorted stores, including missiles, may be carried

Right: An F-14 performs its interceptor role when it sees-off a Soviet Il-38 maritime patrol aircraft.

Right: An overhead view of an F-14 with wings fully swept back revealing the aircraft's high-speed delta-shaped design.

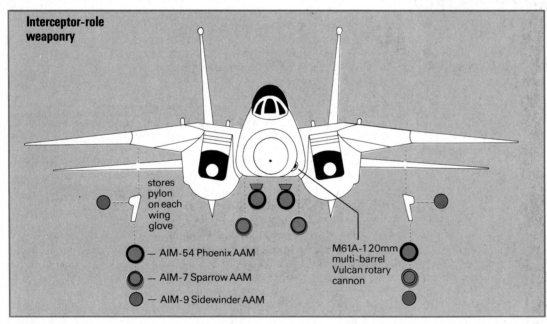

Interceptor-role weaponry

stores pylon on each wing glove

— AIM-54 Phoenix AAM

— AIM-7 Sparrow AAM

— AIM-9 Sidewinder AAM

M61A-1 20mm multi-barrel Vulcan rotary cannon

Left: One of the Tomcat's most important features is the power and flexibility of its weaponry. A variety of configurations can be carried, though the most usual consists of four long-range Phoenix AAMs, two medium-range radar-guided Sparrow missiles and two short-range heat-seeking Sidewinder missiles.

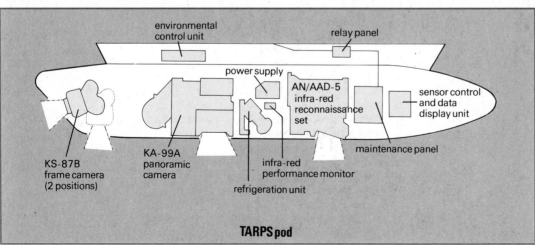

environmental control unit

relay panel

power supply

AN/AAD-5 infra-red reconnaissance set

sensor control and data display unit

maintenance panel

infra-red performance monitor

refrigeration unit

KS-87B frame camera (2 positions)

KA-99A panoramic camera

TARPS pod

Left: When the TARPS pod is fitted to the F-14 fuselage the aircraft can be transformed to carry out a reconnaissance role without recourse to expensive structural modifications. This capability is unique in carrier-borne aircraft and further extends the operational possibilities of the versatile F-14.

On the brink
The tense climax of the Cold War

The early 1960s were dangerous years to live in. Crisis and confrontation between the two great powers, the USA and the USSR, grew on a rising scale from the U-2 spy plane scandal of 1960 through the Bay of Pigs fiasco and the Berlin Wall crisis in 1961 to what was so nearly the final showdown – the Cuban missile crisis of 1962. Two dynamic leaders, President John F. Kennedy and Premier Nikita Khrushchev, asserted their opposed ideologies and interests with vigour, and the nightmare of nuclear holocaust was close to becoming a waking reality.

In retrospect, the years 1960-62 can be seen as the climax of the first period of the Cold War, which had threatened global peace since the 1940s. Amid the ruins of a Europe devastated by six years of fighting, a de facto division had emerged along the lines of occupation of the Allied forces – Soviet to the east, American, French and British to the west.

Each side viewed the other as bent on territorial expansion and, ultimately, the overthrow of its rival and the imposition of its own ideology throughout the world. This was not entirely fantasy: but in their own eyes both the Soviets and the West were bent on self-defence. To the Russians, their domination of eastern Europe was a necessary buffer against attack from the West, especially after German rearmament began in 1954. To the West, the Russian presence in eastern Europe was an example of the expansionist tendencies of the 'Soviet empire'. The rearming of Germany seemed to the West a necessary security move, not an aggressive policy. And so every action based on mistrust provoked a reaction which in its turn served to confirm the original suspicion, and the powers slid ever deeper into paranoia.

A constant background to the series of flashpoints – the Berlin blockade, the Korean War, the Soviet invasion of Hungary – was a deep fear of nuclear attack. The US was profoundly shocked by the speed with which the Soviet Union broke the American monopoly of atomic weapons after the war. The people of America were not used to the idea of their country being vulnerable to direct enemy attack. The Russians were also understandably afraid. After their heavy losses in World War II, they found themselves the target of an arsenal of fearsome weapons.

In the immediate postwar years, the tyrannous cruelty of Stalin's rule in the Soviet bloc appeared to be a major obstruction to any conciliation. But Stalin's death in 1953 and subsequent moves towards a liberalisation of communist regimes posed new problems.

Coexistence or conflict?

When Nikita Khrushchev, who had succeeded Stalin as First Secretary of the Soviet Communist Party, made his famous speech at the 20th Communist Party Congress in 1956 denouncing some of the worst aspects of Stalin's rule, the immediate effect was to undermine the authority of Moscow-trained officials who had been appointed to rule in eastern Europe. The result was that in the autumn of 1956 the Polish and Hungarian peoples rose in revolt.

After 1958, with eastern Europe in a firm grip and his position as leader secure, Khrushchev turned his attention increasingly to an active foreign policy. Where Stalin had been suspicious and inherently conservative in foreign policy, obsessed by Soviet security, Khrushchev welcomed the world stage as a platform for his flamboyant personality. He never achieved a coherent and purposeful foreign policy,

Below: Wreaths and crosses at the side of the Berlin Wall in memory of a failed escape to the West. The erection of the Wall symbolised the political stalemate that had existed between East and West since the end of World War II.

however. On the one hand he proclaimed the doctrine of 'peaceful coexistence' of communism and capitalism and obviously enjoyed his contacts with Western statesmen; at the same time he was capable of declaring that the Soviet Union would 'bury' the capitalist world, and never tired of boasting of Russia's might.

In 1959 he made a much-publicised visit to the United States and in 1960 a similar visit to France. But that same year hopes of an improvement in East-West relations were dashed by the U-2 incident. Khrushchev presented himself at a summit meeting of world leaders with the knowledge that the Soviet Union had captured the American pilot of a high-altitude spy plane. The Soviet leader broke the news in such a manner as to cause maximum embarrassment to US President Dwight D. Eisenhower, and wrecked the summit.

Eisenhower was serving the last of eight years in office, and in that year foreign affairs became an acute embarrassment for the US government. The emergence of Castro's regime in Cuba seemed to bring communism nearer home than ever before. The mishandling of the U-2 affair constituted a public humiliation. But the most fundamental issue in the public eye was the so-called 'missile gap'.

When the Soviet Union became the first country to launch a space satellite in 1957, Americans received the impression that the US was behind in rocket technology. A scare story spread, fuelled by intelligence reports which subsequently proved quite false, that Russia was ahead of the US in strategic nuclear missiles. It is now clear that, especially in the late 1950s, the Americans vastly overestimated Soviet nuclear capacity. Throughout the 1950s – and indeed the 1960s also – US superiority in nuclear weaponry was overwhelming. But the missile gap was a major issue in the 1960 US presidential elections which brought John F. Kennedy to power.

Kennedy had an idealistic view of the role of the USA in the world. Less cynical than his predecessors, he took both the defence and promotion of freedom very seriously. His more active approach to foreign policy was intended to combine a vigorous anti-communism with the pursuit of political and economic reforms.

Neither Kennedy nor Khrushchev were happy with the stalemate that had persisted since World War II. They wanted things to move. But their summit meeting in Vienna in 1961 produced scant results and shortly afterwards the Berlin Wall was erected by the communists to seal off East Germany from the West. This action added to the tension in superpower relations.

In 1962, Khrushchev and his advisers decided on a move to break the stalemate and achieve a real change in the strategic balance. Their plan was to place batteries of nuclear missiles in Cuba, which was by then closely associated with the Soviet Union. It was an extremely risky gambit which the Americans could not permit to succeed. As soon as he was alerted to the danger Kennedy reacted swiftly, forcing the Russians to retreat, and withdraw the missiles.

The Cuban missile crisis brought the world closer to nuclear war than ever before or since. At one time during the crisis American missile crews were on 'maximum alert', 90 B-52s carrying multi-megaton bombs were airborne over the Atlantic, and all commands were in the highest state of readiness.

As the shock of the crisis receded, some moves were made to avoid another major confrontation. In June 1963 the 'hot line' between Moscow and Washington was set up for use in future crises. In July

Contrasting reactions to the missile crisis, from American students in Washington (above) and British demonstrators in London (right).

The series of crises while Khrushchev and Kennedy (right, and below, as the British *Daily Mail* saw them) were in power contrasted strongly with the state of world politics 20 years later, when the older, more conservative leaders Reagan and Brezhnev (below right, left and right) presided over a far more rigidly defined world order.

the United States, the Soviet Union and Britain signed a treaty banning certain kinds of nuclear tests. And in October 1964 Khrushchev was removed from the leadership of the Soviet Communist Party, accused of 'harebrained scheming, hasty conclusions, rash decisions and actions based on wishful thinking'. By then, Kennedy too was no longer on the world stage, having been assassinated in November 1963.

But the new era of 'detente' did not signal the end of the Cold War. The basic ideological division of the world remained, even if the split between Russia and China showed that the communist bloc was not the unified threat it had once seemed. The US and the

USSR continued their territorial rivalries, although transferred to the Third World, and there were frequent misunderstandings. Above all the fear of nuclear attack persisted, as the Soviet Union concentrated on equalling the nuclear might of the US – with considerable success by the mid-1970s.

The difference after 1962 was a new caution in great power relations. Events had shown how difficult it was to achieve any significant change in the status quo. All the crises of the early 1960s had resulted in the defeat of forces for change; and the main long-term legacy was the Berlin Wall – the symbol of a permanently divided world. **R.G. Grant**

Below: A US soldier stands guard in front of eight B-47 medium jets during the Cuban missile crisis.

Eyeball to eyeball

On Sunday, 14 October 1962, an American U-2 reconnaissance aircraft flown by Major Rudolf Anderson, USAF, conducted a high-level photographic sweep over the area of San Cristóbal to the west of Havana, Cuba, where it was known that Soviet military bases were being constructed. The flight was uneventful, but the photographs it produced were dramatic. Instead of showing defensive surface-to-air missiles (SAMs) as expected, they provided the first clear evidence that Soviet technicians were preparing sites for nuclear-capable medium-range ballistic missiles (MRBMs). Once operational, these missiles – each with an effective range of 2200km (1200 nautical miles) – would pose a potential threat to American cities as far north as Washington, DC.

Three days later a similar sweep discovered launch-platforms for intermediate-range ballistic missiles (IRBMs) at Guanajay, to the east of San Cristóbal, and this extended the arc of threat by a further 1850km (1000 nautical miles), covering the whole of mainland USA. Within a week another two sites, at Sagua la Grande (MRBMs) and Remedios (IRBMs), both to the east of Havana, had been located.

They posed a threat which the US authorities could not ignore. At a local level, the United States could become wary of defending her interests in the Caribbean and Latin America for fear of nuclear retaliation from Cuba. At a global level, the threat of even one warhead being fired against the homeland could undermine her resolve and weaken her stand against communism. This in turn would affect relations with her allies (especially in western Europe), who looked to the unfettered strength of the United States for their

protection. The removal of the missiles was therefore essential if the United States was to retain her predominant role in world affairs – and was important to President John F. Kennedy as he approached the mid-term elections, due to take place on 6 November.

It is perhaps surprising that the Americans were not more aware of the nature of the threat, for it had been developing for some months. As early as July 1960 Soviet Premier Nikita Khrushchev had indicated his support for Castro, and at the time of the abortive, American-sponsored Bay of Pigs invasion in April 1961 he had warned Kennedy of possible Soviet armed intervention if American forces attacked Cuba. He felt able to make these moves because he was convinced that Kennedy lacked resolve. As this was reinforced by events in 1961 – Kennedy's abandonment of the Bay of Pigs invaders in April, his poor showing at the Vienna summit in June and his lack of positive response to the building of the Berlin Wall in August – Khrushchev became more daring. By the middle of 1962 he was pouring military equipment into Cuba – SAMs, MiG fighters, coastal patrol craft, tanks, artillery and smallarms – partly to support a fellow-Marxist state against possible American aggression, but also to test the strength of the White House.

The potential advantages to the Soviet Union of such a policy were enormous. Success in Cuba, less than 160km (100 miles) from the American coastline, would not only break the American hold on the area but also enhance Soviet prestige and influence in Latin America, a region which, since Castro's revolution, looked ripe for communist expansion. By the same token, a lack of American response to the provocation of missile deployment so close to home

Above left: Soviet delegation members urgently discuss their next move at a UN meeting in 1962. Above: Khrushchev gives a fulsome hug to Castro during a public display of solidarity. Such warm personal feelings did not survive the missile crisis; Castro was furious at the Soviet climbdown (on which he was not consulted), and broke a mirror in a rage when he heard the news. Above right: Kennedy addresses US troops in Florida during the crisis.

Preparations for war over the siting of Soviet missiles in Cuba. While the US began to deploy a defensive missile screen along the Florida coast (right above), the Cuban army manned Soviet anti-aircraft machine guns in order to defend cities and other major installations against air attack (right).

The Cuban missile crisis

would destroy her nuclear monopoly and indicate the extent to which the Soviets might be able to apply pressure elsewhere, especially over the vexed question of Berlin. Indeed, many commentators regard the Cuban missile crisis as an attempt by Khrushchev to force a 'trade' with the Americans: in exchange for his withdrawal of the missiles, they would abandon West Berlin, permitting its incorporation into East Germany or, at the very least, agree to dismantle their Jupiter IRBM sites in Turkey and Italy.

Debate and decision

In fact, the Americans were well aware of Soviet support for Castro, choosing to ignore the build-up of arms so long as the weapons involved were essentially defensive and offered no direct threat to American interests. But as soon as the photographs taken on 14 October 1962 had been analysed, the situation changed dramatically. Late on 15 October, as photo-interpreters reported the discovery of missile erectors and launch sites at San Cristóbal, selected members of Kennedy's administration were informed. The president himself was left to enjoy a good night's sleep before being told at 0800 hours on the 16th. He immediately ordered the creation of an *ad hoc* group of advisers, soon to be known as the Executive Committee of the National Security Council, or 'ExCom'.

Initially composed of 14 key people, including Secretary of State Dean Rusk, Secretary of Defense Robert McNamara, Chairman of the Joint Chiefs of Staff General Maxwell Taylor, Director of the CIA John McCone, Attorney-General Robert Kennedy (the president's younger brother) and National Security Adviser McGeorge Bundy, ExCom was to meet almost continuously for the next 13 days.

From the start, the members of ExCom were split over the nature of the American response. Some suggested that the threat could be ignored – it did not, after all, alter the reality of American nuclear superiority – while others advocated a purely diplomatic approach. But these ideas were quickly rejected for it was realised that the crisis amounted to a test of American resolve.

Accordingly, the emphasis was placed firmly upon military action. This created problems, however. The Joint Chiefs, for example, favoured an all-out invasion of Cuba to destroy the missile sites and topple Castro, but they received little support. Such a move, although always viable as a last resort, seemed a recipe for World War III and would demand a huge commitment of military resources that would weaken American strength elsewhere. Cuba could, it was argued, be nothing more than a feint, designed to divert American forces from Europe or elsewhere preparatory to a communist attack; the fact that at the height of the crisis Chinese troops invaded India, merely reinforced the point.

This left two possibilities: a surgical air strike to destroy the missile sites before they became fully operational, or a maritime blockade of Cuba to cut the island off from Soviet support. Both had disadvantages. An air strike would cause civilian casualties (Robert Kennedy estimated 25,000) and could not be guaranteed to destroy all the missiles in a single raid, leaving a few which might then be fired against American cities in retaliation. The blockade would take time to organise, be difficult (and probably illegal under international law) to impose and, as the

The Cuban blockade

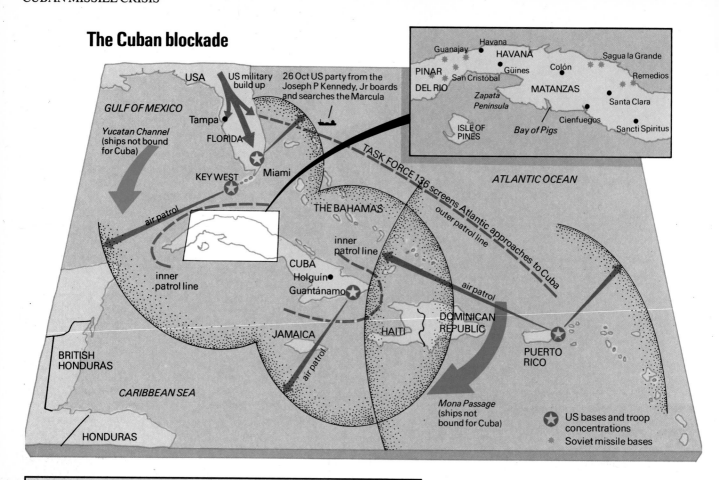

The moment of truth

The quarantine around Cuba came into effect at 1000 hours on Wednesday 24 October 1962. In his book *13 Days*, Robert F. Kennedy related the events of that time.

'It was now a few minutes after 10 o'clock. Secretary McNamara announced that two Russian ships, the *Gagarin* and the *Komiles*, were within a few miles of our quarantine barrier. The interception of both ships would probably be before noon Washington time....

'Then came the disturbing Navy report that a Russian submarine had moved into position between the two ships. It had originally been planned to have a cruiser make the first interception, but, because of the increased danger, it was decided in the past few hours to send in an aircraft carrier, supported by helicopters, carrying antisubmarine equipment, hovering overhead. The carrier *Essex* was to signal the submarine by sonar to surface and identify itself. If it refused, said Secretary McNamara, depth charges with a small explosive would be used until the submarine surfaced.

'I think these few minutes were the time of gravest concern for the president. Was the world on the brink of a

holocaust? Was it our error? A mistake? Was there something further that should have been done? Or not done? His hand went up to his face and covered his mouth. He opened and closed his fist. His face seemed drawn, his eyes pained, almost gray. We stared at each other across the table....

'One thousand miles away in the vast expanse of the Atlantic Ocean the final decisions were going to be made in the next few minutes. President Kennedy had initiated the course of events, but he no longer had control over them. He would have to wait – we would have to wait. The minutes in the Cabinet Room ticked slowly by. What could we say now – what could we do?

'Then it was 10:25 – a messenger brought in a note to John McCone. "Mr President, we have a preliminary report which seems to indicate that some of the Russian ships have stopped dead in the water." Stopped dead in the water? Which ships? Are they checking the accuracy of the report? Is it true? I looked at the clock. 10:32. "The report is accurate, Mr President. Six ships previously on their way to Cuba at the edge of the quarantine line have stopped or have turned back towards the Soviet Union."'

missiles had been delivered already, would not really solve the problem.

As the debates over these options continued, Ex-Com was effectively deadlocked for six days. During that time, reconnaissance photographs charted the steady process of preparation at the missile sites. In order to display at least an appearance of resolve, the American base at Guantanamo in Cuba was substantially reinforced, naval vessels were deployed into the Caribbean, air force, marine and army units were concentrated in Florida and American nuclear forces were placed on full alert.

Against this background of sabre-rattling, President Kennedy went on nationwide television at 1900 hours on 22 October, disclosing for the first time to the American public the nature of the crisis. He reviewed the options and announced his chosen course of action: if the Soviets did not show signs of dismantling the missile sites and halting the arms build-up by 1000 hours on 24 October, a 'quarantine line' of naval vessels would be imposed around Cuba. Any Soviet, Soviet-chartered or East European ships which tried to cross the line thereafter would be stopped, searched and, if found to contain proscribed military cargoes, ordered to turn back.

Task Force 136, comprising 17 destroyers and two cruisers under the command of Admiral Alfred Ward, was already moving to block the navigable channels to Cuba from the east. It was hoped that this would be sufficient to force the 25 Soviet-controlled vessels known to be *en route* to the island to return home. Unfortunately this did not happen. At 1906 hours on 23 October, Kennedy signed the Quarantine Proclamation and a direct superpower confrontation seemed inevitable.

But the Russians were under increasing pressure.

American military preparations implied that the blockade was only the first step in a process of controlled escalation leading to all-out war, while on the diplomatic front substantial opposition to Soviet policies was beginning to emerge. On 23 October the Organisation of American States unanimously backed the blockade and the Nato allies pledged their support to Kennedy. Two days later, in a dramatic incident in the Security Council of the United Nations, Ambassador Adlai Stevenson publicly disproved Soviet denials of missile deployment by producing copies of the San Cristóbal photographs. By that time, in fact, some of the Soviet ships had been recalled and the rest had stopped short of the quarantine line – a discovery which occasioned Dean Rusk's famous comment: 'we're eyeball to eyeball and I think the other fellow just blinked.'

Stop and search

This proved to be only temporary, however. By late on 25 October, with Soviet ships resuming their passage to the Caribbean, the Americans had no choice but to show their resolve more clearly. They decided to stop and search the *Marucla*, a Panamanian-owned vessel flying the Lebanese flag and known to be under charter to the Russians, as she entered the quarantine zone. At 0700 on 26 October she was boarded by sailors from the destroyer *Joseph P. Kennedy, Jr*, checked for proscribed material and, when none was found, allowed to proceed.

It seemed to have the desired effect. As the day progressed the first signs of a Soviet climb-down became apparent, based upon a face-saving formula whereby Khrushchev would agree to dismantle the missile sites in exchange for an American promise not to invade Cuba. Relief in Washington was short-lived, however, for within a matter of hours the Kremlin suddenly insisted upon the withdrawal of American missiles from Turkey as well.

Kennedy refused to accept this and on 27 October the tempo of the crisis built up to the very brink of war. It was not eased by reports that a U-2, flown by the same Major Anderson who had taken the original San Cristóbal photographs, had been shot down over Cuba and another, on a routine flight over Alaska, had inadvertently strayed into Soviet air space. In desperation the members of ExCom decided to ignore the new Soviet demands and accept the original formula of 26 October, hoping that Khrushchev would grasp at any opportunity to avoid a nuclear confrontation.

The gamble worked. Early on 28 October the Kremlin agreed to withdraw the missiles from Cuba as soon as America promised to demobilise her invasion forces. Kennedy quickly responded. As the two sides climbed down, a new and mutual respect entered the superpower relationship and a slight thaw in the Cold War occurred. The world was still divided into two rival camps but the missile crisis, by confronting the leaders with the horrors of nuclear war, forced upon them a new awareness and sense of responsibility. In this sense the trauma of the 13 days in October 1962 acted as a watershed in the history of post-war world. **John Pimlott**

Below: A US Navy patrol plane shadows a Soviet freighter as the destroyer USS *Barry* moves alongside during the enforcement of the blockade around Cuba.

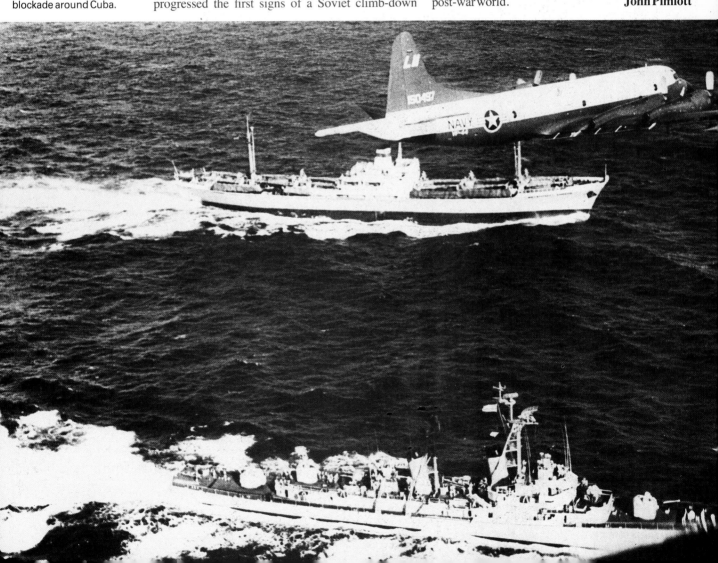

Credibility and capability: ways of avoiding World War III

Nuclear deterrence

On 6 August 1945 an estimated 75,000 men, women and children were killed by a single atomic explosion in the Japanese city of Hiroshima. It represented the realisation of a nightmare which had haunted mankind since the end of World War I. During that conflict, for the first time, civilian populations had suffered the effects of indiscriminate aerial bombardment, designed to destroy a country's social and economic infrastructure rather than its front-line forces. Between 1915 and 1918 German airships and bombers had mounted a series of raids on targets in England and, although the results were not decisive, significant evidence of civilian panic and diminished industrial output had emerged.

The conclusion was drawn that, as aircraft ranges and payloads increased, a position would be reached in which future wars could be decided not by battle but by the amount of civilian and industrial destruction wrought by fleets of bombers flying virtually unmolested over the enemy state. In 1938 it was estimated that there would be 70,000 casualties a week in London alone if war began, and such fears were sufficient to help persuade the British government to accommodate the expansionist demands of Adolf Hitler towards Czechoslovakia rather than face the apparently formidable Luftwaffe.

There proved to be a limit to British appeasement, however, and in September 1939, despite continued fears, the nightmare was faced. It soon emerged that bomber capabilities had been grossly exaggerated and, as unforeseen practical problems of mounting a sustained strategic offensive were experienced, first over Britain (1940-41) and then over Germany (1940-45) and Japan (1944-45), the impact of aerial bombardment was largely absorbed. Huge death-tolls and widespread devastation could be achieved – as the destruction of Dresden on 13/14 February 1945 and the fire-raid on Tokyo a month later made clear – but this was rare, requiring hundreds of bombers to drop thousands of tonnes of bombs in tight concentrations to produce a fire-storm. In the vast majority of raids the damage was spread thinly over a large area and the civilian population, despite casualties, was able to carry on.

The revolution in strategy

Hiroshima was different, simply because it proved that atomic technology could guarantee instantaneous devastation using one bomb delivered by a single aircraft. The ramifications were dramatic. Thereafter, anyone foolish enough to provoke a state in possession of atomic weapons would be effectively committing suicide. Because of this, traditional strategies of war-fighting, at least between the superpowers, had to be reassessed.

In a 'revolution in strategy' which has characte-

Above: Deterrence has become a sophisticated set of theories that depend upon credible response at all levels to work properly. So all aspects of Nato's armed forces are geared into an interlocking system to prevent any form of attack being considered worthwhile and these US F-4 Phantom multi-role fighters have an essential part to play in the overall pattern.

rised the period since 1945 but which had its roots in the fears of the 1930s, war-prevention has become the key to survival. It is based upon an ability to deter a potential aggressor from carrying out hostile acts rather than an ability to respond to hostility after it has taken place. The concept of deterrence has replaced that of victory through force of arms as a mainstay of great-power relations.

The nature of the threat
Deterrence may be defined as 'the ability to prevent aggression by persuading a potential enemy that the gains to be had from undertaking a particular course of action are outweighed by the losses he will incur if he persists'. From this the basic characteristics of the concept can be discerned. The aim is to influence the actions of another, persuading him that the policy he is contemplating or pursuing is not in his best interests and should be abandoned. This is achieved by introducing a threat that, if he should continue, certain punishments will be meted out. The idea is to present this in such a way that he is forced to make a psychological 'cost-gain' calculation: 'is what I am hoping to achieve worth the penalties that will be imposed?' If the answer is 'no' – in other words, if the costs outweigh the gains – then he will probably be deterred, and will choose some other, less disastrous way of achieving his objectives, or abandon them altogether as unattainable.

Such a concept is not unique to the nuclear age, for we all experience deterrence at a variety of levels throughout our lives. To a religious man, the prospect of eternal damnation may be sufficient to deter him from sin; to the moralist it may be the voice of his own conscience with its promises of self-disgust and sleepless nights. Similarly, as members of society, we should be deterred from committing crimes by the threat of legal punishment.

The same pattern can be seen in inter-state relations. If one state wishes to influence the policies of another, it can use a wide range of deterrent threats. At a diplomatic and political level it may threaten to withdraw support from a government unless that government agrees to revise its policy. Precise examples are not easy to find, but it would appear that the Americans attempted something along these lines in South Vietnam in 1963 when they sought to persuade President Ngo Dinh Diem to moderate his policies towards the Buddhists and so prevent the embarrassing spectacle of an American-aligned state forcing its repressed members to burn themselves to death in public. More commonly, the state may threaten economic sanctions if a particular policy is initiated or continued. A prime example of this was the Arab threat of an oil embargo in 1973, designed to persuade Western states to modify their support for Israel in the Yom Kippur War. Finally, the threat of conventional military force may be used, accompanied by appropriate mobilisations and deployment.

Certain requirements have to be satisfied if deterrence is to succeed. Top of the list is credibility, for it is no good trying to deter someone if he does not believe that you will carry out your threatened response. Put in simple terms, if I say, 'You hit me and I'll hit you back harder,' and I am a well-known pacifist who has devoted his life to a non-violent creed, then you are unlikely to believe that I will lift a finger against you. Similarly, a state that has no tradition of violence or obviously fears the ramifications of such a response

will lack credibility in the eyes of its opponent.

At the same time, it is essential that the deterrer has the proven capability to carry out his threat. Just as Soviet missiles could hardly influence the policies of the United States in the 1950s because they clearly lacked the range to hit American cities, so the man who says, 'You hit me and I'll hit you back harder,' will not pose a threat if his arm is in a sling and he is leaning on crutches. If, however, he was to accompany his threat with a demonstration of his capability – by driving his fist through a nearby door, for example – his deterrent stance would be considerably strengthened. Military parades, publicised weapons testing and success in minor wars will have much the same effect at the level of state relations.

Communications and quarantine
But credibility and capability are only two of the ingredients for success. Of equal importance is communications, for unless the nature of the proscribed action is clearly defined and the form of punishment unequivocally laid down, the potential aggressor may not understand the deterrent and go ahead regardless. In 1950, for example, the Chinese attempted to deter the United Nations' forces from advancing as far as the Yalu River on the border with North Korea by threatening to intervene militarily if they did so, but a

Despite the fact that the systems for the control, monitoring and launch of both home and enemy attacks are extremely complex and sophisticated (below, the strategic air command operations centre), they are operated by human beings always capable of error. The 'failsafe' system shown at bottom requires both of the missile launch control officers to press their buttons before a missile can be launched.

lack of clear communications between the two sides failed to get the message across and the threat had to be carried out.

Twelve years later President John F. Kennedy tackled a similar problem more carefully, laying down a precise 'quarantine line' around Cuba and clearly stating that any Soviet vessel which tried to cross it would be stopped, searched and, if necessary, turned back by force. In this case the deterrent worked, but only because Kennedy was dealing with a 'rational' man in Premier Nikita Khrushchev, who made the cost-gain calculation and concluded that his deployment of missiles in Cuba was not worth the prospect of a superpower confrontation to the point of war. This need not always happen, for the last requirement for success must be rationality, involving people who fear the consequences of failure and value the things under threat.

The importance of these four requirements – credibility, capability, communications and rationality – may be seen in the nuclear context by a brief examination of how deterrence works between the superpowers. Immediately after 1945 the process was simple: the United States, as the sole possessor of atomic weapons, clearly satisfied all four requirements. The bombing of Hiroshima and Nagasaki in August 1945 proved that the will to use the weapons (credibility) as well as the weapons themselves (capability) existed; the threat of their use was clearly communicated to all potential enemies and those enemies, having just experienced the trauma of a world war, were rational men, fearful of the consequences of atomic devastation. The Korean War (1950-53) may have implied that the threat was inapplicable to conflicts in peripheral theatres, but the introduction of a strategy of 'massive retaliation' in 1954, whereby the Americans promised to punish even the smallest misdemeanour with instant nuclear response against enemy cities, soon closed the gap.

Unfortunately massive retaliation began to lose its credibility in the late 1950s as the Soviets developed their own nuclear weapons and intercontinental delivery systems. In such circumstances it became less likely that a deterrent threat by the United States would have the desired effect. If, for example, Soviet troops merely crossed the East-West border in Europe, it would seem irrational for the Americans to respond with nuclear attacks against Moscow or Kiev when that would lead inevitably to the destruction of New York or Boston. In short, no-one could believe that the United States would commit suicide in cir-

cumstances short of a direct assault upon her home territory.

Deterrence thus entered a new phase, characterised by the ability of both sides to threaten unacceptable damage to their opponents. This situation, soon to be known by the acronym MAD (mutually assured destruction), has persisted to the present day. It is a complex phenomenon, in which the maintenance of the four requirements for success is by no means guaranteed.

MAD is based upon the ability of a state to absorb a nuclear attack – a 'first strike' – and still retain sufficient weapons with which to hit back in a 'second strike' and impose unacceptable damage. The idea is to deter any use of nuclear weapons, particularly in a pre-emptive move designed to disarm a potential opponent, and is dependent upon the survivability of delivery means despite a first strike.

MAD and madness

If, for example, the Soviets were to launch a nuclear attack against American weapons sites, they could not guarantee to destroy all the intercontinental ballistic missiles (ICBMs) in their hardened silos and would not be able to 'take out' the manned bombers already in the air or the submarine-launched ballistic missiles (SLBMs) hidden in the depths of the oceans. The United States would thus have sufficient weapons left with which to devastate the Soviet Union. In a rational world, this should be sufficient to deter.

But the system is by no means perfect, being subject to a variety of pressures which could lead to failure. There is a distinct possibility, for example, that one side may achieve a technological breakthrough which gives it the capability to destroy all the opponent's weapons in a first strike or to protect its homeland against a second-strike response. If one side was to perfect the means to track and target the other's missile-carrying submarines, it could threaten to destroy them in a pre-emptive strike, effectively disarming the enemy's retaliatory force; if, by deploying anti-ballistic missiles (ABMs) or laser/charged-particle beams, it could create a protective 'shell' over its homeland, capable of destroying all incoming missiles before they reached their targets, it could deny to the enemy all advantage of having a second-strike ability. Either way, deterrence would cease to be effective.

Similarly, the process of MAD applies to the superpowers only, and in an age of nuclear proliferation, with other states gaining access to nuclear weapons, this may be insufficient to deter attacks from elsewhere. Such attacks may, in turn, be initiated by men who are not 'rational' in the accepted sense: a religious or political fanatic, for example, may be prepared to sacrifice his state to nuclear devastation if he sees a greater advantage in terms of a spread of his particular creed.

Finally, and most worryingly, the entire deterrent edifice depends upon the people who control it, and they may make fatal mistakes. In the 1950s a flock of geese was mistaken by American radar operators for a squadron of Soviet bombers heading for Alaska; in November 1979 a faulty computer tape led to an American nuclear alert. We live in a precarious world. Although deterrence has protected us thus far from the horrors of nuclear holocaust, it is, in the words of the theorist Albert Wohlstetter, 'a delicate balance of terror'. **John Pimlott**

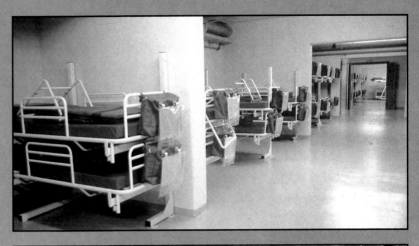

Above left: An AGM-86B cruise missile is air-launched from a USAF B-52 strategic bomber. Below left: Cruise missiles can also be launched, as here, from submarines. Top: The clinical and depressing interior of a fallout shelter, man's only real hope of survival should nuclear war erupt. Above: A meeting of UN experts confers in an attempt to regulate international nuclear testing. Right: The possibility of nuclear holocaust led to opposition to the possession of nuclear weapons, especially in western Europe. Here, French students call for disarmament.

The Berlin Wall

How a city was divided

In the early hours of Sunday 13 August 1961, under the cover of tanks and heavily armed troops, East Berlin was sealed off from West Berlin by barriers, fences and barbed wire entanglements. During the next few months concrete made this partition more permanent, and it quickly became known as the Berlin Wall.

The border between East and West Germany had, apart from a few officially recognised crossing points, been sealed since 1952. By means of the Paris Agreements of 1954 the Western allies had ended the occupation regime in West Germany, recognising it as a sovereign state. Then, in May 1955, the Federal Republic had become a member of Nato. Berlin, however, remained a delicate problem, situated as it was within East Germany. Even though West and East Berlin had been incorporated into the Federal and German Democratic Republics respectively, the city remained ultimately under Four Power control.

Even after the sealing of the border in 1952, free passage between East and West Berlin was still permitted. Indeed, more than 50,000 East Berliners worked in West Berlin, and 7000 West Berliners had jobs in the East, while it was estimated that 500,000 people crossed the sector borders each day. So, during the 1950s, with travel between East and West

Above: Checkpoint Charlie, the crossing point for members of the Diplomatic Corps, Western Occupation Forces and non-German civilians. Right: One of the early casualties of the Berlin Wall, Peter Fechter, lies mortally wounded, shot by East German guards after an abortive escape attempt.

Germany increasingly restricted, Berlin became the one route by which those discontented with the communist regime could flee to the West. After the 1953 uprising in East Berlin, it was estimated that some 150,000 refugees each year arrived in West Berlin.

On 10 November 1958 Soviet Premier Nikita Khrushchev announced that the USSR wished to terminate the existing status of Berlin, and that all powers previously exercised by the Russians in East Berlin, including control of the routes from the Federal Republic to Berlin, would be handed over to the East Germans. Furthermore, the Western powers were to withdraw their troops from the city, and a six-month ultimatum was given. The Western powers replied that Berlin could only be discussed in the context of Germany as a whole and rejected the Soviet proposal. Khrushchev then temporarily climbed down.

During the next 18 months attempts to resolve the problem came to naught, and East-West relations worsened with the shooting down of Gary Powers' U-2 reconnaissance aircraft over Soviet territory in May 1960. The June 1961 summit between Khrushchev and John F. Kennedy in Vienna highlighted the divergent views between East and West on Berlin. On 15 June, Khrushchev announced Russia's intention to conclude a separate peace treaty with East Germany by the end of the year which would have the effect of terminating the West's right of access to Berlin. A month later the Russians stated that they were increasing defence expenditure by one third, and President Kennedy retaliated by requesting a substantial build-up of Nato forces. 'We cannot and will not permit the communists to drive us out of Berlin, either gradually or by force,' he said. Then, on 7 August, Khrushchev threatened to increase the strength of the Red Army on the frontiers of western Europe and to call up reserves.

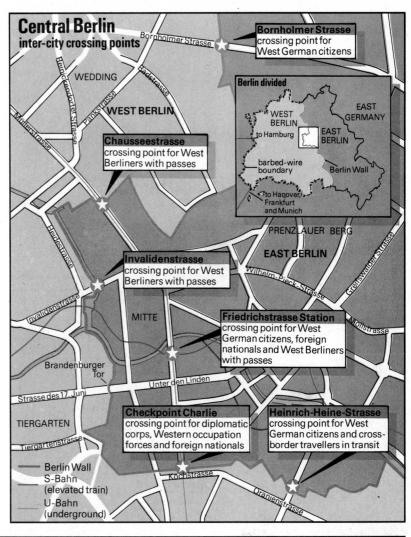

Central Berlin
inter-city crossing points

Bornholmer Strasse
crossing point for
West German citizens

WEDDING

WEST BERLIN

Chausseestrasse
crossing point for West
Berliners with passes

Berlin divided

WEST BERLIN — to Hamburg — EAST GERMANY — EAST BERLIN — barbed-wire boundary — Berlin Wall — to Hanover, Frankfurt and Munich

PRENZLAUER BERG

EAST BERLIN

Invalidenstrasse
crossing point for West
Berliners with passes

Wilhelm-Pieck-Strasse

MITTE

Friedrichstrasse Station
crossing point for West
German citizens, foreign
nationals and West Berliners
with passes

Brandenburger Tor

Unter den Linden

Strasse des 17. Juni

TIERGARTEN

Checkpoint Charlie
crossing point for diplomatic
corps, Western occupation
forces and foreign nationals

Heinrich-Heine-Strasse
crossing point for West
German citizens and cross-
border travellers in transit

Tiergartenstrasse

Kochstrasse

Oranienstrasse

— Berlin Wall
— S-Bahn (elevated train)
— U-Bahn (underground)

Right: Shortly after the communists began building the Berlin Wall, this East German soldier successfully escaped to the West by leaping over a barbed wire barricade.

This was followed by the physical partition of Berlin by the East Germans.

The Wall was built, said the official announcement, to 'effectively check the subversive action against the countries of the Socialist camp and install a reliable watch and control around the whole of West Berlin, including its boundaries with Democratic Berlin'. Until such time as West Berlin is transformed into a demilitarised neutral Free City, citizens of the capital of the GDR shall require special permission in order to cross the borders to West Berlin'.

Below: One of 57 East Berlin escapees makes his way to freedom through the tunnel constructed by students in 1964.

Escape to the West

When the Berlin Wall went up on 13 August 1961, families, friends and relations found, overnight, that they had been separated. There began, soon after, attempts by those trapped on the eastern side of the Wall to reach West Berlin.

One of the earliest escapes was made by Harry Deterling, who worked for East German Railways. After careful manoeuvring, he secured himself a job as driver on the Albrechtshof-Spandau line, which ran from East to West. On 5 December 1961, with 25 members of two families aboard, he drove his train at full speed past the astonished border guards and into West Berlin.

Tunnels were a more popular method. On 5 May 1962 a tunnel dug by an 81-year-old man and his friends enabled eight men and four women, all of mature years, to reach West Berlin. Perhaps the most famous was Tunnel 57, so-named because 57 East Berliners were brought safely

through. It was begun in April 1964 by 35 people, mostly students, from the French sector of West Berlin and was to finish in the backyard of a derelict house in East Berlin. The tunnel was to be 129m (140 yards) long and just wide enough for one person to crawl along. On 3 and 4 October, all the refugees successfully escaped – just hours before the police arrived.

Many unusual escape methods were developed. In one instance, Heinz Meixner, a West German intent on bringing his fiancée to the West, found that by removing the windscreen from his Austin Healey Sprite and letting some air out of his tyres he could drive under the booms at Checkpoint Charlie. He drove legally into East Berlin, loaded up his fiancée and future mother-in-law, and then sped back into the West at top speed, ducking as he whizzed under the boom. Then there was the latter-day Trojan Horse, although it took the form of a stuffed cow: on two occasions, refugees were transported to the West in the belly of the model.

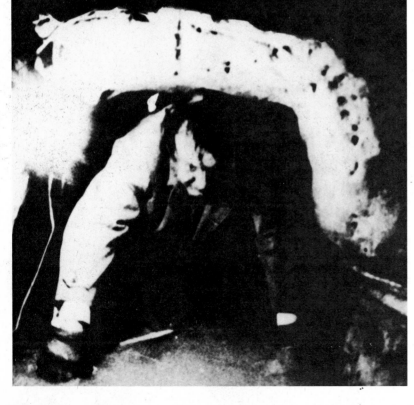

In effect, East Germans were banned from visiting West Berlin and those with jobs there lost them at one blow. People living adjacent to the border in East Berlin were forcibly evicted from their houses, which were pulled down to create a no-man's-land devoid of cover. Anyone found in this cleared strip was liable to be shot on sight.

The mounting crisis had resulted in more than 100,000 refugees flooding into West Berlin in the first six months of 1961 alone, and in the next few weeks before the Wall went up another 50,000 had joined them. But the Wall did not prevent others from attempting to escape. Cutting through the wire, tunnelling, trying to dash through the few remaining official checkpoints were among the methods; some were successful but many were not. In the first 18 months after the building of the Wall, at least 47 people are known to have been killed while trying to escape to West Berlin: very many more were injured. Perhaps the most notorious case was that of Peter Fechter, an 18-year-old building worker who was shot on 17 August 1962 while attempting to scale the Wall. He lay for more than an hour, grievously wounded, on the East Berlin side. The border guards made no attempt to come to his aid, and when he was eventually removed he was dead. The incident resulted in demonstrations by West Berliners.

Kennedy at the Wall

The Wall did not deter the federal government in Bonn from continuing to invest money in West Berlin, which was fast becoming a modern, highly industrialised and prosperous community – in marked contrast to war-scarred East Berlin. Indeed, the glaring economic difference between the two parts of the city had been a major influence in attracting refugees to the West. Now, however, even more than before, West Berlin became a symbol of freedom, the Wall itself a symbol of communist repression. In February 1962, Robert Kennedy carried to Berlin a message from his brother, the president, which said: 'Although West Berlin is situated on the edge of the totalitarian system, it will not be attacked, for an attack in West Berlin is an attack on Chicago, New York, Paris, London.' The following year President Kennedy himself visited the city and declared before the people of West Berlin, 'As a free man I take pride in the words: Ich bin ein Berliner (I am a Berliner)!' Pilgrimages were also made on the other side of the Wall. Khrushchev visited it in January 1963 and called the Wall 'a great and heroic socialist achievement'.

At times throughout the remainder of the 1960s the communists temporarily closed the autobahn routes from the Federal Republic to Berlin, and the West reacted by sending military vehicles in order to reaffirm right of access to the city. On these occasions it was East German authorities who dealt with civilian traffic, Soviet personnel handling the military – and honouring the right of British, American and French military vehicles to proceed. Indeed Western military personnel were ordered to deal with the Soviet authorities only, for the Western powers did not acknowledge the right of East Germany to control the access routes to Berlin. The coming of East-West detente in the early 1970s produced an easing of communist restrictions. It became easier for West Germans to visit Berlin, and for West Berliners to visit their relations in the East. Nevertheless, Berlin remains a physically divided city. **Charles Messenger**

The
F-104 STARFIGHTER

The F-104 was conceived in 1952 at a time when US Air Force fighter pilots in Korea were opposed by the Soviet-designed MiG-15 which had a much better altitude performance than their F-86 Sabres. Consequently the overriding characteristic demanded of the new fighter was an outstandingly good flight performance. This, Lockheed designer 'Kelly' Johnson certainly produced: his F-104 was the first operational fighter capable of achieving sustained speeds of more than Mach 2, and at one time it held both the aeroplane world speed and altitude records.

The first of two prototype XF-104s took off on its maiden flight on 7 February 1954. The aircraft was powered by a 4535kg (10,000lb) thrust afterburning Wright J65 turbojet and achieved a top speed of Mach 1.79. The more powerful 6710kg (14,800lb) thrust General Electric J79-GE-3 became available to power the 15 service-test YF-104As and it was one of these that first reached a speed of Mach 2 on 27 April 1955. Early in 1958 the USAF's 83rd Fighter-Interceptor Squadron began to equip with F-104s, and pilots of this unit set up a number of speed and altitude records.

The F-104's remarkably high performance was achieved by a radically new design, aptly described as 'the missile with a man in it'. The Starfighter combined high engine thrust with very low airframe drag. It was a small aircraft, with a long slender fuselage and a wing of extremely small span and exceptional thinness. From the wing's fuselage attachment points to its tip it measured just 2.31m (91in) and its thickness varied from 106.68 to 49.78mm (4.2in to 1.96in). Such a design led to other unusual features. As there was no room for internal stowage of fuel or the retracted main undercarriage, these had to be

accommodated within the fuselage (although additional fuel could be carried in wing-tip and underwing drop-tanks). Another problem was the fast landing speeds associated with the F-104's high wing loading. Leading and trailing edge flaps helped to improve low speed handling, and the fitting of a boundary layer control system, which piped air – bled from the engine – at high speed over the wing trailing edge, cut landing speeds by 32km/h (20mph).

The Starfighter's fuselage consisted of three main sections. The forward section housed the radar in the extreme nose beneath a pointed radome. The F-104A interceptor had the AN/ASG-14 air-to-air radar, while the widely used F-104G had the NASARR (North American search and range radar) with both air-to-air and air-to-ground capability. The pilot's cockpit was located well forward, immediately behind the radar installation. Visibility from the cockpit was exceptionally good for a fighter of the Starfighter's generation; the instrument layout was also well designed, as the gauges could be easily read and the switches were within easy reach.

Less well conceived were the downward-operating ejector seats fitted to early Starfighters. This unusual arrangement was considered necessary in order to achieve successful ejection at speeds above Mach 1.8, when a conventional upward-ejecting seat would not clear the aircraft's high-mounted tailplane. However, as successful ejection at low level was found to be more desirable than the high speed requirement, a conventional upward-ejecting seat was substituted.

Behind the cockpit in the rearmost part of the forward fuselage section was the avionics bay, which contained such electronic systems as the inertial

Previous page: A front view of a US Air Force F-104 that has just finished refuelling from a KC-135 tanker. Above: An F-104E banks over to reveal its under-fuselage drop tank. Although the wing hardpoints are empty the Starfighter can carry up to 1134kg (2500lb) of ordnance.

navigation set, UHF communications, TACAN (tactical air navigation) and PHI (position homing indicator) navigational aids. These systems were neatly packaged in so-called 'jeep cans', which resembled the petrol cans carried by World War II jeeps and were shaped to fit the avionics compartment. Access to the avionics systems was by means of a hinged hatch immediately behind the cockpit and the equipment's serviceability could be quickly and simply checked using a built-in self-test system. The other important system occupying the forward fuselage section was the built-in 20mm M61 Vulcan rotary cannon and its ammunition stowage. Mounted in the lower fuselage and offset to port, the six-barrelled Vulcan had a rate of fire of up to 6000 rounds per minute.

The main fuselage section housed fuel tanks, powerplant and main undercarriage. There was a forward as well as an aft main fuel tank, the auxiliary fuel tank forward and saddle fuel tanks mounted

Above right: While on shore patrol two F-104Gs of the Royal Netherlands Air Force fly along the Dutch coastline.

Right: The Starfighter's long slender fuselage led to the aircraft being called the 'missile with a man in it'. This US Air Force Starfighter is one of the F-104G variants that were developed for the new German market.

Above: A two-seat TF-104G trainer of the Belgian Air Force. The Belgians employed the Starfighter as an all-weather interceptor. The national markings – red, yellow and black – are painted on the tailplane, and on the wings as a roundel.

Left: Two USAF Starfighters fly in formation over California, with the stub wings very apparent.

Above: Partners in arms, a British Jaguar and German Starfighter undertake a combined combat air patrol. Given the multiplicity of arms and equipment within Nato national cooperation at all levels is essential if military efficiency is to be maintained.

Below: As the pilot leaves his Starfighter ground crew prepare to take over. Due to its relatively simple design maintenance duties are kept to a minimum.

above the engine to port and starboard. With wing-tip drop-tanks fitted, the F-104 had sufficient fuel to fly a 1045km (650 mile) radius combat mission. The main fuselage section was virtually tailored around the General Electric J79 afterburning turbojet. In its developed J79-GE-11A version, this powerplant produced 4535kg (10,000lb) of thrust dry and 7166kg (15,800lb) with afterburning. Its installed weight was 1580kg (3485lb) and overall length 5257mm (207in). The rear fuselage section, which could be unbolted and removed from the aircraft to provide easy access to the powerplant, carried the vertical tail fin with an all-moving tailplane mounted on the top in a 'T-tail' arrangement.

Four variants of the Starfighter served with the USAF: the F-104A interceptor and its two-seat training counterpart the F-104B, the F-104C ground attack fighter and equivalent F-104D two-seater. In all, 154 F-104s were built for Air Defense Command (ADC) and were initially armed with two Sidewinder AAMs and later with four. Despite its many virtues, because the interceptor version lacked the ability of the much larger F-106 Delta Dart to carry a heavy load of missiles and elaborate radar and other avionics, its service in defence of North American air space was short-lived. It entered service with ADC in 1958 and was temporarily withdrawn from regular units two years later. However, the Cuban missile crisis of 1962 showed the need for a fast-reacting interceptor to defend US airspace, and F-104s returned to service from 1962 until 1969. Tactical Air Command's

F-104C – of which 77 were produced – was fitted with an in-flight refuelling probe and could carry tactical nuclear weapons. This version entered service with the 479th Tactical Fighter Wing at George air force base, California, in 1959 and was retired in 1967.

It was with the air forces of America's Nato allies in Europe that the Starfighter was to see most wide-ranging service. No fewer than nine Nato air forces operated the F-104 – Canada, West Germany, the Netherlands, Belgium, Italy, Turkey, Greece, Norway and Denmark – and the aircraft was built under licence by consortiums of Belgian, Dutch, Italian and German companies and by Canadair. The version operated by these nations was the F-104G, the so-called Super Starfighter, which had an uprated powerplant, NASARR radar, strengthened structure and new mission equipment. It was operated as a multi-role fighter in Europe, carrying out air defence and air superiority missions as well as those of ground attack reconnaissance and tactical nuclear strike. In many ways this was an over ambitious requirement for a small and lightweight fighter which had been specifically designed for an air superiority role.

Many air forces had problems operating the Starfighter, but in West Germany, both in the Luftwaffe and Marineflieger, F-104G losses reached crisis levels. By 1969 West Germany had lost more than 100 Starfighters in 10 years. Many factors conspired to produce this state of affairs. In the first place, West Germany was the world's major Starfighter operator, having taken delivery of 866 aircraft; the United States, by comparison, had 294, Canada 238 and Italy 149. German losses were therefore the highest in terms of numbers, although as a percentage of the total force the losses were no worse than those of some other Starfighter operators.

There can be no doubt that the Starfighter was a very demanding aircraft to fly and, while by no means an unsound design, it was unforgiving of pilots' mistakes. Furthermore, in European service it often flew in the low level strike role, for which it had not been designed and which often pushed the fighter beyond the limits of its capability. Add to this the notorious vagaries of European weather and the 'experience gap' in the Luftwaffe (which had trained no military pilots whatever between 1945 and 1955), and Germany's Starfighter losses are easier to comprehend.

Outside Europe the major operator was Japan, which produced 230 F-104J single-seat and DJ two-seat Starfighters under licence. The F-104J was similar to the F-104G and entered service with the

Right: A team of German and British aircrew members congregate by an F-104 at an airfield in West Germany. The Starfighter had a bad name in the Luftwaffe — being dubbed 'the widow-maker' — but this was largely unjustified. Starfighters had roughly the same proportion of crashes per hours' flying time as other Nato aircraft.

Japanese Air Self-Defence Force in 1964. Ex-USAF Starfighters were supplied to Pakistan, Nationalist China and Jordan, while Spain received 21 F-104Gs and TF-104G trainers from the United States in 1965 in return for American use of Spanish air bases.

The Starfighter did not see extensive combat during its service life, but it was nevertherless involved in a number of conflicts. Shortly after it entered service with the USAF in 1958, the type was despatched to Taiwan during the confrontation between Communist and Nationalist China over Quemoy. Thereafter the Chinese Nationalist Air Force operated Starfighters, which participated in numerous combats with Chinese communist fighters. During the Indo-Pakistan War of 1965, the Pakistan Air Force's single F-104A squadron was used for air defence, scoring several victories for the loss of one fighter in combat. In Southeast Asia the USAF employed F-104C Starfighters from 1965 to 1967, initially to counter North Vietnam's fighter force. As it happened, however, most sorties flown from Da Nang in South Vietnam and Udorn in Thailand during this period were ground attack missions.

In the early 1970s the USAF formulated a requirement for a lightweight fighter aircraft for the 1980s and 1990s. Lockheed offered a developed version of the F-104, the Lancer, to meet this requirement; but a new fighter did not come about, the USAF choosing to adopt General Dynamics' F-16 as its lightweight fighter. It was left to Aeritalia in Italy to produce the ultimate version of the Starfighter; this was the

Above: Attached to this German Navy Starfighter is a Kormoran air-to-ship missile. One of the latest advanced missiles the Kormoran is fitted with both anti-radiation and active-radar homing and has a range of 65km (40 miles). Left: A German Luftwaffe pilot climbs out of his Starfighter. Below: One of the more spectacular experiments carried out on the Starfighter was the ZELL launcher which attempted to introduce an extremely short take off.

F-104S, which currently serves with the Italian and Turkish Air Forces. The F-104S has an increased all-up weight and more powerful engine, allowing a heavier warload in the attack role; for all-weather air defence it possesses two AIM-7 Sparrow AAMs plus four AIM-9 Sidewinders.

During its long service life the Starfighter has been adapted for a variety of experimental and special purpose duties. In 1960-61, 24 F-104As were converted as unmanned, high-speed target drones with the designation QF-104. In the mid-1960s the USAF and Luftwaffe conducted trials with an F-104 launched by rocket motors from an inclined ramp under the ZELL (zero length launch) programme. Perhaps most important was the NF-104A Starfighter, fitted with a 2720kg (6000lb) thrust rocket motor, which could climb to altitudes well above 30,480m (100,000ft) to provide prospective astronauts with training in the use of thrust reaction controls.

F-104G Starfighter

Type Single-seat multi-role fighter
Dimensions Span 6.68m (21ft 11in); length 16.69m (54ft 9in); height 4.11m (13ft 6in)
Weight Empty 6390kg (14,088lb); maximum take-off 13,054kg (28,779lb)
Powerplant One 7166kg (15,800lb) General Electric J79-GE-11A afterburning turbojet

Performance Maximum speed Mach 2.35 or 2333km/h (1450mph) at 10,970m (36,000ft)
Range Combat radius 1200km (745 miles)
Ceiling 17,680m (58,000ft)

Armament One 20mm M61 Vulcan rotary cannon and up to 1134kg (2500lb) of ordnance, including AIM-9 Sidewinder air-to-air missiles, Kormoran and Bullpup air-to-surface missiles, free-fall bombs and unguided rockets

Left from the top: The distinctive colour scheme of a Canadian 'Red Indian' Starfighter; an F-104 of the Danish Air Force speeds past a parked and disassembled model; and a Dutch F-104 painted in the dark camouflage colours typical of military aircraft based in northern Europe. Right from the top: An F-104 in the colours of the Canadian Tiger squadron; a TF-104G of the Norwegian Air Force; and one of the F-104s that make up a fighter/bomber wing for the Greek Air Force.

Fighting for a homeland

The tragedy of nationalism in the Middle East

'An empty dream? An illusion? Then let it be a dream so long as it is *our* dream. Let it be a mistake so long as it is *our* mistake.' *Gostan Zarian, an Armenian writer*.

The search for independence and self-determination is one of the longest and most bitter struggles in the Middle East. The area is a crossroads for numerous civilisations, ethnic communities, cultures and religions; Muslim and Christian Arabs, Jews, Armenians, Kurds and a myriad of smaller communities.

After the collapse of the Ottoman Empire in 1918 and the decline of European imperialism as the century wore on, the national communities sought to attain the goal of nation-statehood, so they would be able to form their own political institutions, to make their own decisions autonomously and to refuse the cultural assimilation which others sought to impose on them. But the modern political boundaries in the Middle East were in fact arbitrarily established with little regard for national aspirations. Most modern Middle East states consist of more than one ethnic or religious group and the minorities have had to

struggle to assert their cultural and political entities.

The particular bitterness and intractability of Middle Eastern nationalism stems from a number of factors. Centuries of religious and cultural division have been exacerbated by recent events that have generated their own momentum, their own special hatred; then the vast disparities of the Middle East – between sparsely populated areas with incredible wealth, like Saudi Arabia, and over-populated regions like the Nile Delta in Egypt, or between the Europeanised cities such as Tel Aviv and the primitive villages of the Yemen – add another level of complexity; while the concern of the superpowers to maintain their influence in this strategically vital part of the world has led them to back one national group against another. And finally, there is the fact that although nationalism is a seductive goal for many groupings, nationalism as such is often overlaid by other, linked concepts that confuse or intensify the issues – for example, the internal conflicts within religions such as Judaism and Islam, or the religious communities that seek to dominate existing states, like the Maronite Christians and the Druze in Lebanon.

Above: Protests in Tel Aviv in September 1982 as Israelis object to what they saw as their government's complicity in the massacres of Palestinians at the Sabra and Chatila refugee camps – a further divisive episode in the seemingly endless conflict between Arab and Jew.

The massacre of civilians has been a regular feature of the history of nationalism in the Middle East during the 20th century, leaving a legacy of bitterness and hatred. Above left: Turks survey the scene after the massacre of an Armenian family in 1909. Above: The village of Deir Yassin where Jewish terrorists murdered over 200 Arab civilians.

The fight for Palestine

The most bitter national struggle in the Middle East is that involving the Jews in Palestine. Following the Balfour Declaration of November 1917 European Jews sought to secure a national home for all Jews in the British-mandated territory of Palestine and Jews resident in other Arab countries were encouraged to settle there by the Jewish Agency. For centuries Jews had lived in Muslim Arab countries reasonably peacefully and had enjoyed a special status as 'people of the book'. But the Arab peoples, who after centuries of rule by the Turkish Ottoman Empire were developing their own concepts of nationalism, were outraged by Zionism and the waves of Jewish settlers arriving in Palestine.

The climax came in 1948, when first of all there was vicious fighting between the Palestinian Arabs and the Jews, and then the neighbouring Arab states sent in troops to try to crush the nascent state of Israel. Both sides were well aware of what victory or defeat could mean. In this regard two episodes stand out: firstly, the desperate struggle by the Jews to supply the beleaguered Jewish enclave in Jerusalem in March, through a countryside in which every rock seemed to hide an Arab with a rifle and where the bodies of any Jewish casualties that were abandoned were mutilated as a matter of course; and secondly, the massacre of over 200 Arab civilians at the village of Deir Yassin on 9 April 1948 by members of the Irgun and the Lehi, Jewish terrorist groups.

Events such as the massacre at Deir Yassin raised religious and racial antagonism to a level from which it has rarely fallen. The mere fact that Menachem Begin, who controlled the Irgun in the 1940s, later became Prime Minister of Israel is an affront to the Palestinians, while the stand of the Palestinian leaders is totally unacceptable to the Jews – the first PLO leader, Ahmad Shuqayri, for example, pledged to 'drive the Jews into the sea'. This kind of rhetoric fuels a remorseless spiral; a history of intense unavoidable conflict is being created which makes any attempts at defusing the tension ever harder, so that by the early 1980s Israel was ruled by a politician whose terrorist activities and extremist attitudes had shocked and horrified the first leaders of the Jewish state, while the Palestinian leader, Yassir Arafat, was unable to find a way of compromising his stand on the destruction of the state of Israel without risking open revolt in the PLO.

Armenia and the Turks

Armenia lies in the area between the Caspian, Black and Mediterranean Seas and is one of the oldest civilisations in western Asia with a history stretching back almost 5000 years. It is also one of the oldest Christian communities in the world, predating Byzantium. Some Armenian legends maintain that it is the Garden of Eden mentioned in the Bible and that its highest peak, Mount Ararat, is where Noah's Ark came to rest after the Flood. Despite the fact that

Armenia has its own language and cultural identity, since the 1920s it has been divided between Turkey and the USSR. For a brief period after the collapse of the Ottoman Empire in 1918 it enjoyed nation-statehood but this ended when Turkish and Soviet troops took over the young Armenian Republic.

Armenians claim that their cultural uniqueness merits nation-statehood independent of the USSR and Turkey and they have consistently championed this claim since before the demise of the Ottoman Empire. Armenians secured key positions in the Ottoman civil service and as lawyers, artists, businessmen and intellectuals were important throughout the Empire, and yet the government in Constantinople refused to recognise their nationalist demands. Indeed, there were widespread massacres of Armenians during World War I, and some sources estimate that over one-and-a-half million Armenians were killed. Since then Armenian nationalists have sought to force the Turkish government to accept responsibility for this act and to recognise the Armenians' right to self-determination based on their ethnic and cultural homogeneity. In the late 1970s ASALA (the Armenian Secret Army for the Liberation of Armenia) emerged as the organisation charged with pursuing this task through acts of terrorism against the Turkish state.

The Turks' allies in many of their attempts to subjugate the Armenians in the days of the Ottoman Empire were another of the empire's ethnic minorities, the Kurds, whose homeland cuts into historical Armenia. A fierce mountain people occupying the rugged mountains on the borders of Iraq, Iran and Turkey, the Kurds are a nation of 17 million people who have never achieved modern statehood. Today this population is divided between five states – Turkey, Iraq, Syria, Iran and the USSR.

Although they are Muslims, the Kurds consider themselves Aryans, as opposed to the Semitic Jews and Arabs of the rest of the Middle East, and speak an Indo-European language. According to the Kurdish nationalists it is this which justifies the establishment of an independent republic of Kurdistan and has fostered conflicts with the governments of the states in which the Kurds now find themselves. The longest and most bitter struggle has been in Iraq where the Kurds occupy the oil-rich northern province around Mosul. All attempts to secure Kurdish autonomy in this region have met with failure in the face of Baghdad's determination to rule Iraq as a unitary state regardless of the ethnic and religious minorities within its borders.

Nationalism and the superpowers

Elsewhere in the Middle East the same pattern of culturally distinct national communities seeking self-determination within arbitrarily defined borders emerges. Perhaps the most extreme example is Lebanon. When French forces withdrew and the Lebanese state was established in 1946 the Maronite Christians of Mount Lebanon, east of Beirut, held all the positions of influence and importance. They considered that their virtual monopoly of wealth and education and their entrepreneurial skills entitled them to run Lebanon in their interests and determine the nature of the state regardless of the fact that the borders of the country embraced other communities. By the late 1960s this was becoming unworkable. The Sunni and Shi"ia Muslim, Druze and non-Maronite Christian groups were openly resentful, and when the PLO set up its headquarters there in the early 1970s, political violence rapidly became the norm, and continued into the early 1980s.

The final ingredient that has kept the pot boiling in the Middle East has been the intervention of the superpowers. The protection that the USA has given Israel and the mass provision of arms to many Arab states by the Soviet Union have encouraged extremist stands on both sides, while the Kurds and the various groupings in the Lebanon have, from time to time, become pawns in the game of global superpower confrontation.

There seems little prospect for peace while there are so many factors making for nationalist conflict in the region; and it is sadly ironic that the world's two most powerful states, the US and the USSR, that are themselves symbols of supra-national identities, have contributed so much to nationalist antagonisms in the Middle East.   **Leigh Douglas**

Refugee camps are the sad resting place of the many displaced persons who are victims of nationalist warfare. Yet even these civilian refugees are not spared the horrors of war. Far left: The corpses of Palestinians lie scattered in the Sabra camp in testimony to the ruthless savagery of Lebanese Christian Phalangists.

Islam and pan-Arabism are unifying factors in the Arab world; though in contrast there are many disparities of political opinion and wealth – between, for example, the crowded slum dwellers of cities such as Amman (left) and the wealthy rulers of the oil states (below, members of the Saudi royal family assemble for evening prayer).

A mountain people's struggle for self determination

The Kurds have been recognised as a distinct national group at least since the 12th century, but the 647,000 square km (250,000 square miles) of Kurdistan, a largely mountainous region rising to over 4600m (15,000ft) at Mount Ararat, has constantly been the prey of more powerful neighbours. There are at present some 17 million Kurds, the largest proportion living in Turkey (8.7 million) with other major concentrations in Iran (4.5 million) and Iraq (3 million) and smaller groups in Syria and the Soviet Union.

An agrarian people, the Kurds have their own language and costume. In recent times they have evolved into two discernible categories, the plains Kurds and the mountain Kurds. The plains Kurds' economy is maintained through a mix of pastoral and agricultural farming (sheep and goats form the bulk of the livestock, and barley, rice and tobacco are the principal crops) while in the rugged mountainous terrain, the Kurdish population depends almost entirely upon rough grazing flocks and illicit cross-border trading. There are over 30 main tribes, and nationalism has often been subordinated to tribalism.

Autonomy had been promised to the Kurds, then subjects of the Ottoman Empire, by the victorious Allies after World War I, but a Kurdish state did not appear. Turkish and subsequently Iraqi nationalism proved much more potent. The inter-war years were therefore marked by a series of Kurdish tribal uprisings in Turkey, Iran and Iraq, the most significant being those of the Barzani tribe in Iraq under the leadership of Sheikh Ahmed and his younger brother, Mullah Mustafa Barzani.

World War II gave the Kurds new opportunities to assert their nationalism after British forces occupied Iraq in April 1941 and British and Soviet forces partitioned Iran in August 1941. Escaping from house arrest in Iraq in June 1943, Mullah Mustafa Barzani joined a Kurdish uprising in Turkey and subsequently organised tribes within Iraq to revolt against the Iraqi government. By 1945 his forces had been driven into Iran. Once there, Barzani became the main prop of a Soviet-inspired Kurdish state, which was proclaimed as the Mahabad Republic in January 1946. When Soviet forces withdrew from Iran, however, the new republic swiftly collapsed, and in an epic march Barzani led his followers to the Soviet Union in June 1947. With Barzani remaining in exile, the political leadership of the Kurds inside Iraq devolved upon the Kurdish Democratic Party (KDP). The party had been formed in August 1946 and its politburo was dominated by left-wing urban intellectuals such as Ibrahim Ahmed and Jelal Talabani.

After the Iraqi monarchy was overthrown in July 1958 and a republic established by Brigadier Abdul

Kurdistan

Kassim, the KDP was legitimised and a new constitution proclaimed that Arabs and Kurds would be partners in the new state. Barzani, who had been named as president of the KDP, returned to Iraq in October 1958 and immediately started to purge the party of its more extreme elements. Increasingly worried by Barzani's growing power, Kassim began to play off against each other old tribal rivals in Kurdistan, closed down the KDP's newspaper in February 1961 and arrested leading party members.

In June 1961 the Kurds petitioned Kassim on a wide range of grievances. In particular, there was considerable resentment against Kassim's land reform programme, which was aimed at reducing the size of private landholdings, and against new land taxes. That same month, Kurdish landlords raised a revolt around Sulaymaniyah. Barzani had had nothing to do with the rising, but in August he presented an ultimatum demanding restoration of democratic liberties in Iraq generally and full recognition of Kurdish autonomy. The government responded by launching a full-scale offensive against Kurdistan, including the bombing of villages, in September. Somewhat reluctantly the KDP politburo joined the revolt in December.

War in the mountains

Over the course of the next 14 years the Kurdish demands remained fairly constant: autonomy within Iraq, rather than independence from it; official recognition of the Kurdish language; a proportional share of political posts, including a Kurdish vice-president; and separate Kurdish units in the army together with a Kurdish assistant chief of staff. Successive Iraqi governments feared that autonomy would be but a short step to the breaking up of the state, and no agreement could be reached on the boundaries of an autonomous region for the Kurds within Iraq. The Kurds themselves habitually demanded at least a third of the revenues from the Kirkuk oil field, which the Iraqis did not consider part of Kurdistan.

An added difficulty for the Kurds was that Barzani did not enjoy the total allegiance of all Kurds within Iraq, and the government initially armed his tribal enemies. Barzani quickly became aware of a growing threat from the various border tribes who were old enemies of the Barzanis. Although support was given by such tribes as the Syrian Goyani and the Mangur Kurds from Iran, other Kurdish tribes such as the Zibari and the Baradost prepared to take up arms with the Iraqi government against the Barzanis. However, as the movement gained momentum, tribal differences were forgotten and, for the first time, there was a genuine sense of nationalism among the Kurds. Only one small group (3000 strong) made up mostly of urban Kurds, fought on the side of the government after 1965 and this was called the Jash ('Little Donkeys').

There were other differences within the rebel movement. Barzani controlled the forces in the northern mountains, but those around Sulaymaniyah and Kirkuk were led by Ahmed and Talabani. It was the latter who first established a rudimentary administration in Kurdish areas and who raised the first elements of what became a standing Kurdish military force – the Peshmarga ('Those Who Face Death'). In 1964 Barzani's forces drove the followers of Ahmed and Talabani into Iran and both were expelled from the KDP. Talabani was subsequently allowed to return but was again ejected in 1966 and by 1968 was openly fighting alongside government forces. Despite such internal friction, however, the Kurdish forces steadily grew in numbers from some 4000 when the fighting began to around 50,000 by 1975, when they controlled about 40,000 square km (15,500 square miles) at the height of the revolt.

To the world outside, the revolt was little known. The Iraqis succeeded in keeping out journalists, and the Kurds constantly failed to interest the United Nations in their cause. The course of the war itself followed an almost ritual pattern. The Kurds were unable to export their campaign from the mountains to the plains, while the Iraqi Army was unsuited to carrying the war into the mountains.

As late as 1970, however, the Kurds possessed just 140 heavy weapons and were always short of ammunition. For the Kurds, the war became a matter of isolating government garrisons in the mountains and ambushing relief forces. Trained and equipped mostly for conventional war, the Iraqis tended when fired upon to go to ground and await air support, which proved the main offensive weapon against the rebels.

The Kurds claimed that in the initial government offensive of September 1961, 500 villages were destroyed from the air and more than 8000 people made homeless, and that in the first two weeks of the government's offensive in June 1963 some 167 villages were bombed. By 1970 the United Nations calculated that 40,000 houses had been destroyed and 300,000 people made homeless. Yet airpower was not particularly effective in halting the revolt, since the Iraqi pilots were notorious for their inaccuracy. The campaigning was also restricted by the annual onset of winter in Kurdistan. Attempted government winter offensives in January 1966 and January 1969 lasted days rather than weeks before weather prevented the Iraqi forces from exploiting any initial tactical surprise they might have achieved.

The alternative to trying to defeat the Kurds mili-

Far left: Kurdish rebels at the entrance to one of their mountain hideouts. The rugged nature of the terrain and the relative safety of the caves from air-attack made it particularly difficult for government units to make inroads into rebel territory. Far left below: Kurdish rebels with a captured anti-aircraft gun. The failure of the rebel leaders to gain international sympathy for their cause meant that such weapons were extremely rare acquisitions. Above: In the sultry glow of a paraffin lamp, Iraqi Kurds plan an ambush against government forces.

tarily was to negotiate with them, and several truces were called while talks were held. After the overthrow of Kassim in February 1963 the new Ba'athist government offered a measure of decentralisation but soon concluded that the Kurds were asking too much, and launched a new offensive in June. This rapidly ran out of steam, one divisional-size formation taking eight weeks to clear the strategically important Rawandiz gorge. The Ba'athists were themselves overthrown in November 1963 and a ceasefire was negotiated the following February. A new constitution spoke vaguely about recognising Kurdish rights within 'the Iraqi national unity', but the Kurds grew impatient for genuine concessions and so the government went onto the offensive again in April 1965.

Battle for Mount Handrin

Next year, despite the deployment of more than 40,000 troops and 100 aircraft and the capture of the Rawandiz gorge, the Iraqis were not only unable to crush the Kurds but lost one brigade which was totally routed by Barzani at Mount Handrin on 11/12 May 1966. Their offensive capability was effectively blunted for over two years.

A new prime minister, Abdul Rahman al-Bazzaz, had come to power in the meantime and his government agreed a 12-point programme which conceded most of the Kurdish demands – but Bazzaz was then forced out of office in August 1966. When the Ba'athists returned to government in July 1968 they announced that they would resurrect the Bazzaz programme, but their support for Talabani led to renewed guerrilla fighting and an attempted winter offensive by the government. Re-equipped with Soviet T54 and T55 tanks, the renewed Iraqi offensive involved

Left: Mullah Mustafa Barzani who led the Kurdish rebels against the Iraqi government, but who was unable to reconcile tribal differences within the Kurdish people. Right: Colonel Abdul Salam Aref who, with his Ba'athist allies, planned a successful coup in Iraq in February 1963. He launched an offensive against the Kurds in June of that year but could make little headway.

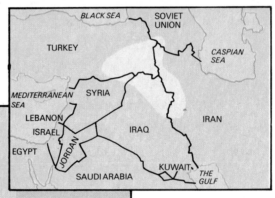

Right: Iraqi troops preparing to defend a lonely outpost against Kurdish attack.

70,000 men against Barzani's 15,000 in August 1969, but again there was a failure to achieve any major objectives and new negotiations were opened in December.

Agreement was finally reached in January 1970 and an armistice concluded in March. It promised full recognition of Kurdish nationality and autonomy within four years, a Kurdish vice-president and a plebiscite on Kirkuk. Almost immediately there were problems, however, and the government rejected the Kurd nominated as vice-president by the KDP. While the government accused Barzani of trying to establish his own administration in Kurdistan and of not dissolving the Peshmarga, Barzani charged the government with not honouring its commitments on representation and the plebiscite and of trying to assassinate him. In March 1973 the government rejected the KDP plan for autonomy and in September produced its own, which failed to satisfy demands on the extent of the autonomous region and the powers of a Kurdish assembly. Talks broke down in early 1974, the government giving the Kurds 15 days to comply with its own version of autonomy. On 6 April, Kurdish ministers were dismissed from the government and fighting began once more.

Hostilities were to take a rather different course

Above: The main phase of the Kurdish revolt ended when agreement was reached between Iraq and Iran in March 1975 and the Iranian border was closed to rebels. Here Kurds march toward an assembly point after an amnesty was announced by Iraq.

from that of earlier years. Both sides were now far better equipped, particularly the Iraqis who committed some 120,000 troops and 20,000 police to a new offensive in August 1974 designed to push the Kurds back from the Rawandiz gorge along the Hamilton road to the Iranian frontier. With the Kurdish forces forced into a far more conventional static defence of their territory and civilian population, the Iraqis got to within 32km (20 miles) of the Kurdish headquarters at Chouman by December. At this point the Shah of Iran, who had given covert assistance to the Kurds in the past, provided them with artillery and anti-tank missiles and, in January 1975, sent in a limited number of troops with 130mm guns and Hawk surface-to-air missiles.

The Shah withdraws support

In March 1975, however, the two states recoiled from the prospect of war and the Shah reached agreement with the Iraqis over outstanding territorial disputes between them. In return for Iraqi concessions on these, the Shah withdrew his support for the Kurds. Iran announced that the frontier would be closed after 1 April, and with some 50,000 Kurds passing into Iran before the deadline, the revolt finally collapsed. The Iraqis admitted to 60,000 government casualties since 1968.

Barzani went to the United States, where he died in March 1979. His exiled followers were resettled around Mahabad and Sanandaj in Iran where they split into two factions. Talabani re-emerged to head a Kurdish Patriotic Union (KPU) while Barzani's two sons led a KDP (Provisional Leadership).

After the fall of the Shah in January 1979, the once clandestine Iranian KDP began to demand the same kind of autonomy that the Iraqi Kurds had sought. Limited concessions from the Khomeini government failed to satisfy these demands and fighting began with Talabani joining the Iranian Kurds in their struggle. By October 1982 all four main Iranian Kurdish tribes were in revolt against the Ayatollah.

The situation has, of course, been complicated by the Gulf War between Iran and Iraq since both sides have endeavoured to exploit the Kurdish factor. Several early Iranian air raids were specifically aimed at Kurdish areas of Iraq, while pro-Iranian Kurds appear to have been responsible for sabotaging Iraqi oil pipelines in January 1982. Although the majority of the Iraqi Kurds appear to be tiring of conflict, events in Iran and the growing unrest among Turkish Kurds suggests that the age-old problem of accommodating a Kurdish national identity is far from resolved and that the focus of violence will merely shift elsewhere. **Ian Beckett**

The Imam's war
Royalist and republican in the Yemen

The name Arabia conjures up for most people a picture of desert: miles of desolation and the occasional oasis of date palms. But the Yemen, in the southwest corner of Arabia, is a green and fertile land. For more than a thousand years this remote country was ruled by the Hamid ud-Din dynasty, the Imams of the Yemen who styled themselves 'The Sword of Islam'. Until the 1960s they kept their land isolated and remote from developments in the outside world. In a country more than twice the size of Scotland there were few tarmac roads and no railways. Life was little changed from medieval times.

The Yemen's eastern and southern borders with the Federation of South Arabia (ruled as a British protectorate from Aden and known as the People's Democratic Republic of Yemen since independence in 1967) were always ill-defined. Successive Imams maintained a historical claim to Aden and to suzerainty over the tribes whose territory lay between Aden and the Yemen border. Anglo-Yemeni relations were therefore usually bad. Similar border disputes in the north and northwest kept relations cool with the Yemen's other neighbour, Saudi Arabia.

But the Imam's attention was largely focused on the need to maintain an often disputed authority over the various mountain tribes and the people of the walled cities of Sana (the capital), Sadah and Taiz. The dynasty came from the northern and central mountains and were members of the Zeidi sect of the Shi'ia branch of Islam, which made up about 40 per cent of the population. Like most mountain men, the Zeidis are tough and independent. The northern mountains rise to 3000m (10,000 feet) or more, every track a defile and open to ambush. The inhabitants carry arms almost from childhood.

The rest of the population, most of whom lived in the south, were Shaffeis of the Sunni branch of Islam

Above: Egyptian troops shell royalist positions with a recoilless cannon. Although the Egyptians were dominant in positional warfare, sorties into the rebel-held mountain areas often resulted in high casualties for the republicans.

Below: Civilians stand and stare as military vehicles patrol Sana after the successful coup, led by Brigadier-General Sallal, which overthrew the Imam in September 1962.

and they did not recognise the religious authority of the Imam. But the Zeidis were much the better fighting men.

Political turbulence under the Imams was normally provoked by personal disenchantment – the hurt pride or unfulfilled financial expectations of a tribal leader or prominent official. But the country could not remain for ever insulated from the political tides that were sweeping the Arab world. In Egypt, President Gamal Abdel Nasser was propounding a left-wing Arab nationalism directly hostile to conservative religious rulers like the Imams.

At the time of Nasser's rising influence in the 1950s, the ruler of the Yemen was the Imam Ahmed. His cruelty was legendary. But his son, Mohammed al-Badr, had travelled widely on foreign missions for his father and had fallen under Nasser's spell. In September 1962, after surviving innumerable assassination attempts, Imam Ahmed died in his bed. Badr succeeded his father, but his rule was destined to be brief.

On 26 September 1962 there was a coup in Sana. It was planned by some young army officers, led by Brigadier-General Sallal, the army's chief of staff and a protégé of Badr. Ironically, the coup was immediately supported by Egypt's President Nasser, whom Badr had so admired. Within a few hours of Sallal's proclamation of a republic, an advance guard of 3000 Egyptians was landing at Sana airfield. By April 1963 their strength had grown to 30,000.

The rebellion had been heralded by the shelling of Badr's palace, and the damage had been such as to suggest that the Imam must have been killed. In fact he escaped and after various adventures got away to the mountains where the Zeidi tribesmen rallied to his side. The royalists, as they came to be known, were supported by the conservative Arab rulers King Faisal of Saudi Arabia and King Hussein of Jordan. Saudi Arabia became the main base for the Imam's forces. The royalists could count on the Bakil and the Hashid, the two most important Zeidi tribal confederations, but they lacked weapons and training. Badr appointed Amir Mohammed Hussein, one of the Hamid ud-Din family, as commander-in-chief, and he proved

The Imam Ahmed of Yemen (left), whose cruelty and reactionary politics were legendary, was succeeded by his widely-travelled and far more liberal son, Mohammed al-Badr (below) in September 1962. Whatever changes may have been in the mind of the new Imam were never put into practice; he was ousted by a military coup shortly after his accession.

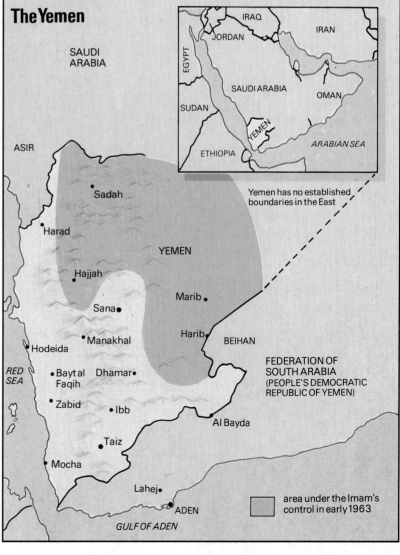

The Yemen

Yemen has no established boundaries in the East

area under the Imam's control in early 1963

reasonably effective.

The war that followed Sallal's bungled attempt to kill the Imam was to last for nearly seven years. It was hard, bloody and cruel. The Egyptians ruled the skies, bombing and machine-gunning at will both in the Yemen and beyond its borders in Saudi Arabia and the Federation of South Arabia; both chemical warfare and napalm were used on occasions. Egyptian tanks controlled the main roads and the royalists were no match for them in positional warfare. But it was a different story in the mountains and foothills where armoured patrols of the Egyptians and their republican allies were regularly ambushed.

British involvement

Inevitably the fighting spread across the ill-defined border with the Federation of South Arabia, some of whose traditional rulers (who were also federal ministers) were assisting the royalists with arms and men. The Federal Regular Army (British commanded and with a large British element) was engaged in frequent actions along the border from October 1962 onwards. Most of the fighting occurred in Beihan state, in the north of the Federation, where the ruling family was closely associated with the royalist cause.

Once established in Sana and Taiz to the south, the Egyptians tried to seal off the border and prevent support reaching the royalists in the Yemen. In October 1962 Egyptian aircraft strafed the Amir's palace at As-Saylan, well within federal territory. The British provided a battery of light anti-aircraft artillery to help defend Beihan. Shipped from Hong Kong to Aden, the battery was flown up to Beihan by the RAF.

Towards the end of 1962 the Egyptians launched an offensive designed to isolate the desert area of the northeast from the mountains. Marib, the ruined capital of the Queen of Sheba, was the objective. The brigade employed was commanded by Brigadier

Shazli, later to plan the Egyptian crossing of the Suez Canal in the Yom Kippur War of 1973. Marib was taken after some tough fighting and the republicans turned southeast to capture Harib which lay opposite Beihan across the 3km (2-mile) wide Wadi Ayn. This brought them into the border area that was disputed with the Federation of South Arabia, and there were clashes with British troops.

By the end of 1964, the Egyptians could claim to control most of the country apart from the northern mountains. The royalist situation began to improve early in 1965, however. The Saudis stepped up their supply of arms and ammunition, and a team composed of foreign mercenaries, several of them ex-SAS, improved the royalists' training and tactics. The royalists were also given better advice, some of which they accepted; Colonel David Smiley, a former commander of the Sultan's army in Oman from 1958 to 1962, paid several visits to the Yemen where his influence was considerable. The royalists were firmly established in the mountains of northern, central and eastern Yemen, their guerrilla tactics isolating the Egyptian garrisons which had now grown to 60,000 troops. An Egyptian offensive against Harad in the extreme northwest proved to be a costly failure, losing half the armoured cars involved and 10 tanks. Nasser was losing interest in a war which was becoming increasingly unpopular in Egypt as casualties mounted. In August 1965 Nasser and King Faisal negotiated a ceasefire agreement which required the Egyptians to withdraw all their troops within 10 months from November 1965.

By the following March about 40,000 Egyptians had left the Yemen, but the bombing of royalist positions was then resumed. This volte-face followed the publication by the British government of a White Paper on Defence in which they announced their intention of withdrawing from Aden by 1968. This confounded all their friends and delighted all their enemies in south Arabia; it was like giving burglars advance notice of one's intention to be away from home. Within months the Egyptian strength had been increased once more to 60,000.

Egyptian withdrawal

The stalemate continued, interrupted by occasional guerrilla activities, until the Six-Day War between Egypt and Israel broke out in June 1967. Under the influence of Egypt's disastrous defeat in that conflict, Nasser decided to withdraw all his forces from the Yemen. The last Egyptian troops had left the country by the end of October 1967.

The immediate consequence of the Egyptian withdrawal was the fall of Sallal, the republican leader. Widely regarded as an Egyptian puppet, Sallal had few supporters left on the republican side. On 5 November, while he was out of the country, he was quietly deposed in a bloodless coup. The man who emerged as his replacement, Hassan al-Amri, was an implacable enemy of the Imam who had also fallen foul of the Egyptians and Sallal. He represented a political position which had wide appeal: no return of the Imam, but no Egyptian interference.

In late 1967, however, Amri's rule seemed set to be short-lived. Without the Egyptians, the Yemeni Army of about 7000 ill-equipped troops of doubtful morale looked no match for the royalist tribesmen, better armed and organised than ever before. Amri hastily turned to the Soviet Union for support. By December the republicans were besieged in Sana as Soviet arms began to arrive by air. The besieging army led by Mohammed Hussein comprised some 5000 trained soldiers and perhaps 30,000 tribal warriors, backed by a few hundred foreign mercenaries handling the more sophisticated arms.

The relief of Sana

Amri hastily organised a 10,000-strong militia, the Popular Resistance Force (PRF), which deterred a direct assault on the city. The arrival of 30 Russian aircraft in January 1968 once more gave the republicans a free hand to bomb and strafe the royalists, who had no cover. Further support came from the National Liberation Front, rulers of the newly independent Aden since November 1967, who claimed to have driven out the British and were equally opposed to the Imam. As the siege of Sana wore on, Hussein's tribesmen began to drift away, harassed by air attacks and bored by inactivity. On 8 February a strong column of republican troops, advised by the Russians, fought its way up from Hodeida and relieved Sana. The royalists had lost their last chance to win the war and restore the Imam.

King Faisal, the Saudi Arabian leader, was alarmed at the Soviet presence in the Yemen; he would even have preferred Nasser. The Saudis had never had any great love for the Imams, and Faisal had long since given up Badr as a hopelessly broken reed. In March 1968 Saudi Arabia ceased to provide arms and money to the royalists, and began to work towards a compromise agreement with the republicans. Among the Zeidi tribesmen also there was no great devotion to the Imam. The tribes had always been open to bribery from either side. When the republicans captured the royalist stronghold of Hajjah in December, the war was virtually over and the fighting gradually died down.

Diplomacy finally resolved what the fighting had failed to do. The Imam went into exile and settled in Bromley, Kent. The ruling family, the Hamid ud-Din, were excluded from government, most of them leaving the country. A kind of coalition of royalists and republicans was patched together, and the Russians were quietly elbowed out. Many of the Yemen's mountain tribesmen remained fiercely independent of the government, but the Imams had apparently gone for ever from the land they had ruled so long.

James Lunt

The dispossessed

How the Palestine Arabs lost their homeland

The Palestine problem is essentially the result of a conflict between two peoples, Arabs and Jews, each claiming rights in a land known as Filastin in Arabic and as Eretz-Israel in Hebrew.

The Jewish national movement emerged in the form of Zionism in the late 19th century as a result of the process of enlightenment and emancipation and the reaction to it in the European societies in which most Jews had been living for generations. Their traditional manner of life was completely changed and they came to be regarded as fellow countrymen sharing the same national identity, entitled to the same political rights and bearing the same burdens of citizenship. As the process of emancipation gathered momentum many western European Jews succeeded in assimilating themselves culturally, socially and even in matters of religion.

But many Jewish thinkers found themselves confronted by two problems. The first concerned the future of Judaism. It seemed almost impossible to preserve the traditional Jewish identity, based mainly on a particular manner of life, in the wider world which, for all the blessings it brought Jews as individuals, posed a mortal threat to Judaism as a religion, a way of life and an historical entity.

Even more important, many Jews were alarmed at the hostile reaction to the gradual integration of Jews into the societies in which they were living. At first anti-Jewish attitudes were expressed mainly in Christian terms, but they were later put in racial terms, with the result that the doors of society were closed in the face of the Jews.

It was in this context that the Zionist idea and movement arose. Palestine, though coveted by the Jews, had been an Arab and a Moslem country since the 7th century. It was inhabited by a population that had no sympathy for the Jewish cause. Indeed, as early as the 1890s, the Palestinian Arabs had made preparations for the restriction of Jewish immigration, fearing that an influx of Jews would alter the nature of Palestine and sever the territorial continuity of the Arab world.

The national feelings of the Palestine Arabs thus became part of the general Arab nationalist movement, sharing the basic goals of independence and unity in opposition to the Ottoman Empire that controlled much of the Levant; but at the same time it fought against Zionism, appealing to the solidarity of all other Arabs. All who spoke Arabic were regarded as Arabs and the whole area inhabited by Arabic-speaking people was considered to be the Arab homeland. Palestine had therefore to be defended against the Jews, not only as a token of solidarity with the Palestine Arab cousins but also as an obligation deriving from the notion of Arab nationalism.

These two contradictory movements – Zionism and Arab nationalism – were bound to come into conflict with one another, and the political history of Palestine since 1918 and the essence of Israel's relations with its Arab neighbours since 1948 is the story of this conflict. During the British Mandate (1918-48) the Palestine Arabs tried in various ways to forestall the process of Jewish immigration and settlement. They attempted to persuade the British public that Britain's Palestine policy was futile and harmful to British interests in other parts of the Arab and Islamic worlds. They exerted pressure by organising strikes, demonstrations and petitions.

Partition and defeat

In the 1930s, when the pace of Jewish immigration increased considerably as a result of the wave of anti-Semitism sweeping through central and eastern Europe, they resorted to force in an effort to make the British government change its policy and to deter the Jews from coming to Palestine. And, when all these efforts had failed, they appealed to the Arab states to defend their rights. In 1936 the Arab countries were asked to use their diplomatic leverage on Britain, but in 1948 their intervention took the form of military action aimed at preventing the implementation of the United Nations Resolution of 29 November 1947 concerning the partition of Palestine between Arabs and Jews.

This action did not, however, save the Palestine Arabs from disaster. The 1948 war led to the establishment of a Jewish state occupying about 75 per cent of the area of Palestine, while the majority of the Palestine Arabs became refugees. Continued Arab hostility, terrorism and even full-scale wars did not result in the destruction of Israel or even prevent Israel

Left: Although the Palestinians may have lost their homeland, the struggle continues. This Palestinian guerrilla brandishes an AKMS assault rifle. Below: A victim of the 1948-49 war, a homeless Palestinian refugee sits among the rubble of a refugee camp in the Gaza Strip. Right: The Arab exodus. Thousands of refugees made their way to Arab-held territories as the war raged in 1948.

The Arab exodus – 1948

▲ Arab refugee camps outside Israel

Arab refugees

Total Arab population of Palestine – mid 1948
1,400,000

Total Arab refugees
846,000

Distribution of refugees

Syria	82,000
Jordan	100,000
Gaza Strip	200,000
West Bank	360,000
Lebanon	104,000

from absorbing the majority of the Jewish survivors of the holocaust and of the Jews who had been living in Arab countries but whose life had become intolerable because of the conflict over Palestine.

On the other hand, after 10 to 15 years of relative inactivity, the Palestine Arabs themselves began to take the initiative again. From the late 1950s several Palestinian organisations, of which the best known is the Fatah, came into existence for the purpose of mobilising Palestinian refugees and carrying on an armed struggle against Israel until Israel is destroyed, all Palestine Arabs have returned to their homes, and all the Jews who settled in Palestine have been expelled or have renounced Zionism and agreed to live in a state of Palestine, preserving only their religious identity.

Birth of the PLO

Palestine-Arab resistance to Israel was strengthened after the Six-Day War of 1967 which took from Arab control those parts of Palestine that had remained Arab after the 1948 war. It also united under one rule, however hated and alien that rule might be, the majority of the Palestine-Arab people and thus, perhaps paradoxically, strengthened the sense of unity and internal cohesion among the Arabs. The fact that after 1967 Israel aimed to hold on to some parts of Arab Palestine, mainly along the Jordan Valley and for reasons of security, and established Jewish settlements there to strengthen its hold over the area – this served only to exacerbate Arab resentment and resistance.

One organisation which grew as a result of this resentment was the Palestine Liberation Organisation (PLO). Discussed as an idea at Arab conferences in 1964 – where some £400 million was allocated prior to its formation – the PLO was officially founded at a Jerusalem conference in 1965. Its charter was established at the same time and declared the establishment of the state of Israel to have been 'entirely illegal'; 'the Palestinian people,' it declared, 'possess the legal right to their homeland . . . armed struggle is the only way to liberate Palestine.' Although initially the aim of the PLO was the destruction of the state of Israel, this was extended in 1968 to include King Hussein's Jordan. Indeed, it is the uncompromising and destructive nature of the charter that has led various Arab nations away from supporting the PLO.

In its early days the PLO used Jordan as an operations base. This soon became dissatisfactory and both Lebanon and Syria flirted with various factions of the PLO. Today the PLO has become a loose coalition of seven or eight groups which, while theoretically led by Yasser Arafat as 'chairman', have individual territorial aims. In spite (or perhaps because) of being associated with acts of horrifying violence against uninvolved civilians during the 1970s, the PLO has managed to force a message through to the world that the Palestinian Arabs are a dispossessed people who have a fierce desire to return to their homeland; and that until this desire is suppressed or satisfied – neither of which appears likely in the near future – then there can be little hope for lasting peace in the Middle East. **Yehoshuah Porath**

Palestinian refugees were the ones to suffer most during the civil war in Lebanon. Christian Phalangists clear a Palestinian enclave during the troubles of 1976, where a woman begs for both her home and her life.

Key Weapons

RIFLE GRENADES

The history of the modern rifle grenade can be traced back to 1908, before World War I. They were developed as a means of hurling a modest explosive charge towards an enemy emplacement without unduly exposing the user. During World War I, troops experimented with many devices to project a grenade further than a hand could throw; catapult and cross-bow were among the more common and less elaborate devices. The early rifle grenades did not serve any specialised function.

Today, however, the story is different. The rifle grenade has undergone many alterations to turn it into a very effective addition to the infantryman's armoury. Currently produced rifle grenades fall into four categories: anti-tank, anti-personnel, smoke and illuminating. These four roles were developed during World War II and refined through subsequent conflicts.

The rifle grenade comes in two distinct design forms; the purpose-built rifle grenade and the ordinary hand grenade which can be adapted for rifle firing by fitting a special fin-stabilised tube to the base. This fitting can either be screwed on or gripped firmly to the grenade by housing clamps.

The rifle grenade is not a universally accepted weapon, and attitudes to it are divided. There are those who doubt its effectiveness and potential role in any conflict. An example of this school of thought is Great Britain, which ceased to use rifle grenades several years ago. The Soviet Union also rejects the weapon, and Poland is the only Warsaw Pact member to employ them.

It is true that the four roles of the rifle grenade can be filled by mortars or disposable anti-tank weapons. But on the credit side, rifle grenades are easier for the infantryman to carry and use. They are also seen by some as filling the gap left between the maximum range of a hand grenade and the minimum range of a light mortar.

A number of countries, such as France, Austria, Belgium, the USA, Spain and certain Latin American countries, do not agree with Great Britain and Russia and still produce quantities of rifle grenades. These countries appreciate their potential for use against lightly-armoured APCs (armoured personnel carriers), AFVs (armoured fighting vehicles), soft-skinned vehicles and troops emplaced in buildings.

To use a rifle grenade requires little modification by an infantryman to his standard issue rifle. There are two methods of launching rifle grenades: the ballistite cartridge and the bullet trap. The ballistite cartridge is in effect a very powerful blank round of ammunition, which produces a large quantity of gases. These gases travel along the barrel, as they would when firing a bullet, and force the grenade away from the muzzle.

The other system, called the bullet trap, is gradually replacing the ballistite method of launching as it dispenses with the need to carry specialised ammunition. The bullet trap, which comprises a series of collapsible baffles, can either be built directly into the grenade or fitted over the muzzle prior to firing. The infantryman loads and fires an ordinary round of ammunition; the baffles trap the bullet, but allow the gases released by firing to launch the grenade.

The rifle is not always held at the shoulder when firing a grenade, because the recoil forces imparted can exceed 15kg (35lb). Types of rifle grenade which can be fired from the shoulder, although they are not as powerful, can be aimed more accurately. There are three types of aiming device. First is the type which is fitted to the muzzle of the rifle and can be used many

Previous page: The portability of the rifle grenade is illustrated in this photograph of a Palestinian guerrilla in the Bekaa Valley. Attached to his AKMS assault rifle is a Yugoslav M60 anti-tank rifle grenade. Above left: During World War II the German Army favoured the use of rifle grenades; here a senior NCO slots the grenade into the launcher cup. Above: A South Vietnamese soldier stands on guard with a grenade launcher containing the US Mk 2 fragmentation grenade, while (inset) a similar, though more modern, grenade launcher is shown – the Austrian SprG 74. In both systems the grenade is clipped onto an expendable stabilising tube.

times over. Next is the type which is a built-in part of the rifle, as in the FN MAS 5.56mm. Lastly, there is the type which is clipped on to the grenade just before it is fired, as in the Austrian Spr G 73, and which is completely expendable. Although some grenades can be projected to 500m (550yd), the sights are only graduated from 50m to 200m (55 to 220yd).

The smoke variant of the rifle grenade is filled with either of two smoke emitting chemicals, white phosphorus or hexachlorethane. White phosphorus is somewhat hazardous to store and use, and hexachlorethane is now generally preferred.

Smoke rounds provide cover for troops moving over open ground. Smoke-emitting time depends on the manufacturer, but a barrier of smoke grenades each lasting one minute will suffice effectively to blanket any advance.

Illuminating rifle grenades are the other pyrotechnic variant. They come in various sizes and burn with varying degrees of intensity. A typical example of an illuminating round is the Luchaire 58mm; with a range of 250m (270yd), it burns for 20 seconds at 150,000 candle power – bright enough to turn night to day for some 500m (550yd) around. Normally, once the illuminating grenade has reached a high point of its trajectory a parachute unfurls. Light floods from the grenade's illuminating pot as it slowly floats down to earth.

The anti-personnel grenade comes in a wide range of calibres, 34mm, 58mm and 55mm, and is the

Left and below: Specifically designed to fire rifle grenades, the M79 grenade launcher was widely used in Vietnam by US ground troops. Firing a special 40mm grenade (in helmet band, left) the M79 was considerably more accurate than the standard rifle-grenade launcher.

version of the rifle grenade most likely to be used in combat encounters. With its pre-fragmented head the anti-personnel grenade can inflict more casualties than a hand-thrown grenade. It allows an infantryman to engage troops ensconced in strong defensive positions such as machine-gun posts and houses. An infantryman can fire a rifle grenade with good effect against a defensive position from up to 300m (330yd) but for pin-point accuracy, such as firing through a window into a room, he should be within 50m to 80m (55 to 90yd) of the target. The anti-personnel grenade comes into its own during the extremely dangerous task of house-to-house fighting.

The anti-tank grenade can serve in two roles; its title role of anti-tank, and also for blasting entrances through walls in house-to-house fighting. It is armed with a HEAT warhead, which has a shaped-charge effect giving high penetration. A typical anti-tank rifle grenade will weigh between 500gm (1.1lb) and 700gm (1.5lb), and penetrate 100mm to 300mm (4 to 12in) of armour, depending on the weight carried by the shaped-charge warhead. Used against buildings, such rounds can penetrate 600mm to 1100mm (25 to 45in) of concrete. Some anti-tank grenades can be fired to ranges in excess of 200m (220yd). But any grenade fired to that range to kill an MBT or APC would either be wildly off mark, or fail to penetrate far enough to do any serious damage.

The last type of rifle grenade to be considered is that known as dual-purpose: hand grenades which can be converted, with no effort, to use from a rifle. These grenades are essentially the defensive (anti-personnel) type, which can be fitted to a fin-stabilising launching tube. The grenade is either screwed to the device or clipped in a special housing, depending on the manufacturer. While not new in conception – the Americans were using a design like this in World War

II – it goes to prove how versatile the hand grenade is.

The Belgian 60mm dual-purpose grenade is launched by the bullet trap system. The launcher tail is threaded to allow it to be screwed on to the base of the 60mm hand grenade. The infantryman pulls out the safety pin as soon as the grenade is firmly fixed to the launcher. A recess on the launcher device holds the striker spoon in place when the safety pin is removed. The time fuse will not start up until the striker spoon is released by the recoil when the grenade is fired.

The Austrian SprG 74 60mm dual-purpose grenade is different altogether from its Belgian counterpart. The launching method is by ballistite cartridge, and the tail assembly is clipped on. The launcher device has four retaining springs, one of which is slightly longer than the others, and shaped like a right angle fish-plate. This longer spring has a sleeve which holds the striker spoon in place.

Above: A Swedish soldier fires an FFV smoke grenade from his German manufactured G3 rifle. The FFV has a range of around 300m (330yd) and is intended to provide the infantryman with a means of rapidly laying down a small but effective smoke screen to cover his movements from enemy observation.

Left: British troops in Cyprus fire rifle grenades from adapted SLR rifles, shortly before the decision to cease using them.

The safety pin is not removed until the grenade is firmly secure in the launcher device. On firing, the fish-plate is bent back by the recoil, the sleeve flies backwards and releases the striker spoon. A fuse of four or five-and-a-half seconds length can be fitted; with either, an airburst is likely to occur.

Grenade launchers, such as the American M79 and the British L1A1 differ from the standard rifle grenade in being shotgun-type weapons specifically designed to fire only grenades. Although a seperate weapon they have proved popular with the troops in the field. And in addition to their military use they can be employed for crowd control and form part of a growing arsenal of anti-riot equipment that has become commonplace in the armouries of the police forces of western Europe.

Besides the M79 the Americans have produced the XM148 grenade launcher. Although it works on the same principle as the M79, and has the same calibre of 40mm, the launcher is attached to the underside of the M16 assault rifle. Not a complete success, however, it was later replaced by the more reliable M203 which is now the standard US rifle-mounted grenade launcher. Other grenade launchers outside the rifle-grenade category are those fitted to the turrets of APCs and MBTs, their function being to fire smoke grenades for local defence.

Rifle grenades and grenade launchers will continue to be a topic of debate by military planners for some time to come. But it seems clear that the armies which currently employ them will continue to do so. The infantryman certainly needs some weapon to fulfil the function of such grenades, especially the anti-personnel variant, and the rifle grenade and grenade launcher provides a relatively simple and efficient solution.

Right: The Israeli 5.56mm Galil rifle is a complete smallarms weapon system, capable of rapid modification through its various attachments, including bipod, bayonet, magazines and rifle grenades. Despite the proliferation of hand-held rocket launchers the Israeli Army still feels there is a place for the rifle grenade.

Below: An American soldier prepares to fire an M203 grenade launcher – fitted to the standard M16 rifle – as part of a training exercise in Germany.

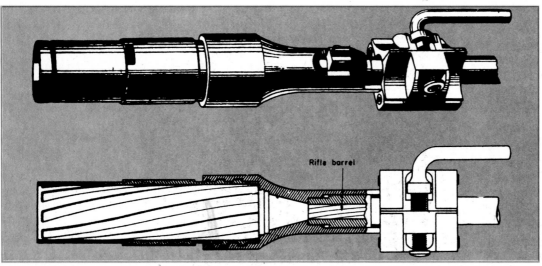

Left: Two views of a German rifled discharger cup showing the method of bolting it onto the rifle. A simple bolt-on system enables the infantryman to convert his rifle into a grenade launcher with both ease and rapidity.

Rifle barrel

Right: Four types of rifle grenade manufactured by Mercar of Belgium – from left: anti-personnel, delayed action anti-personnel, smoke, and parachute flare.

Below: The somewhat unusual Smith and Wesson tear-gas grenade launcher known as the 'Mighty Midget'. Below right: An FN Fal with a Mercar anti-personnel grenade attached.

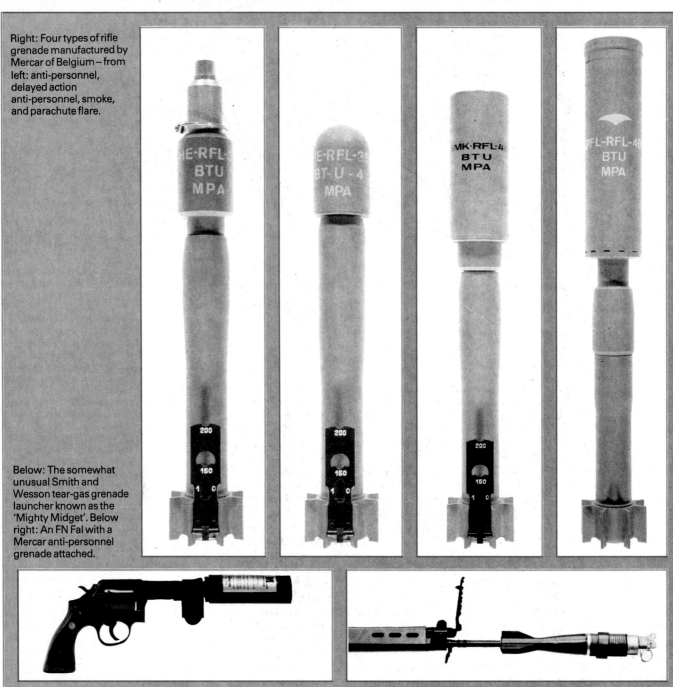

Nightmare in the Congo

The birth pangs of a nation

Of all the African colonial territories which achieved independence after World War II, none experienced the degree of confusion, turmoil, inter-tribal rivalry, bloodshed and disorder that beset the former Belgian Congo between 1960 and 1967.

The Congo (now renamed Zaire) occupies a territory almost the size of Western Europe and in 1960 its population comprised only some 14 million people. Towns were few and far between and communications in most regions were of a very primitive nature. All of this meant that even under normal conditions central government would have been hard pressed to establish its authority throughout the land. The task was made even more difficult by the fact that the 14 million inhabitants were divided into some 200 distinctly different and often mutually hostile tribes.

In 1960, following the somewhat hasty move to grant sovereignty to many French and British African colonies, the Belgians took the 'panic' decision to give independence to the Congo in the June of that year. This allowed a period of only five months for the Congolese to prepare to govern themselves. Such speed was, with hindsight, bound to lead to problems. When it is considered how little the Belgians had done to prepare the people of the Congo for independence before 1960, it is not surprising that the central government of the new state collapsed within days of acceding to power.

The Congo in chaos

When independence came on 30 June 1960 the country fell almost instantly into a state of disorder bordering upon chaos. Politics functioned, but only at tribal level. Joseph Kasavubu, the newly installed president, and his prime minister, Patrice Lumumba, found themselves totally unable to command the allegiance of their people. Within less than a week mutinies broke out in army garrisons and government virtually disintegrated.

There were still some 100,000 Belgians in the Congo after independence. In the disorder many were threatened or attacked and panic spread rapidly among their community. A number of Belgian army units were still in the country by agreement with the new government; these troops were immediately reinforced from Belgium (without Congolese agreement) and the total force was deployed to protect Belgian civilian lives. Most Belgians fled or were evacuated by US aircraft and thus, when their expertise could have been most beneficial, it was lost to the newly-born state.

Previous page: A para-trooper of Mobutu's forces parades through the streets of Stanleyville. Above: The two leaders of post-colonial Congo – Patrice Lumumba (left) and Joseph Kasavubu.

Below right: A Congolese is clubbed to the ground by men of another tribe. Violence was endemic in the Congo during the 1960s and was intensified by fierce tribal disputes.

As chaos descended on most of the country, local leaders in the mineral-rich southern provinces – source of 8 per cent of the world's copper, 60 per cent of the West's uranium, 73 per cent of the world's cobalt and 80 per cent of the world's industrial diamonds – seized the opportunity to go their own way, backed by the mining companies. In south Kasai, Albert Kalonji set up a 'kingdom' based on wealth from the mining of industrial diamonds. His rule was short-lived, but the secession of neighbouring Katanga province was to dominate the first years of Congo's independence.

Moise Tshombe, the president of Katanga province, declared the region an independent state 12 days after the end of colonial rule. His action was designed to allow Katanga, the richest province by far in the whole country, to keep its wealth for itself. Union Minière du Haut Katanga, the major mining company, was ready to pay its revenues and taxes to Tshombe instead of to the central government. This gave Tshombe the money to pay for the effective defence of his 'state', and helped bankrupt the central government – some 50 per cent of total central government revenues came from Katanga.

No sooner had law and order broken down in the Congo than external powers became involved. Both the US and the Soviet Union were anxious that their own interests should not be jeopardised. The Cold War was at its height and each superpower was intent on preventing the other from gaining undue influence in black Africa as colony after colony emerged into independence. Kasavubu and Lumumba made appeals to the US and the USSR and also to the UN for assistance in coping with the disaster which confronted them.

The UN intervenes

On 14 July 1960 the UN Security Council authorised its Secretary-General, Dag Hammarskjöld, to arrange for military assistance to the Congo. Offers of help to mount a UN force were rapidly forthcoming from many states and this led to a UN presence in the Congo for the next four years. The resolution which thus authorised military assistance also demanded the withdrawal of Belgian troops. The UN military force was to be made up of contingents from Africa, Asia and neutral European countries.

The UN forces, when they arrived, were given four main objectives: to restore and maintain law and order; to prevent foreign intervention; to resurrect the economy; and to restore political stability. In the event it proved extremely difficult to achieve these aims, so severely constrained were the actions of the UN troops. They not only had to have Congolese government approval for anything they did but they had also to consult with all governments providing

The Belgian Congo

Map showing the Belgian Congo (Zaire) and surrounding countries: Central African Republic, Sudan, Cameroon, Gabon, Congo, Uganda, Rwanda, Burundi, Tanzania, Angola, Zambia. Cities and features marked include: Uele River, Buta, Lake Albert, Lisala, Stanleyville (Kisangani), Mbandaka, Lake Edward, Lake Kivu, Bukavu, Lake Leopold II, Port Francqui (Ilebo), Lusambo, Brazzaville, Leopoldville (Kinshasa), Matadi, Kasai River, Kwilu River, Kabalo, Lake Tanganyika, Kamina, Katanga, Kolwezi, Elisabethville (Lubumbashi), Lusaka. Inset map of Africa showing the location of the Belgian Congo.

troops for the force before committing themselves to a course of action. Lastly, the Security Council instructions allowed actual military force to be used only in self-defence. Under the anarchic conditions pertaining in the Congo this made it virtually impossible for the UN troops to function with any degree of effectiveness.

Throughout the whole period of UN involvement in the Congo the US gave the UN actions their unstinted support. Indeed, without the massive US logistic and material aid the whole initiative might have foundered. The Russians, on the other hand, while not going so far as to veto resolutions in the Security Council, complained bitterly of the failure of the UN forces to take decisive action against Katanga. They also intervened by providing military assistance to whichever contender in the Congo power struggle seemed most likely to side with Soviet aims.

A further external influence which made itself felt throughout the upheaval was that of the Belgians, who persistently played a role of their own. Their initial offer to provide more troops to assist the Congo government was rejected and eventually the Belgian government professed itself to be in complete agreement with the aims of the UN. Yet Belgian forces remained in Katanga in strength and many Belgian officials who stayed on in the province as advisers to Tshombe were distinctly hostile to attempts by the UN to deploy troops there. The reason for this ambivalent attitude is not hard to find. There remained considerable Belgian economic and financial interests in Katanga: the main mining corporations were largely Belgian-owned and Belgian mining engineers and their families remained there long after most of their compatriots in the rest of the Congo had departed. This continued Belgian presence in Katanga and the apparent disinclination of the UN to end Katanga's secession caused much friction between the UN and the central Congolese government. Lumumba, the prime minister, was anti-Belgian and anti-American; he began to look increasingly to

Power, politics and personal ambition

Tshombe of Katanga

Moise Tshombe was born in 1917 into the Balunda tribe from southern Katanga. He first turned to politics in the early 1950s, becoming one of the few Congolese to serve on the Katanga provincial council. In 1959, only a year before independence, he became president of the Confédération des Associations Tribales du Katanga (Conakat). The Balunda tribe dominated Conakat and the movement exercised a persuasive authority throughout southern Katanga. The Belgian-owned Union Minière du Haut Katanga, which held the monopoly of the rich Katangan copper mines, also supported the party and this made its leader a very powerful man within the province.

In May 1960 Tshombe was elected to the post-independence Katanga assembly and immediately became president of the Katanga provincial government. He declared Katanga independent the following July and remained at the head of the breakaway state until January 1963 when he finally succumbed to UN pressure and fled into exile in Spain.

Recalled from exile in 1964 by President Kasavubu to be premier of the Congo government, he was dismissed in 1965, ostensibly for using white mercenaries in his attack on the rebels but there were those who thought it was because he coveted the presidency.

He returned to Spain only to be kidnapped in 1967 and taken to Algiers, where he died of a heart attack in 1969. Ironically, his kidnapping was carried out by a white mercenary.

Katangan leader Moise Tshombe (above) returning from a meeting with Dag Hammarskjöld. Right: Patrice Lumumba shortly before his execution.

Lumumba the nationalist

Patrice Lumumba was born in 1925 in the Sankuru district of Kasai. Politically active at an early age he became involved with trades unions and emerged as one of the leaders of the educated Congolese. In 1956 he was arrested and imprisoned on charges of embezzling post office funds. After release from prison he worked as a sales director of a brewery in Leopoldville and became even more active in politics. In 1958 he created the first national Congolese political party, the Mouvement National Congolais (MNC). All other political groups were at that time tribal-based and led by powerful tribal leaders. Lumumba came from one of the smaller tribes and made a successful bid for power across tribal lines.

In elections prior to independence the MNC gained far more votes than any other party and as leader Lumumba was asked to form the first government. When Mobutu assumed power in the post-independence chaos, Lumumba escaped his clutches initially by seeking UN protection. When attempting to escape from the capital to Stanleyville, however, he was captured by Mobutu's men; after a short delay, he was sent down to Katanga where he was murdered in February 1961.

The Congolese Army

At independence the Armée Nationale Congolaise (ANC) numbered 23,000 Congolese soldiers and 1000 Belgian officers. The troops were largely illiterate and poorly paid, and the racial division between officers and men had long been a source of discord.

Instead of acting as a stabilising force, the army was itself the immediate source of upheaval in the newly independent Congo. On 6 July members of the army tried to force a way into parliament to protest at the confirmation of Belgians in top defence posts. The following day, the cabinet of Patrice Lumumba agreed to replace the Belgian commander of the army and to promote all Congolese

NCOs by one rank.

Nevertheless, on 8 July the army mutinied in Leopoldville, and over the next three days the revolt spread. On the day of the Leopoldville mutiny, Joseph-Désiré Mobutu was appointed chief of staff with the rank of colonel. Mobutu realised the urgent need to create an African officer class to replace the Belgians. He toured the country arranging for the appointment or election of Congolese officers, and quickly gained the support of the most disciplined units and the older career soldiers. By September Mobutu felt sufficiently strong to announce that the army had taken power. Two months later he restored the government to the politicians, but in September 1965 he again intervened; this time for good.

the Russians for help in bringing down Tshombe's government.

The UN was tied hand and foot by its decision not to use force other than in self-defence, but on 12 August 1960 a token contingent entered Katanga where they took over duties from some Belgian troops. At almost the same time Lumumba, having obtained military equipment from the Soviet Union, launched what turned out to be a totally unsuccessful attack on Katanga in an attempt to force Tshombe into submission. This single-handed action brought utter confusion to the Congo central government. President Kasavubu dismissed Lumumba who in turn 'sacked' the president. Central authority almost ceased to exist and in September 1960 yet another contender for power emerged: Colonel Joseph Mobutu, the chief of staff of the Congolese Army. He arrested Lumumba and announced a temporary military takeover. There was some confusion as to whether Lumumba was being protected by the UN, but in November he fled, only to be recaptured by Mobutu's men. In February 1961 he was transferred to Katanga, ostensibly for reasons of safety, and on his arrival there Tshombe had him shot.

Threat from Stanleyville

Lumumba's death was greeted with horror in many capitals of the world and especially in Moscow where it was seen as a blow to the Russians' main hope of sustaining their interests in the Congo. His place however was taken by his close associate, Antoine Gizenga, who built up a power base at Stanleyville in Eastern Province where he set up an alternative government in active opposition to Mobutu who was establishing his power in

Right: Well-armed Congolese troops trudge back from the battle zone. Their Belgian FN rifles are supplemented by rifle grenades and belts of machine-gun bullets.

Leopoldville. His authority was enhanced to a considerable degree when his government was recognised by the USSR and communist China. Mobutu meanwhile closed Eastern bloc embassies in Leopoldville and expelled Soviet military personnel.

In August 1961, after a number of earlier abortive attempts, President Kasavubu succeeded in bringing together all contending factions in the Congo, except Tshombe in Katanga, and a new government was formed under the premiership of Cyrille Adoula. Even Gizenga cooperated with Adoula in the formation of this government, but in November he returned to Stanleyville and subsequently opposed every move that Adoula made.

Adoula's single main objective was to obtain control over Katanga and to this end he put continuous

pressure on the UN to help him. In Katanga itself Tshombe was building up his own strength to withstand the expected onslaught. Recognising his own troops' limitations in such a serious situation he began recruiting a white mercenary army composed mainly of French, Belgian and southern African whites together with a mixture of other Europeans. These soldiers of fortune were easily a match for any of the other ill-trained and ill-equipped Congolese forces, but when at last the UN troops went into action against Katanga, political and military pressures were such that Tshombe was forced onto the defensive.

The initial UN operations in August and September 1961 were only marginally successful, but they were followed by a second major operation in December of that year which was sufficiently effective to force

Below: Rioters surge across the streets of Leopoldville during the early stages of the conflict in the Congo. The ineffectual central government was unable to enforce public order, even in the capital.

Hostage rescue in Stanleyville

The revolt in eastern Congo in 1964 was one of the bloodiest episodes in the crisis. When rebels led by General Olenga swept into Stanleyville on 4 August 1964 they took over 1000 whites hostage. Tales of rape and murder in other areas led to desperate fear for the hostages' safety.

On 23 November, with Premier Tshombe's approval, 600 Belgian paratroopers flew from Ascension Island to Kamina in the Congo. The following day they took off for Stanleyville on board 10 US transport planes. Within 35 minutes of landing they had secured Stanleyville airport. Meanwhile, the rebels had forced some 250 hostages to sit in the street in the centre of the town. As the paras approached, the rebels sprayed the hostages with bullets before fleeing. Thirty hostages were killed.

The dramatic Stanleyville rescue illustrates several of the most distinctive features of the warfare in the Congo. The actual fighting was relatively light, because faced with a superior enemy, men would either flee into the country or quickly change sides. But large numbers of men, women and children were massacred when their enemies, tribal, racial or ideological, were temporarily in control. In the month before the paras' attack, an estimated 4000 Congolese, mostly political leaders or the educated elite, were killed by the rebels. In the aftermath of the rebels' defeat in Stanleyville, it was the turn of the Congolese Army to butcher anyone vaguely suspected of aiding the rebellion. The national police chief, Victor Nendaka, was alone responsible for the execution of more than 500 people. Although the Western news media concentrated on attacks on whites, in most cases the victims were black.

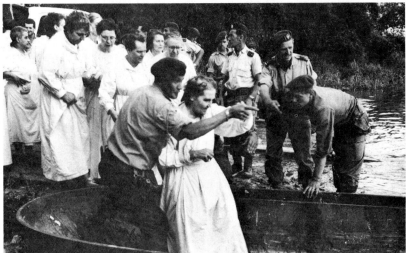

Tshombe to the negotiating table. Agreement was thought to have been achieved, but then Tshombe procrastinated and a stalemate ensued which lasted for a whole year.

During this lull the UN forces were built up in strength and finally, in December 1962, they moved to end secession once and for all. On 21 January 1963, Tshombe finally capitulated. The UN forces remained in the Congo until June 1964 when the last troops were withdrawn. During this last 18 months the UN contented itself with low-key operations protecting vulnerable points and maintaining communications. It was as though the accession of Katanga marked the end of the Congo problem. This was far from being the case, however.

In July 1964 Moise Tshombe was invited back from exile by President Kasavubu to take control of the central government in Leopoldville and to confront a rebellion in the east of the country and in the Kwilu region of the southwest. Led by former supporters of Lumumba and Gizenga, notably Pierre Mulele who had received training in China, the rebels captured Albertville and Stanleyville. Their crack troops, the Simbas (lions), who were mostly young tribal warriors or schoolchildren, struck terror into the government forces with their fearless attacks (many Simbas believed witchcraft had made them immune to bullets). The brutality of the government troops in their efforts to reassert control was sufficient to guarantee the rebellion wide support.

During the second half of 1964 Tshombe waged war against the Stanleyville rebels with aid provided by the US and Belgium. He also raised a new mercenary force which provided a lead for his own troops. The campaign was bloody but successful up to a point and the rebels were temporarily routed. In the early part of 1965 Tshombe worked hard to consolidate his position but remained unable to extend his authority throughout the country. He was eventually dismissed by President Kasavubu, but Kasavubu was overthrown in his turn by the army chief of staff (now General) Mobutu in November 1965. After a further year filled with crisis on crisis, Mobutu managed to assert his authority. The rebellion in the east fell apart through internal dissension and loss of external support. From mid-1967, when he survived a revolt by former mercenaries, Mobutu's rule was largely unchallenged. Gradually a state of law and order came to prevail, even if only as a result of the imposition of authoritarian military government.

So ended a nightmare period in which every sort of horror was committed, ranging from murder and the taking of hostages to rape and cannibalism. The Congo was not prepared for independence and when it came there were many who sought to gain advantage from the shambles that ensued. **Major F.A. Godfrey**

Top: Rebel Simba prisoners come under the strict scrutiny of one of Tshombe's government soldiers. Centre: mercenaries help European refugees to safety. Above: General Mobutu – the eventual victor in the bloody struggle for power in the Congo.

Hammarskjöld's army

How the UN became involved in the Congo

The UN was set up at the end of World War II as a body through which the victorious Allies could exercise a benevolent tutelage over the rest of the world. Decisive action could be undertaken only with the agreement of all members of the UN Security Council, which included the US, Britain, France and the USSR. Into the 1950s, as the Korean War showed, the UN was generally dominated by Western views and attitudes, although the Soviet veto in the Security Council prevented much action.

In 1953 the UN elected a new Secretary-General, Dag Hammarskjöld, a Swedish civil servant. Hammarskjöld advanced a new concept of the UN as a force independent of the Eastern or Western blocs, representing the emerging 'non-aligned' nations. Following an active policy which made him a major world figure, he identified the UN not only with the cause of peace but also with anti-colonialism.

When President Kasavubu and Prime Minister Lumumba appealed to the UN for help in restoring law and order and in defending the newly independent Congo from Belgian military intervention, Hammarskjöld rose to the challenge. At a UN Security Council meeting held on 13 July 1960, he expressed his belief that the UN should involve itself in 'preventive diplomacy' to avoid the involvement of the superpowers in incidents which might lead to escalation. He argued that the Congo – an area outside the

immediate spheres of influence of the two blocs – should be offered UN assistance as a 'fire brigade' to prevent the trouble spreading. He persuasively identified the presence of Belgian troops as a source of both internal and international tension and called for the creation of a UN force to go to the Congo. For once, Hammarskjöld could rely on US and Soviet support; the next day, the Security Council passed a resolution giving the Secretary-General a wide mandate to create an interventionary force. Without actually condemning Belgian aggression, the Security Council also called for the removal of Belgian troops from the Congo.

The decision to intervene

ONUC, the 'Force de l'Organisation des Nations Unies au Congo', was created as a peacekeeping force under Chapter 6 of the Charter to assist in the re-establishment of law and order in the Congo and to secure the departure of Belgian troops. It was to use force only in self-defence and was not to interfere in the domestic affairs of the state. To send UN troops to the Congo in the hope that their presence would settle its problems was optimistic and risky. Nevertheless, the Secretary-General was convinced that the gamble was worthwhile and the UN moved in fast. UN troops, contributed largely by African states, began to arrive in the Congo within 48 hours. About 3500 men

Above left: Dag Hammarskjöld attempted to turn the post of Secretary-General of the UN into a centre of power in world politics. By origin a mild Swedish bureaucrat, he yet brought a fierce conviction to his support for anti-colonial movements. When the Congo crisis broke, he committed a force of largely Third World troops under the UN banner. Above: As the swelling forces flew in to the morass of Congolese politics, each detachment with its own national commander in close touch with political leaders at home, it seemed the UN might become a cloak for hidden ambitions and an agent of war rather than a force for peace.

Accidental death?

Mystery still surrounds the circumstances of the death of Dag Hammarskjöld. Hammarskjöld, aged 56 and Secretary-General of the United Nations since 1953, left Leopoldville aboard a Swedish aircraft on charter to the UN on 17 September 1961. The plane crashed only 10 minutes' flying time from Ndola Airport in Northern Rhodesia (now Zambia). The flight had taken a circuitous route to Ndola to avoid flying over Katanga. Hammarskjöld, his staff, the UN Security guards and the Swedish crew were all killed. Both the UN and the Northern Rhodesian government's investigations ruled out sabotage and suggested that the likely cause was pilot error, confirming some reports that the plane had hit trees with its undercarriage down.

Nevertheless, there are some reports which have brought the official explanations into doubt. For example, one survivor of the crash, who subsequently died on 23 September 1961, claimed that Hammarskjöld himself decided not to land at Ndola and told the pilot to change course. Soon after altering course, he claimed, there were a number of explosions on board the aircraft. The Rhodesian report, however, could find no evidence to support this idea or that the plane might have been shot down. Nevertheless it was confirmed that the plane had made contact with Ndola and had changed course.

According to another version, Hammarskjöld was to have been kidnapped in the air and kept hostage until the UN ended its operations against Katanga, but the hijack went wrong. Other reports claim that an extra body was found in the wreckage but never identified. All sorts of individuals and states have been accused of causing the death of Hammarskjöld but there is little real evidence and the cause of the crash is still unknown.

Dag Hammarskjöld was buried in Sweden on 29 September 1961.

came from Tunisia, Ghana, Morocco and Ethiopia, soon to be followed by a Swedish battalion from UNEF in Gaza. ONUC, which was under the exclusive command of Hammarskjöld (who was himself answerable to the Security Council), set up its headquarters in Leopoldville. Hammarskjöld appointed a special representative in the Congo to take command of ONUC operations.

ONUC was not deployed to Katanga where Moise Tshombe had proclaimed independence from the Congo, but there was fighting between Belgians and the mutineers of the Congolese Army (ANC) and between different tribes in areas where ONUC was present.

By 28 July 1960 ONUC had risen to a force of almost 10,000 men and Dag Hammarskjöld visited his army in the Congo. Hammarskjöld had expected reconciliation and compromise after ONUC's first operations, but he was to be disappointed. A degree of calm and order had indeed been restored to some parts of the Congo but the Congo government and ONUC were still faced with the secession of Katanga, tribal warfare and potential civil war. Accordingly, at the beginning of August 1960 the Security Council agreed to Hammarskjöld's request for authorisation to move ONUC troops into Katanga, in order to carry out the original resolutions of the UN. Tshombe threatened to resist UN intervention by force and although a token body of UN troops moved in peacefully, Hammarskjöld was not then willing to risk the use of force on a large scale.

The UN was heavily criticised for its failure to prevent Lumumba's assassination in February 1961. The Soviet Union wanted the Congo operation ended and Hammarskjöld removed, and ONUC might have collapsed but for firm American support

UN troops take cover behind a disabled armoured car and return fire against Katangan rebels. The soldier in the foreground is firing a Swedish Carl Gustav M45 sub-machine gun.

in the UN. ONUC was placed on full alert and survived the crisis. On 21 February 1961 the Security Council authorised ONUC to use force to prevent civil war and to remove the Belgians and the mercenaries.

Through these political storms, ONUC carried out its peacekeeping function with a measure of success, although it continually faced attacks from the Congolese Army, the body which it had officially been brought in to support. In April 1961 almost an entire company of Ghanaian UN soldiers were murdered by Congolese troops at Port Francqui.

But ONUC's relatively successful police role was subsequently overshadowed by the decision to move against Katanga. From the outset, UN operations against the province were enthusiastically supported by the Afro-Asian bloc, who saw it as a fight against colonialism, but they came in for heavy criticism in some Western countries, notably France and Britain. Certainly, ONUC went beyond a 'peacekeeping' role. Indian, Ethiopian and Swedish troops were accused of human rights violations, including mortar attacks on a hospital in Elizabethville. And the UN was clearly involving itself on one side in an internal political dispute.

Into Katanga

Round One, as it was known, of the battle for Katanga consisted of Operation Rumpunch in August 1961 and Operation Morthor the following month. Neither was especially successful. ONUC occupied certain key points in Katanga and rounded up a number of European officers for repatriation, but Tshombe remained firmly in control. ONUC strength in Katanga was 5000, facing 15,000 Katangese troops.

On the night of 17/18 September 1961 Secretary-General Hammarskjöld was killed in an air crash while on his way to meet Tshombe to try to negotiate an end to secession. His loss was a serious setback to the UN operation, but ONUC continued under the new Secretary-General, U Thant. In December, Round Two of the fighting began.

Despite the use of strike aircraft, including Swedish Saabs and Indian Canberra bombers, ONUC still failed to achieve a decisive military victory, but Tshombe was forced to negotiate with the central government. It gradually became clear that no agreement could be reached, however; a final push by ONUC was needed. Round Three, known as Operation Jacaranda, lasted through December 1962 and January 1963. After heavy mortar and machine-gun battles Tshombe fled and Katangese resistance crumbled away. Katanga's secession was at an end.

The phasing-out of ONUC began soon after the fall of Katanga. As there was still some fighting, the UN authorised part of ONUC – about 5000 men – to stay until 30 June 1964. A huge civilian rehabilitation effort was then launched by the UN with over 2000 civilian personnel providing technical help and a full-scale development programme.

UN operations in the Congo had cost over $400 million and 235 UN lives. ONUC at its peak numbered about 20,000 men, but in total 93,000 men were used from 35 different countries between 1960 and 1964. The legal, moral and political arguments regarding ONUC's use of force in Katanga still continue, but in most respects the UN achievement was considerable, for ONUC limited outside interference, which could have been so dangerous, and enabled considerable progress to be made towards solving the Congo's domestic problems, as well as ensuring the country's continued existence.

David Johnson

Below: Some of the many refugees who found themselves displaced from their homes await the arrival of transport to ferry them to resettlement camps away from the battle areas. The UN forces found themselves as much involved in relief work as in actual fighting. Bottom: Armed with a recoilless rifle, Indian troops of the UN interventionary force wait beside a road block in Katanga.

When empires crumble, bands of mercenaries appear. It is a law as old as history. The European colonial empires in black Africa began to crumble almost a quarter of a century ago, and in the struggle for power that followed, bands of white mercenaries began to appear. The crumbling has not finished; still less has the struggle for power; the role of white mercenaries fighting, at least ostensibly, for black rulers or would-be rulers is far from over.

When Rolf Steiner, the German mercenary (who had served like many mercenaries in that most famous of all 'official' mercenary bodies, the French Foreign Legion) was tried in Khartoum by a Sudanese military court in 1971, he described himself as 'not a mercenary but a soldier of ideals'. In some ways this was probably true: like many of the white mercenaries, Steiner did not hire himself out for the money alone. He fought for adventure, for a cause, for a chance of wealth or power, but probably above all because he was a professional soldier and fighting was the only way of life he knew. The Sudanese foreign minister had, at an earlier press conference, called him 'a criminal hireling of imperialism'. There was certainly that aspect too: in black African eyes white mercenaries represented neocolonial interests – being either the indirect instruments of the former ruling power or else the means by which vast capitalist conglomerates like Union Minière in the Congo attempted, not always successfully, to preserve their profits. White mercenaries were both 'hirelings of imperialism' and 'soldiers of ideals': it is a curious paradox.

They first appeared before the eyes of the world in the Congo in 1960. The British and French colonial empires in black Africa did not collapse; they dissolved in a reasonably orderly fashion. But the Belgian colonial empire did collapse: on 30 June 1960 the vast land mass that King Leopold of the Belgians and his successors had exploited became suddenly, abruptly and without proper preparation independent. As the Belgian-trained army, the ANC (Armée Nationale Congolaise), mutinied and the country dissolved into warring chaos, Moise Tshombe declared the independence of the wealthiest province, mineral-rich Katanga.

Tshombe's Frenchmen
Katanga's main enemy was not the disorganised and primitive ANC, but the United Nations forces that poured into the country at the request of the central government to end the secession – including Irish troops, Swedish troops, Indians and Gurkhas, and most effective of all, Ethiopians. To defend their independence against what they called the 'supermercenaries of the United Nations' the Katangese hired white mercenaries: first, naturally enough, Belgians. But the Belgians were restrained, semi-official, ineffective. Tshombe turned to the most experienced counter-revolutionary fighters of the Western world, the French.

Colonel Roger Faulques became the first great mercenary leader of modern times. He and his Frenchmen were veterans of France's fearsome struggle against the Viet Minh in Indochina and against the FLN in Algeria. They were hard professional soldiers, many of whom had served in those toughest of all regiments, the 1st and 2nd REP, the Legion's paratroops. The 'war' against the United Nations forces continued for over two years with dramatic ups-and-downs but comparatively little bloodshed:

Soldiers
Mercenaries in the modern world

# of fortune

the Swedes, for instance, would never venture out of their armoured cars and a whole battalion of the Irish surrendered to the mercenary Michel de Clary when their water supply was cut off. But the end was inevitable: in January 1963 Faulques' lieutenant, Bob Denard, retreated with the remnants of the Katangese gendarmerie and perhaps a hundred mercenaries across the border into safe refuge in the then Portuguese colonial territory of Angola. Tshombe flew into exile; the mercenary-backed secession of Katanga was at an end.

Tshombe did not remain long in exile. In a surprising reversal of fortune he was called back in July 1964 as prime minister not of Katanga but of the whole country – to be faced with yet another secessionist revolt. This time the whole of the east of the country had broken away. Unlike Katanga, it was an anti-Western communist-backed rebellion. Nuns were being raped, missionaries tortured, whites murdered – and the ANC, faced by the troops of the Mulelists and Lumumbists, the so-called Simbas (Lions) who believed themselves invulnerable to bullets, were turning tail. It looked as if the whole country would be swept away in the turmoil, particularly as the United Nations troops had left. Tshombe decided to call back 'his' white mercenaries. He sent for a man living in Durban, an Irish-born adventurer who had played a small role in the Katanga affair, Mike Hoare.

Mad Mike's mercenaries

Hoare, first known as 'The Major', then as 'The Colonel', then more familiarly as 'Mad Mike', rapidly became the most spectacularly successful and admired mercenary leader of modern times. He had served with the Chindits in Burma, and emigrated after the war to South Africa where he had set up as an accountant. He and his right-hand man, Jeremiah Puren, an Afrikaner and once commander of the Katangese Air Force, organised Five Commando, a whites-only mercenary unit. Recruiting bases were set up in South Africa and Rhodesia, for though the officers were mainly ex-British Army like Hoare himself, the 'volunteers' (as they were officially called) were almost all young white South Africans or Rhodesians who signed up for six months at a time. There were never more than 250 mercenaries in Five Commando at any one time, often less; but in their jeeps and armoured cars they acted as a fast-moving strike column that darted all over the eastern Congo, mowing down Simbas, rescuing nuns and missionaries, and liberating towns and cities. But they liberated more than just people and places; they also 'liberated' possessions and banks. That is how the mercenaries made their fortunes: by loot. They were paid rarely and sporadically (as all white mercenaries in black Africa have been ever since), but Hoare, Puren and most of the other officers made fortunes, and some of the lower-ranking 'volunteers' did very well indeed.

The Simba War was over by the end of 1965; but before its end Hoare had returned to Durban, 'John-John' Peters, a former policeman and a much more sinister character, had taken over as commanding officer of Five Commando, Tshombe had been sent into exile again, and the present ruler of the Congo, General Mobutu, had seized power. The eastern Congo was now occupied by no less than three mercenary groups: Five Commando under Peters (later succeeded by the Afrikaner George Schroeder); Six Commando, a French mercenary group, led by

Above: Jeep-mounted mercenaries blast away into the jungle with 0.3 and 0.5-inch Browning machine guns. Far left: One of the more audacious mercenary leaders, Jean Schramme; he attempted to set up a mercenary-ruled republic in Eastern Congo in 1967. Left: A machine-gun armed mercenary vehicle prepares to embark on a mission.

the rumbustious, mustachioed Bob Denard; and Ten Commando, an outfit commanded by a Belgian planter, 'Black Jack' Schramme.

Eventually Five Commando disbanded despite protests by the local population who relied on its protection, particularly against the dreaded ANC. But Schramme and Denard united in an elaborate plot to restore Tshombe. The plot aborted when Tshombe, on a flight in the Balearics off Spain's Mediterranean coast, was hijacked by another mercenary, François Bodenan, and diverted to Algeria, where he was imprisoned and eventually died. Bodenan was probably hired by the CIA who were now backing Mobutu. The hijacking took place on 30 June 1967. But despite this the mercenaries' revolt went ahead five days later.

At first the revolt looked doomed to failure: Schramme and about 150 mercenaries, with 800 Katangese gendarmes, were wandering around the eastern Congo pursued by hordes of ANC troops and

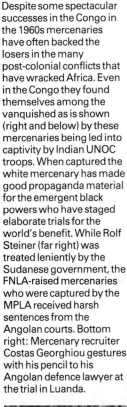

Despite some spectacular successes in the Congo in the 1960s mercenaries have often backed the losers in the many post-colonial conflicts that have wracked Africa. Even in the Congo they found themselves among the vanquished as is shown (right and below) by these mercenaries being led into captivity by Indian UNOC troops. When captured the white mercenary has made good propaganda material for the emergent black powers who have staged elaborate trials for the world's benefit. While Rolf Steiner (far right) was treated leniently by the Sudanese government, the FNLA-raised mercenaries who were captured by the MPLA received harsh sentences from the Angolan courts. Bottom right: Mercenary recruiter Costas Georghiou gestures with his pencil to his Angolan defence lawyer at the trial in Luanda.

by Cuban-exile pilots trained by the CIA. But five weeks later came news that shook all Africa: Schramme and his men had suddenly captured the major city of Bukavu, on the borders of Rwanda, proclaimed a Provisional Government under the nominal leadership of the Katangese Colonel Monga, and called on Mobutu to resign or be thrown out. Remembering what Hoare and his handful of men in Five Commando had achieved, this suddenly seemed on the cards. Denard meanwhile, although wounded, had flown out to Portuguese Angola to launch from there a rebellion in Katanga. Jeremiah Puren, Hoare's associate, flew in and landed on Lake Kivu.

But then this extraordinary attempt by rebellious mercenaries to found their own major mercenary-ruled state (as the Grand Catalan Company of mercenaries had successfully done in medieval Greece) collapsed. Denard's 'invasion' of Katanga on bicycles proved a fiasco. No help came from Hoare or South Africa. Schramme, surrounded and bombarded, did not surrender, but eventually retreated to internment in Rwanda. Months later the mercenaries were all released – their passports stamped 'Not Valid in Africa' – but the Katangese gendarmes, their allies, were repatriated with promises of 'resettlement'.

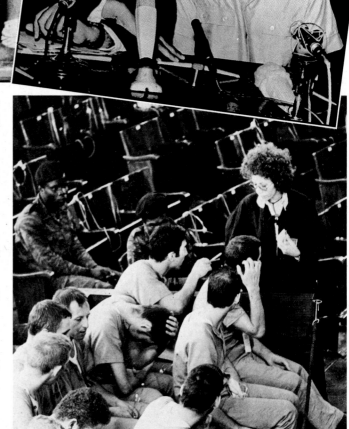

None was ever heard of again.

Nigeria was by this time about to plunge into the throes of civil war. On 30 May 1967 Biafra declared its independence from Nigeria, as Katanga had earlier done from the Congo. Biafra too – and to a lesser extent the central government in Nigeria – set about hiring white mercenaries. Hoare was approached by both sides but refused to intervene on, he alleged, idealistic grounds. It was probably because South Africa had no real interest in the outcome. Colonel Roger Faulques and a large band of French mercenaries were hired by the Biafrans. (Not including Denard: he and various other mercenaries went off to the civil war in the Yemen where they played a minor and ineffectual part as training officers on the losing royalist side.) But the 'French connection' foundered in a welter of arguments between employers and mercenaries about terms, pay and numbers. The French withdrew, leaving a handful of mercenaries to train and command certain of the Biafran forces. These included the Englishman Alexander Gay (said to be the model for Frederick Forsyth's hero in his bestselling *Dogs of War*) and Rolf Steiner, whose overweening pride and ambition led to his dismissal by the Biafran president, General Ojukwu. The only mercenary whose efforts really helped the Biafrans was the old Swedish adventurer, Count Carl Gustav von Rosen, who had flown in 1936 for the Ethiopians against the Italians. He crated-in light Swedish training aircraft and almost destroyed the Nigerian Air Force on the ground in surprise bombing raids. He was to die years later, heroically, in an attempt to rescue by air the princesses of the Ethiopian imperial family imprisoned by Ethiopia's Marxist revolutionary government.

Steiner's lucky escape

Even before Biafra finally collapsed, in January 1970, Steiner and Gay were training the Anya-Nya rebels of the southern Sudan, the next African state to be torn by a separatist civil war. But that rebellion had even less success than Biafra's. Captured in November 1970, Steiner was tried in August 1971 and sentenced to death. Luck was with him, however. First his sentence was commuted by President Nimeiri to 20 years' imprisonment, then, after only three years, he was quietly released 'on humanitarian grounds'.

He was particularly lucky when his fate is compared to that of the mercenaries in Angola. In 1975 the Portuguese colonial empire in black Africa collapsed almost as quickly as the Belgian colonial empire had done 15 years earlier. Independence found three rival Angolan factions struggling for power: Cuban soldiers poured in to support the Marxist MPLA; from the Congo (now Zaire) the CIA backed Holden Roberto's rival right-wing FNLA; the third faction, UNITA, was backed by South Africa.

Holden Roberto's emissaries arrived in London that autumn, their suitcases stuffed with dollar bills, to recruit British mercenaries. They found a new breed of entrepreneurs ready and waiting for them: mercenary recruiters, usually ex-NCOs and often from Britain's paratroop regiments, who, for $500-a-head recruiting money, were prepared to spread the word in the pubs of Aldershot, Camberley and Britain's other garrison towns and recruit former professional soldiers then swelling the growing ranks of Britain's unemployed.

In January and February 1976 up to 300 British mercenaries flew out to Zaire, to the FNLA training camps. It was for most of them a disastrous experience. There were no officers of Hoare's calibre, indeed apparently no ex-officers at all. Their commander in the field, 'Colonel Callan', was an ex-paratrooper from north London, a Greek Cypriot named Costas Georghiou. They found themselves, without armour and lightly equipped, opposed by Cuban tanks. When one particular group mutinied, Callan shot down 14 of them. None ever received anything but the first instalment of his pay. A handful of Americans recruited via the Ohio-based magazine *Soldier of Fortune* fared just as badly. As the FNLA forces disintegrated and the mercenaries disbanded, those who had not escaped or been killed in action were captured.

Thirteen – three Americans and ten British – were put on trial that June in Luanda. This was a show

Above: Many commercial mercenary training camps, like the one shown here, have been set up in the USA. Below: Mike Hoare (right) did well out of the war in the Congo unlike Jean Schramme (left) who was forced to flee into internment in Rwanda.

trial, stage-managed by the Cubans, which I attended. It was a people's court, a revolutionary tribunal, designed to humiliate the mercenaries and condemn '*mercenarismo*' in the eyes of the world. It succeeded in its aim. The psychopathic Callan, the crippled Mackenzie and the unlucky 'Brummy' Barker, plus one American, Gearhardt, were executed on 10 July. The remaining seven British mercenaries were still in jail in 1983; the two Americans by contrast were released earlier that year in a complicated exchange organised by the US State Department. The British then had between nine and 23 years more of their sentences to serve.

It might have been thought that after this tragic fiasco mercenaries would have considered the game not to be worth the candle. On the contrary Mike Hoare, though approaching his sixties, was preparing a comeback. He was encouraged by his old rival, Bob Denard's, example. After the failure of the bicycle invasion in Katanga, Denard attempted nine years later, in 1976, an airborne invasion of the small West African state of Benin. That failed too. But in May 1978 he tried the third element: he launched and led a successful sea-borne invasion of a group of islands near Madagascar, the newly-independent Comoros. With a force of only 50 mercenaries, he overthrew the Maoist-style President Ali Soilih and reinstated ex-President Ahmed Abdallah with himself as minister of defence. It was swift, easy and effective – a classic mercenary coup.

Swangsong in the Seychelles

A few hundred miles to the north of the Comoros lies another Indian Ocean archipelago, the Seychelles. There too the original right-wing President James Mancham had been ousted and driven into exile by a left-wing rival, Albert René. Seychellois exiles hired Hoare to restore a right-wing regime. Hoare had, in the past, yachted around the paradise-like Seychelles and dreamt of retirement there. On 25 November

1981 he and a group of about 50 mercenaries, disguised as peaceful tourists, carrying Czech-made AK-47s concealed in false bottoms in their hand luggage, landed by charter flight on the Seychelles. But, thanks to one drunken mercenary and one astute customs officer, the guns were discovered. The mercenaries seized the airport, but after six hours of sporadic shooting that caused two deaths, one on each side, they hijacked an Air India plane and flew back to South Africa. That hijacking was their undoing. They were charged under South Africa's severe anti-hijacking laws: most were released after six months in prison, but on 29 July 1982 Hoare himself was sentenced to 10 years.

Meanwhile six mercenaries – including Jeremiah Puren, now also white-haired – were left behind in the Seychelles, captured and put on trial for treason. Four – Brooks, Carey, England and Puren – were condemned to death by the Chief Justice of the Seychelles on 6 July 1982. However, the sentences were not carried out (one problem is that there are no gallows on the islands) and the mercenaries were released in 1983.

The mercenary's trade is, and always has been, a very dangerous one. If he escapes death in battle, he may be executed on or after capture. If successful, he risks being betrayed and murdered by his own employer. He will very rarely be paid the wages he has contracted for, and his opportunities for looting will be limited. As a mercenary at the time of the Hundred Years' War told the historian Froissart, 'there are very few of us who have died peacefully in our beds'. Yet what strikes a military historian is not the reappearance of professional mercenaries on the world stage so much as their temporary (as it proved) absence between 1789 and 1960 – that is to say, from the emergence of the 'modern' concept of the European nation state till the collapse of the European world empires. Now, in an era of small wars, they are probably here again to stay. **Anthony Mockler**

A West German mercenary cleans his machine gun after an engagement with Simba forces in the Congo. The operations in the Congo were the high mark of mercenary activity, and they fuelled the mercenary myth to a dangerous degree – subsequent mercenary adventures enjoyed much less success.

Key Weapons
WESTERN FIELD ARTILLERY

Amongst the many improvements made in the design and use of artillery during World War II were advances in mobility and versatility – the latter being the ability of a weapon to fulfil a dual role – the most notable example being the German 88mm anti-aircraft/anti-tank gun. One of the tactical lessons reaffirmed during the war was the importance of airborne or ground-based FOOs (forward observation officers) whose task was to control and coordinate artillery fire by watching the fall of shot and passing corrections to the gun line. The guns themselves ranged from close-support weapons to heavier guns and howitzers capable of longer range counter-battery fire designed to silence the opponent's own artillery.

Since World War II the importance of the field gun has in no way been reduced. Indeed, quite the reverse could be argued, especially with the introduction of shells capable of delivering a nuclear warhead, thereby providing artillery with a new-found strategic role. On the tactical side, conventional artillery played a central part in the Korean War, and even in guerrilla-style conflicts – such as the European involvements in Indochina – its effect has at times been crucial. The French defeat at Dien Bien Phu in 1954 is a good example of the battle-winning power of the field gun. The French positions were destroyed when they were subjected to a massive artillery bombardment which saw over 100,000 rounds pour into Dien Bien Phu. Unable to make an effective reply and with casualties

Page 783: A prototype of the multi-national 155mm FH-70 gun/howitzer on trial in 1974. Left: Although limited in range, the light-weight 105mm Model 56 pack howitzer is particularly effective in mobile warfare since it can be rapidly deployed into position by helicopter.

Below left: Viet Minh artillery pounds French positions at Dien Bien Phu. The Viet Minh victory owed much to the devastating effect of their well-sited artillery. Bottom left: French 105mm guns fire against Viet Minh enclaves in the hills along the Black River. Below: The devastating effects of the Copperhead CLGP (cannon-launched guided projectile). Copperhead has a range of 20,000m (21,900yds) and can be fired from a variety of artillery pieces including the 155mm M109A self-propelled howitzer, the 155mm M198 and the FH-70.

rising, the isolated French position was doomed. The Viet Minh had moved their guns into position by dragging them across the most inhospitable terrain, a feat which caught the French totally off guard and once again demonstrated the importance of mobility in warfare. Although the size and shape of field guns has not radically changed since 1945, they have continued to become more mobile and the latest artillery pieces have a greatly improved ability to be brought to firing positions with minimal delay.

Both the Soviet Union and the United States have devoted much finance and energy to improving their conventional artillery and several new types of gun have evolved. In the West some joint national ventures have been launched, and ammunition trends of more recent years have included the American M712 Copperhead CLGP (cannon-launched guided projectile). This relies on terminal guidance by an FOO who illuminates the target with a laser designator towards which the projectile (which is fin-stabilised and fitted with small wings) is guided by its electro-optical seeker. The round is available for users of the FH-70, M198 and M114 guns and its accuracy is extremely high in all weather conditions. Projects such as the Hughes Tank-Breaker and various extended-range guided projectiles show that development in this field is by no means static.

Artillery bombardments are a highly unnerving experience for those exposed to them and, for example, British artillery fire was a powerful factor in

undermining Argentinian morale in the Falklands War of 1982. The high mobility of the helicopter-transportable Light Gun and the effective use of FOOs enabled the British forces to harass the Argentinian troops from frequently changing positions. The Argentinians were able to respond with 155mm artillery fire, but this was never effectively coordinated and consequently had little effect.

The 155mm FH-70 field howitzer is the result of a joint venture undertaken in the 1960s, initially between Great Britain and West Germany but later joined by Italy. In Britain the FH-70 was intended to replace the well-tried but ageing 5.5in medium guns (dating back to World War II) which were withdrawn from service in 1980. In concept the FH-70 was designed to accept a new series of ammunition and feature an APU (auxiliary power unit) which could be used to bring the gun swiftly into action under its own power without recourse to a tractor. In 1978 the first FH-70s entered service, with the UK ordering 71 for deployment in its 18-gun artillery regiments, West Germany 216 and Italy 164. The 6m (19ft 6in) barrel has a double-baffle muzzle brake and is provided with a semi-automatic wedge breech. The split trail carriage mounts an 1800cc VW APU which allows the FH-70 to be driven at speeds of 16km/h (10mph) and also powers the trail and main wheels. Only two minutes are needed to bring the howitzer into action.

The range of ammunition developed for the FH-70 includes an HE fragmentation shell which weighs

43.5kg (95.8lb), smoke and illumination rounds, and the Copperhead CLGP. A rocket-assisted projectile is also under consideration which would extend the weapon's range to over 30km (18.6 miles). In German and Italian service a digital display unit processes information from a fire-control computer, though the FH-70s of the Royal Artillery do not have this facility. In mid-1982 it was reported that Saudi Arabia had placed an order for the weapon.

In 1974 the 105mm Light Gun replaced the Italian 105mm OTO-Melara Model 56 pack howitzer which had served with the light regiments of the Royal Artillery. It extended the latter's range from 10.5km (6.5 miles) to 17km (10.5 miles) and has subsequently proved to be a very successful weapon. The gun's bow-shaped trail, which carries the turntable while on the move, and light weight of 1858kg (4096lb) allows it to be towed by a Land Rover or carried as an underslung load beneath a helicopter. Up to eight rounds per minute rate-of-fire can be achieved for the first minute, with a rate of three thereafter.

Ammunition types include a 16kg (35.2lb) HE round and it can accept smoke and illuminating rounds. The barrel is fitted with a detachable double-baffle muzzle brake, vertically sliding breech and hydro-pneumatic recoil system. The plus 70-degree elevation and 11-degree traverse – or 360 degrees on its turntable – contribute to its versatility. The Light Gun is in service with Brunei, Kenya, Malawi, Oman and the UAE, while Australia has it under order.

Top: Royal Artillery men crew the now obsolete 5.5in gun/howitzer. Developed in 1939, the 5.5 saw action in Africa from 1941 and remained in service until the late 1960s.
Above: Italian troops prepare a 105mm OTO-Melara pack howitzer for action.

Below: The semi-automatic wedge breech mechanism of the FH-70 field howitzer. The FH-70 is crewed by eight men and is capable of a normal rate of fire of six rounds per minute. Currently under development is a self-propelled variant, designated the SP-70, which is expected to enter service in the late 1980s.

The US Army's 105mm M101 howitzer can date its origins to well before World War II but only after the end of the war did it receive its current designation. The gun's weight is just over 2 tonnes and elevation to plus 66 degrees and traverse to 46 degrees are provided. It is served by a crew of eight who can produce an initial rate of fire of eight rounds per minute which decreases steadily to the sustained rate of 100 rounds an hour. Maximum range is 11km (6.8 miles) and a wide range of ammunition is available, from anti-personnel, HE and anti-tank types to leaflet rounds. The weapon has been sold and exported to over 40 countries. The West German Rheinmetall FH-105(L) is a modified M101 with a longer single-baffle barrel. The FH-105(L) can deliver a 21kg (46.2lb) shell at a muzzle velocity of 600m/sec (1968ft/sec) to just over 14km (8.6 miles). It has a split trail and weighs 2.5 tonnes. The 105mm M102 howitzer was developed in the late 1950s and saw action in Vietnam. Today it provides the airborne and air mobile divisions of the US Army with a light-weight replacement for the M101. The gun has an aluminium carriage, with 360 degree traverse, and this has helped reduce the overall weight considerably to under 1.5 tonnes.

The United States Army's current 155mm howitzer is the M198. Development of this weapon began in the late 1960s and the first production examples entered service in 1978. The US Army has placed an order for 435 guns and the United States Marine Corps has ordered 282. The M198 will also be supplied to Australia, India, Greece, Holland, Pakistan, Saudi Arabia and Thailand. This split-trail weapon has a crew of ten and weighs 7 tonnes. A hydro-pneumatic recoil system is fitted and the 6m (19ft 6in) barrel has a double-baffle muzzle brake. It can accept standard types of ammunition as well as nuclear and Copperhead rounds. With a rocket-assisted projectile the range extends to 30km (18.6 miles) and representative of typical shell weight is the M692 HE round weighing 46.5kg (102.5lb) and containing 36 anti-personnel mines. An APU is under development.

Other types of American 155mm weapons include the M59 gun – known as the 'Long Tom' – (no longer

Top: A French artillery crew on manoeuvres with the American 105mm M101A1 howitzer. With a weight of 2.25 tonnes, the M101A1 is airportable by Chinook helicopter and can be deployed quickly and effectively in mountainous positions. Centre: American troops unpack ammunition for the 105mm M102 light howitzer. Designed to replace the M101, the M102 is lighter and has a slightly increased range.

Right: A British 105mm Light Gun in action against Argentinian positions near Port Stanley. Developed as a replacement for the Italian 105mm OTO-Melara pack howitzer the Light Gun saw extensive service in the Falklands.

Above right: A British 105mm Light Gun on NBC exercise in Germany. Above left: A French 155mm M1950 field howitzer at the Centre de l'Artillerie in Poitiers. The 9-tonne M1950 is the standard 155mm weapon deployed by the French Army with a range of 17,600m (19,250yds) and a firing rate of four to five rounds per minute. Below: The French 155mm TR which first appeared in June 1979 and known as Le Cannon de 155mm Tracte, is planned as the replacement for the M1950. The new piece has a considerably longer range and can fire the Brandt RAP (rocket assisted projectile) in addition to a 43.2kg (95.2lb) HE round, and illuminating and smoke projectiles. The TR is fitted with a double-baffle muzzle brake and can traverse through 65 degrees.

in US service but used by, among other nations, Austria, Japan, Italy and Turkey) and the M114 howitzer, which is retained by the US Army and also widely distributed among pro-Western nations. This latter weapon accepts the Copperhead round. The largest American field gun is the 203mm M115 howitzer. This fires a 92kg (202lb) HE round as well as nuclear shells. It weighs 14.5 tonnes, is served by a 14-man crew and has a range of 16.8km (10.4 miles).

Although France's motorised infantry divisions are currently equipped with 155mm M1950 towed howitzers which date from the late 1940s, plans are in hand to re-equip them with the 155mm TR towed gun, of which 130 have been ordered. Broadly similar to the FH-70 it has a barrel length of 6.2m (20ft 3in), a double-baffle muzzle brake and hydro-pneumatic recoil system. Served by an eight-man crew, the gun has a split-trail carriage and weighs some 10 tonnes. Barrel elevation is to plus 66 degrees and range is dependent upon ammunition type – with the Brandt rocket-assisted projectile, for example, it can extend to over 30km (18.6 miles). The gun is towed by a Renault TRM 6x6 tractor which also carries the 50 rounds of ammunition. A small APU is fitted along the lines of that of the FH-70. The towed gun can be brought into the firing line in five minutes, and an automatic rammer means that three rounds may be fired in the first 18 seconds, after which a rate-of-fire of six per minute is possible for the next two minutes.

The Italian OTO-Melara Model 56 pack howitzer has provided a 105mm weapon for numerous Western nations. Its great advantage is that it can be dismantled into 11 pack loads in three minutes which can then be transported by anything from mules to helicopters, and is thus ideally suited to mountainous terrain. Another advantage of the pack howitzer is its application in the anti-tank role where it is capable of penetrating up to 102mm (4in) of armour. It is served by a crew of seven and overall weight is only 1.29 tonnes. It can deliver a 21kg (46.2lb) projectile to over 10.5km (6.5 miles) and more than 2400 examples have been produced since the first guns appeared in 1957.

Conquest and consolidation

Independent India takes shape

As Hindu India and Muslim Pakistan approached independence, scheduled for 15 August 1947, the prospect of the partition of the sub-continent aroused profound emotions, especially in areas that were to be physically divided. In the Punjab, for example, the Sikhs began a horrifying pogrom of Muslims. And against a background of vicious intercommunal fighting between Hindus and Muslims, the rulers of the sub-continent's 562 largely feudal, semi-independent Princely States were supposed to choose their own destiny.

The Princely States were a product of the British Indian Empire. Either through diplomacy or plain good luck, during the British conquest of the sub-continent the rulers of some areas of India had been allowed to retain their sovereignty on the under-standing that they performed no acts that would threaten the sta-bility of British rule. Early on it became British policy to maintain the states, as a substantial bulwark to the British administration and a foil to the rise of Indian nationalism. Under the British they were free to pursue their own internal policies. But the Indian National Congress, the Indian independence movement, was committed to demo-cracy and the establishment of strong central author-ity. In the month preceding independence most rulers bowed to the inevitable and permitted themselves to be absorbed by whichever nation's borders sur-rounded them. The exceptions were Junagadh, Hyderabad and Kashmir.

The first two were Muslim-ruled but with largely Hindu populations and the Indian government was neither prepared to see them under feudal rule nor to permit potential threats to its internal security posed by enclaves within its borders. The Indian Army invaded Junagadh on 9 November 1947, although the ruler had officially acceded to Pakistan, while the Nizam of Hyderabad, after a vain diplomatic battle for independence, saw his state become the victim of a 100-hour 'police action', Operation Polo, in mid-September 1948. There were 1200 casualties during the fighting as Indian troops occupied Hyderabad.

By contrast, 80 per cent of the four million people of the mountainous state of Jammu and Kashmir were Muslim but the ruler was the Hindu Maharajah, Sir Hari Singh. The largest non-Muslim groupings were in Jammu and the eastern area, Ladakh. The state had evolved in the 19th century when the warlike Hindu Dogras pushed out of their Jammu heartland to take Ladakh and then Baltistan in the north. The Vale of Kashmir was bought from the British in 1846 while the Gilgit Agency, in the extreme north, joined the state only a month before independence (having previously been run by the British).

Kashmir was geographically linked to Pakistan. The various rivers that flowed out from Kashmir into the Punjab were extremely valuable to that province, while Kashmir, locked into the mountains and bor-dered on three sides by Afghanistan, China and the Soviet Union, relied upon access through the Punjab to reach the outer world.

It seemed likely that Kashmir would join Pakistan at independence. On the eve of the British withdrawal the traditional antipathy of the Maharajah's Muslim subjects led to a spontaneous revolt related to tradi-tional problems rather than nationalist fervour and the state verged on anarchy. The Maharajah himself was reluctant to commit Kashmir to either India or Pakis-tan, hoping that Kashmir might emerge as an indepen-dent state, though this view was naive in strategic terms. On the one hand Pakistan would claim the largely Muslim state on religious grounds, while India was concerned with her border security and Kashmir would, naturally enough, play an important part in this. Thus both sides were keen to gain influence and, ultimately, control in Kashmir.

The chance to intervene in Kashmir came with

British-armed and -equipped, Indian troops practice bayonet drill as part of a refresher course for drill instructors. The armed services of both India and Pakistan were initially modelled on the British Army, the dominant force on the subcontinent since the late 18th century.

the Muslim revolt in the Punch district. Arms for the rebels began to come in from sympathetic Pathan tribesmen in Pakistan's North West Frontier Province.

As this popular Muslim uprising grew in strength, events moved very quickly. Hindu and Sikh factions crossing into Kashmir from the newly created state of Pakistan were massacring Muslims by the thousand. The leaders of the 'Free Kashmir' movement (as the Muslim rebels were known) appealed to their friends among the Pathans for help and, while awaiting this, set about destroying the Maharajah's influence in the outlying areas of Kashmir. In a short time the Kashmiri administration had entirely lost control of these outer areas. On 22 October 1947 a spearhead of some 2000 Pathans, who had earlier crossed into Kashmir, began to advance up the Jhelum Valley towards Baramula and Srinagar. That same day the Maharajah requested Indian military aid but was told none would be forthcoming unless he agreed to accede to India.

Takeover in Kashmir

As news of Muslim atrocities filtered through, the Maharajah complied with the Indian ultimatum on 26 October, whereupon Indian Prime Minister Jawaharlal Nehru, himself a Kashmiri Brahmin, authorised the despatch of troops. However, Lord Mountbatten, the governor-general, stipulated that they would not be accompanied by British officers.

The first priority was to relieve Srinagar and clear the Vale of Kashmir. An airlift of 100 Royal Indian Air Force and civilian Dakotas assembled the 161st Brigade there within a fortnight. On 7 November the Indian offensive began, supported by 50th Parachute Brigade which had moved by road to Jammu from the Punjab. Driving the tribesmen westwards with the aid of air and artillery support, the Indian forces reached the line Uri–Punch–Kotli before the appalling winter weather set in. Punch remained besieged but was supplied by air. Good roads were almost non-existent and the tribesmen waged a guerrilla war, frequently cutting communications and compelling the Indians to evacuate the more isolated garrisons such as Jhangar. In the north the Gilgit Agency declared for Pakistan on 2 November after the garrison there had mutinied. Then, with aid from Pakistani tribes, the insurgents occupied Baltistan.

The initial reaction of Mohammed Ali Jinnah, the Pakistani leader, to the Indian intervention had been to commit his own troops but, when the British refused to allow their officers to accompany any units, he changed his mind. Nevertheless a 'Free Kashmir' (Azad Kashmir) administration was created at Muzaffarabad with its own army based on deserters from the Kashmir state forces and aided by seconded Pakistani officers. In the face of overwhelming Indian air superiority the Azad Kashmir forces were unable to cut the main supply route to Srinagar in February 1948, while the Indians strengthened their position in west Kashmir by recapturing Jhangar.

By the spring the Indians had substantial reinforcements in Kashmir: the Srinagar (later 19th Infantry) Division in the Vale of Kashmir and the 2nd Airborne (later 26th Infantry) Division in Jammu. But a renewed offensive westward failed to clear the state and Punch remained besieged despite temporary relief. During the summer and autumn the Indians concentrated on containing the threat from Baltistan, and a parachute brigade, supported by Stuart light tanks,

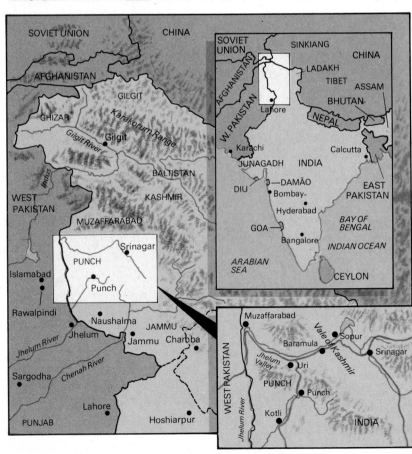

fought a successful two-month campaign, opening and securing communications to Ladakh.

In November 1948 a renewed push westwards, Operation Easy, saw the Indians complete the relief of Punch. The proximity of Indian troops to Pakistan led to the 7th Pakistan Division concentrating near Jammu ready to cut the Srinagar road and isolate the Indian forces which, at a strength of 29 battalions, were a third of the Indian Army. The Indians prepared for a counter-offensive towards Lahore but both sides backed away from a full-scale war and a United Nations ceasefire was negotiated, taking effect on New Year's Day. On 27 July 1949 the two nations agreed at Karachi that a plebiscite would decide the future of Kashmir but neither could agree who was to control the state in the meantime. The Indians, who had lost 6000 men in the fighting, were determined to retain their foothold in Kashmir. The situation was exacerbated by economic problems and disputes over water, leading to incidents which brought both sides to the edge of war in 1950 and 1951. Nehru warned that military action in Kashmir would bring Indian retaliation in the Punjab, and then India formally annexed Jammu in May 1954 and Kashmir in January 1957. No plebiscite was held, despite the avowed Indian foreign policy of self-determination.

Between the ceasefire in Kashmir in 1949 and war with China in 1962, the Indian Army was involved in a small number of minor operations. One was concerned with an uprising by primitive Naga tribesmen in Assam who repeatedly requested autonomy from the Indian government. By the mid-1950s there were at least 1500 Naga rebels, operating from their hill camps, prepared to fight against the Indian Army. Sporadic operations against the Nagas came to an end in 1961 when a degree of autonomy was granted to the tribesmen, but fighting continued.

Another concerned Portugal's colonies in the subcontinent, principally Goa. Although France had willingly given up its territories, Portugal feared a precedent that might destroy its vast African empire. In 1955 *satyagrahis* (non-violent resisters) crossed from India into Goa in an attempt to overcome Portuguese intransigence. At first the Portuguese authorities restricted themselves to deporting the intruders, but as the scale of the incursions grew they

The problems arising from the division of Britain's Indian Empire were resolved by military action. Above: Volunteers rally to the Nizam of Hyderabad in 1948, shortly before Hyderabad was invaded by the Indian Army. Above left: Afridi tribesmen prepare to join the Muslim uprising against the Maharajah of Kashmir. Left: Pakistani planes fly supplies in to the insurgents in Kashmir.

Below right: In their attempt to peacefully absorb the Portuguese colony of Goa into India the *satyagrahis* come under fire from the Portuguese. Below: an American cameraman helps a wounded *satyagraha*.

resorted to force and casualties resulted. India broke off diplomatic relations. For another six years India tried diplomatic and legal persuasion but, with major elections due in February 1962 and border tension rising, the Indian government decided to send in troops on 16 December 1961. Two brigades of the 17th Division and the 50th Parachute Brigade invaded Goa in Operation Vijay. Defended by only four battalions, the colony was overrun in 26 hours at the cost of 75 casualties, the Portuguese losing 51 men and a frigate. The tiny Portuguese enclaves of Damão and Diu were occupied at the same time.

Military expansion

Despite these military activities, the Indian forces were generally given a low priority in the allocation of national resources. Although four armoured regiments and 51 infantry battalions were added to the Indian order of battle, some of these units were militia-style forces absorbed from the former Princely States in 1951.

To Pakistan, however, India seemed to represent a major threat. In May 1954 Pakistan concluded a military agreement with the United States and this was shortly followed by membership of the pro-Western alliances of the Baghdad Pact (later Cento) and the South-East Asia Treaty Organisation (Seato). Ostensibly to prevent a Soviet thrust through Afghanistan, Washington agreed to equip five and a half divisions at a cost of $1500 million. This action was regarded with the deepest suspicion by India which gradually began to develop closer links with the Soviet Union – the Soviets provided diplomatic support for India in its dispute with Portugal.

In 1962 came the Himalayan border war between India and China. Both Nehru, the Indian leader, and his Defence Minister Krishna Menon, were staunch advocates of Sino-Indian understanding. The Chinese victories of 1962 shattered not only their policy and personal prestige but also the reputation of the Indian Army. In the light of the Indian defeat, Pakistan's leaders ignored Indian concessions in Kashmir. They began to see the possibility of a military solution to the problem. The outcome of this line of thinking was to be the major Indo-Pakistan conflict of 1965.   **E. R. Hooton**

Flight of the Dalai Lama
Chinese takeover in Tibet

Absolute theocratic ruler of Tibet the Dalai Lama (inset above) was eventually forced by events to flee to India in March 1959 (left).

Tibet has always been within the sphere of Chinese political and cultural influence, but has only rarely been under the direct control of Peking, protected as it is by its physical remoteness in the Himalayan mountains. After coming to power in China in 1949, the Chinese communists were determined to impose their authority on Tibet and to revolutionise Tibetan society. When the Chinese People's Liberation Army (PLA) invaded Tibet in October 1950, the Tibetans quickly realised that military resistance was useless. Under an agreement between the Chinese and the Tibetan government in 1951, China achieved recognition of an effective occupation of the country, although the Tibetan Buddhist theocracy in Lhasa remained in existence.

Despite their military success, the Chinese did not find it easy to assert their authority; for eight years the Lhasa government was able to impose a bitter stalemate on the Chinese authorities. The main obstacle to the Chinese was the innate conservatism of most Tibetans, reinforced by their mystical respect for the authority of the Dalai Lama, their political and religious leader. The Chinese set about the demolition of these obstacles. Their first step was to disrupt the political unity of the country, by detaching the culturally separate eastern provinces and building up the secular authority of the Panchen Lama, a Tibetan leader backed by the Chinese as an alternative to the Dalai Lama. These measures forced the Dalai Lama to take part in the political process, to the detriment of his traditional position of detachment from the material world.

At the same time the Chinese worked at lower levels to undermine the religious, economic and legal foundations of traditional society. Hospitals and schools were opened and intense propaganda used modern scientific ideas to discredit the religious life and monastic institutions. Measures to increase the productivity of agriculture were accompanied by legal changes to abolish feudal dues, and to reduce rents and rates of interest. The clear aim was to detach the rural lower classes from their noble and monastic overlords. These political, ideological and social activities were firmly sustained by military measures. The Tibetan Army was formally absorbed into the Chinese Army, but was greatly outnumbered by PLA garrisons in all the major centres. A network of major trunk roads was constructed, airfields were built and a telephone system and long-range wireless communications network set up.

These material achievements undoubtedly impressed the people of Tibet, but also alienated substantial numbers of them. The technology was useful, but the Maoist ideology was regarded with suspicion. The presence of so many Chinese overstrained local resources, causing shortages and inflation, and then led to deep resentment. In the first few years of the Chinese occupation, most Tibetans maintained a passive psychological resistance to attempts to reform them. The Dalai Lama successfully retained the respect of his subjects, despite persistent attempts to discredit him. The Panchen Lama and Ngaboo, the

Below: Chinese cavalry ride past the Winter Palace at Lhasa as part of the force bringing Tibet within the Chinese sphere of influence. The Panchen Lama (inset) was installed in place of the Dalai Lama.

Mountain warfare

The nomadic Khambas were often very successful in harassing Chinese troops, as the following account by a participant in the conflict shows: 'Our scouts discovered that the Chinese camp was down in a valley and had a constant garrison of 500 soldiers. But they grazed their horses high up on the hills, a few miles away from the camp. We managed to get close to the large herd and spotted only about 20 guards. Cautiously we crept up undetected and let loose a hail of bullets at them. Every one of them fell down dead, and we were able to drive away 70 horses with us. We headed back fast to Trodha Nyoko. As we rode around a bend in a narrow ravine, we suddenly encountered eight

Khamba guerrillas clean their weapons.

mounted Chinese soldiers. All of us (including the soldiers) were taken by surprise. We stared at each other for a brief moment and just as we prepared to fight, one Chinese raised his hands in surrender. A few seconds later the rest of the soldiers nervously followed suit. Most of them were raw recruits having no battle experience and they begged us to spare their lives. Some young men in our band wanted to kill them, and one lad went so far as to break a soldier's arm with the blunt side of his sword. But the older men and I told them to stop and said it was a sinful thing to do. We stripped the soldiers of their horses, guns and clothes and sent them away, free and naked as the day they were born.'

From Horsemen in the Snow *by Jamyang Norbu.*

Governor of Chamdo, served Chinese political interests, but had no popular following.

As the Chinese, frustrated, baffled and enraged by their failure to make progress in reform, increased pressure on the bases of society and on the position of the Dalai Lama, some Tibetans became more active in their opposition. The transition from political opposition to violent insurrection was started in the east by the Khambas. These bellicose nomads began a persistent war of raids and ambushes in 1954. The PLA responded with devastating attacks against the monasteries, which were regarded as centres of reactionary inspiration. The persecution of the monks and villagers alienated Tibetans in the rest of the country but failed to reduce the scale of guerrilla activity. The strategic roads through Chamdo became a focus for Khamba raids and the PLA was forced to make extensive use of air transport.

Reform and resistance

By 1957, the Chinese realised that they had been attempting to force too much reform on Tibet too swiftly. Chou En-lai announced that Tibet would be allowed more time to opt for socialism, and with less obtrusive help from Chinese advisers. Many Chinese went home, and the level of tension eased. However, a stream of refugees from Chamdo had carried the spirit of revolt into Lhasa, and Tibetan resistance was encouraged, not appeased, by the concessions.

In 1959, the Chinese brought on a Tibetan revolt by their tactless treatment of the Dalai Lama. The PLA garrison commander in Lhasa invited the Dalai Lama to attend various entertainments at an inconvenient time, and showed his anger when his invitation was refused. The people of Lhasa were fearful that the Chinese intended to kidnap the Dalai Lama; inspired by the example of the Khambas and influenced by what had occurred in Chamdo, they occupied the Summer Palace to guard their ruler, and refused to let him leave. The Chinese, determined to win what they saw as a trial of strength, adopted a menacing attitude which resulted in a series of attacks on Chinese officers, one of whom was stoned to death by a Tibetan crowd. The Dalai Lama was unable to conform to Chinese demands, but did not approve of his subjects' use of force to protect him. To escape from his dilemma, he secretly left the palace and fled to exile in India. Soon after his departure, PLA artillery shelled the Summer Palace, killing large numbers of Tibetans. This was the signal for the Khambas and their local allies to attack the Chinese garrison in Lhasa. Swords and stones did not avail against machine guns and the attackers suffered heavy casualties. The PLA brought in reinforcements and dispersed the rebels in the central provinces; Tibetan deaths in the following months have been estimated as approaching 100,000. Those who were not killed fled to remote and inaccessible areas, where resistance continues to this day. With no encouragement from the Dalai Lama, no formal organisation and no clear aims, the rebels were doomed to failure from the start.

It is quite clear that the PLA allowed the Dalai Lama to escape to Assam. His flight (described by the Chinese as an abduction by imperialists), removed one of the greatest obstacles to Chinese indoctrination of the Tibetan people and was used to justify the abolition of the Lhasa government. The central government of Tibet ceased to exist, and Peking tightened its grip on the whole country. **Nigel de Lee**

The Sino-Indian War

Two Asian giants clash in the Himalayas

The Sino-Indian War was fought in remote and barren places with small forces and was over in less than two months, but it had wide-ranging implications. The conflict undermined Indian claims to a policy of non-alignment, and added bitterness to the developing Sino-Soviet struggle for influence in Asia.

The causes of the war can be traced to the early 20th century and Britain's desire for secure frontiers in India. In 1904 Britain recognised the Dalai Lama in Tibet as an autonomous ruler, thereby making Tibet a buffer state between India and China. In 1914, at a conference in Simla, British and Tibetan officials concluded an agreement to define the northeast frontier of India along what was known as the McMahon Line. The Chinese government sent a delegate to the conference, but never accepted the Simla Convention or the McMahon Line as binding.

The territories about which disagreement arose were in the west in Kashmir, in an area known as the Aksai Chin which lay between the Karakoram mountains and the Kuen Lun, and in the east the province called the North East Frontier Agency (NEFA) situated east of Bhutan and between Assam and Tibet. The McMahon Line, delineating this frontier between India and Tibet, followed the mountains south of Migyitun and Rima. The area between the Thag La Pass east to the Bomdila Pass remained under Tibetan control. When India became independent in 1947, it adopted the McMahon Line in the east, and Indian maps showed the Kuen Lun range in the west in Kashmir as Indian territory.

In 1950, however, the Chinese People's Republic sent the People's Liberation Army (PLA) to occupy Tibet and restore it to China. The McMahon Line then became a matter of contention. The Chinese desire to restore the ancient frontiers of China, including Tibet, and reverse all 'unequal treaties' inflicted by imperialist powers, ran contrary to Indian nationalism and determination to retain all the territory of British India.

Until the late 1950s serious trouble was averted by mutual self-restraint. China rejected the McMahon Line in principle but respected it in practice as a matter of political convenience. India, in support of the cause of non-alignment, was careful to avoid provoking China. It accepted Chinese authority over Tibet and supported China's claim to a seat in the United Nations.

But by the late 1950s the atmosphere had changed; the goodwill and minimal understanding required to avoid violent conflict had evaporated. Chinese suppression of the Tibetan rebellion of 1959 was a source of apprehension and concern to India and public opinion was critical of the PLA's vigorous and brutal campaign. The Dalai Lama fled to India, as did about 80,000 refugees, and anti-Chinese sentiment was aroused. The Chinese were upset and alarmed by Indian attitudes and concerned by increasing Soviet

The clash between India and China in the Himalayas represented a conflict between two major Asiatic powers that was to be decided in the latter's favour. Top: Chinese artillery pounds away in support of an infantry advance. Above: Armed with a British-made Bren gun an Indian light-machine-gun team prepares to defend its position against an impending Chinese attack.

cordiality shown to India's Prime Minister Jawaharlal Nehru. Accordingly both countries became more interested in their shared frontier.

China began to press hard for alterations in the frontier between Assam and Tibet, but India held fast to the McMahon Line and refused to negotiate any changes. The western portion of the common border, that in Kashmir, also now became a matter of dispute. Despite numerous diplomatic signals to the contrary, the Indian government refused to believe that Chinese objections to the frontiers were serious. Above all, the Indians were convinced that the Chinese would never take up arms against India. This miscalculation led to a dangerous complacency and the adoption of a much more provocative policy. In particular, in some areas of the eastern sector, the Indian government claimed territory on the Chinese side of the McMahon Line, on the grounds that the frontier should be strategically secure. From the Chinese point of view, these modifications looked like aggressive expansionism and added to the suspicion that India was being used as an instrument of superpower policy.

This increasing tension led to military measures by both sides. India replaced its frontier police with the army, in the belief that a firm policy would deter the Chinese. The PLA, however, simply built up larger and better-armed posts. Tension was temporarily defused by an agreement to observe the status quo

Above: A contrast in styles – the Chinese People's Militia parades through Peking (above) while an Indian Army regiment conducts a ceremonial march past in 1961 (left).

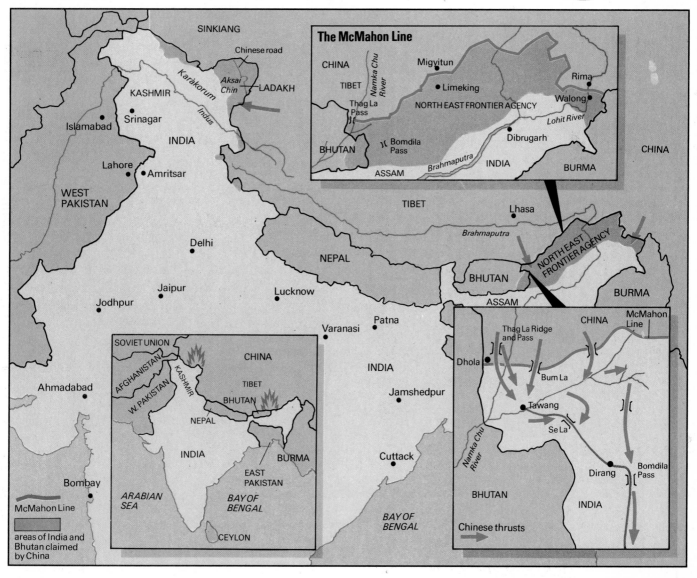

The McMahon Line

McMahon Line

areas of India and Bhutan claimed by China

Chinese thrusts

along the frontiers reached in 1959.

No general conflagration occurred until 1962, when fighting was sparked by Indian policy. In December 1961 the Indian government decided on a forward policy and began patrolling regularly right up to a modified version of the McMahon Line. This policy entailed the establishment of posts on the Chinese side of the line as drawn on the map in 1914.

One such post was set up at the junction of the frontiers of Assam, Tibet and Bhutan, a most sensitive area. In this region the McMahon Line ran below the dominant ridge of Thag La, but the Indian government decided that the ridge itself should be the only acceptable boundary. Accordingly, in early June 1962, a patrol post was set up by the Namka Chu River, south of Thag La ridge but north of the old McMahon Line. It was called the Dhola Post, although it was a day's march from Dhola itself. Chinese local forces asked the Indian troops to leave and, when they refused, constructed positions to dominate the post. In September, Nehru rejected Chinese protests and refused to discuss the matter. He accused the PLA of crossing the 'true' border and threatening Indian security. Reports of the PLA presence at Thag La created demands that the Chinese should be evicted, which forced the Indian authorities to prepare for action.

The Indian government and public were ignorant of the extremely difficult conditions in the North East Frontier Agency and were complacent in their underestimation of the PLA. The Chinese troops were much more numerous than their Indian opponents; they were better acclimatised, they had battle experience, and they occupied higher ground. They were also warmly clad. The Tibetan military road network meant they could be reinforced and supplied without difficulty. The Indian troops had little to sustain them but the inflated confidence of their national leaders. In particular, logistic support and movement were extremely difficult due to the broken terrain and lack of roads. The nearest roadhead to Thag La was at Tawang, six days' trek away. Tawang itself was five days' drive from the foothills, even when the roads were not buried deep under snow. The Indians at Dhola had to rely on airdrops

for their supplies, and winter weather made this process very difficult. In consequence, the troops were lightly equipped, short of ammunition, unable to dig proper fieldworks and forced to subsist on hard rations. Most of the soldiers who took part in the fighting at Thag La were not acclimatised to the cold at 4875m (16,000 feet) and wore summer uniform. For all these reasons, local Indian commanders objected to the prosecution of active operations at Thag La, but their arguments were overruled. They were ordered to be ready to launch Operation Leghorn on 10 October, for the politicians in New Delhi were convinced that the Chinese would fall back in the face of a determined show of force.

By 9 October the Indian Army had deployed the three battalions of 7th Brigade along the Namka Chu, an 11km (7-mile) front that took three days to march. The plan of attack was to send a battalion across the river to occupy Tseng-jong, a knoll from which the strong Chinese positions on the southern slopes of Thag La could be outflanked. A patrol of 50 Punjabis moved to this feature on 9 October. On the morning of the 10th they were followed by a battalion of Rajputs, heading towards the Namka Chu. The Rajputs were stopped by mortar fire, however, and a PLA battalion assaulted Tseng-jong. This assault was beaten off and the Punjabis withdrew, without opposition from the PLA, back across the Namka Chu.

Despite this proof of China's determination to resist, Nehru continued to insist that the PLA should be cleared from the North East Frontier Agency. At the same time China decided that a more spectacular proof of its resolute approach was required. In mid-October the Indian 7th Brigade was reinforced with another battalion plus some mortars and artillery, which added further to the strain on supply. The brigade was ordered to hold the Namka Chu and prepare for active operations, but the troops were deployed in an extended screen along the river rather than in well-ordered defensive positions.

On the night of 19/20 October the Chinese formed to assault the 7th Brigade and the centre of the Indian position was infiltrated. In the morning the positions of the 1st/9th Gurkhas and 2nd Rajputs were heavily bombarded, then overrun by waves of infantry. The 4th Grenadiers and 9th Punjabis, on the flanks, were engaged with fire but not assaulted. Having broken the Indian centre, the PLA moved down the trail to Hathung La, where it blocked

Below: As leader of the Chinese people Mao Tse-tung was determined to secure China's ancient borders, even if this meant conflict with India.

Below: Indian troops haul a 25-pounder gun/howitzer and vehicle up a treacherous mountain track in the Himalayas.

Above: Alarmed by the success of the Chinese offensive, Indian premier Pandit Nehru attempts to placate Indian fears at a political rally.

the retreat of the flanking battalions. The 7th Brigade was destroyed and its commander captured. The events at Thag La caused a political crisis in New Delhi, but no change of policy. Encouraged by sympathy from the West, Nehru decided to fight on.

Meanwhile the Chinese had advanced on Tawang in three columns and the Tawang garrison fell back to the pass at Se La. This was a good defensive position, but was never occupied in sufficient strength and was too difficult to supply. It was 95km (60 miles) from Bomdila and the road was frequently closed by snow or landslide. It was served by good dropping zones, but these were often inaccessible in winter. Bomdila, close to the plains, would have been a more suitable position to hold, but it was politically impossible for the Indian Army to yield ground. The PLA built a new road from Bum La to Tawang, and on from Tawang to Se La. Chinese patrols explored the Indian position, and their preparations were soon complete.

At that time the route from Se La to Bomdila was held by the Indian 4th Division, Se La itself by the 62nd Brigade with five battalions, and Bomdila by the 48th Brigade of three battalions. Divisional HQ was at Dirang, in a valley between the two passes. It deployed two battalions, some tanks and artillery, but was not in a defensive position.

The 4th Division was made vulnerable by the Bailey Trail, a difficult route over the mountains which could be used to bypass Se La and reach Tembang, a spur dominating the road between Bomdila and Dirang. This trail was only lightly held, because Indian commanders did not believe that it could be used by large numbers of troops. Reports that the PLA was on the trail in battalion strength were discounted as implausible. However, on 16 November a battalion was sent from Bomdila to occupy Tembang, and the following day Tembang was attacked by a Chinese force of 1500. The Indian garrison ran out of ammunition, attempted to withdraw and was destroyed. By this manoeuvre the PLA cut off Se La and Dirang from Bomdila.

As the attack on Tembang went in, the PLA drove in outposts north of Se La. The Indian commander decided that the strong brigade at Se La should abandon its position, fall back to Dirang to collect Divisional HQ, then move to make a stand at Bomdila, which was held by just two battalions. But this plan was put into effect too late. As a battalion of the 62nd Brigade left its positions during the night, the PLA moved into them, and so compromised the brigade that it was forced into a precipitate withdrawal under fire. Early on 18 November, before 62nd Brigade could reach Dirang, the 4th Division HQ came under machine-gun fire and dissolved into chaos. Only one battalion managed to fight its way back out of the mountains as a formed unit. The 62nd Brigade ran into an ambush on the road to Bomdila and was eliminated.

The PLA strikes

The garrison at Bomdila had been reduced by *ad hoc* detachments to a mere six companies attempting to hold a position designed for 12. A few minutes after this garrison had sent two companies down the road towards Dirang, Chinese troops attacked the position. The Brigade HQ and administration area soon came under fire, and Bomdila was evacuated. The surviving remnants of the brigade fell back down the road towards the plains until they were finally overwhelmed by an attack on 19 November.

The annihilation of the 11th Brigade at Walong in the Lohit Valley was accomplished by similar means. The PLA generally allowed the Indian Army to make the first offensive move, knowing that the attack would be made by inferior numbers of troops lacking ammunition and other essential supplies. Once the Indian troops had been exhausted by futile attacks, they would be counter-attacked.

In the western sector, meanwhile, both sides had long been consolidating their positions. In March 1956, China had begun to build a road through the Aksai Chin to link the province of Sinkiang with Tibet, and India had responded by improving access to the border areas in Kashmir. By mid-1962 more than 40 new Indian posts had been set up along the frontier, many inside territory that had been claimed by China. When fighting broke out, the Chinese technique was simply to bring overwhelming bombardments down onto Indian posts, then swamp them with huge numbers of infantry.

By 20 November the PLA had won a victory. The Indian Army in the North East Frontier Agency had been dispersed and the plains of India lay open to invasion. In the west, the Chinese had secured their claim. India was panic-stricken. Parts of Assam were evacuated; members of the Indian Communist Party were arrested and Nehru called on the United States to help defend India against the Chinese. At this point, China announced that the PLA would institute a unilateral ceasefire and withdraw from Assam to the original Chinese claim line. Having humiliated the Indian Army, the Chinese settled for a modest advance they considered just. The imagined Chinese invasion of India did not materialise. The Indian Army was lucky to escape with only 1383 killed.

Nigel de Lee

Above: A military convoy wends its way up to the strategically vital passes held by the Indian Army before the Chinese offensive.

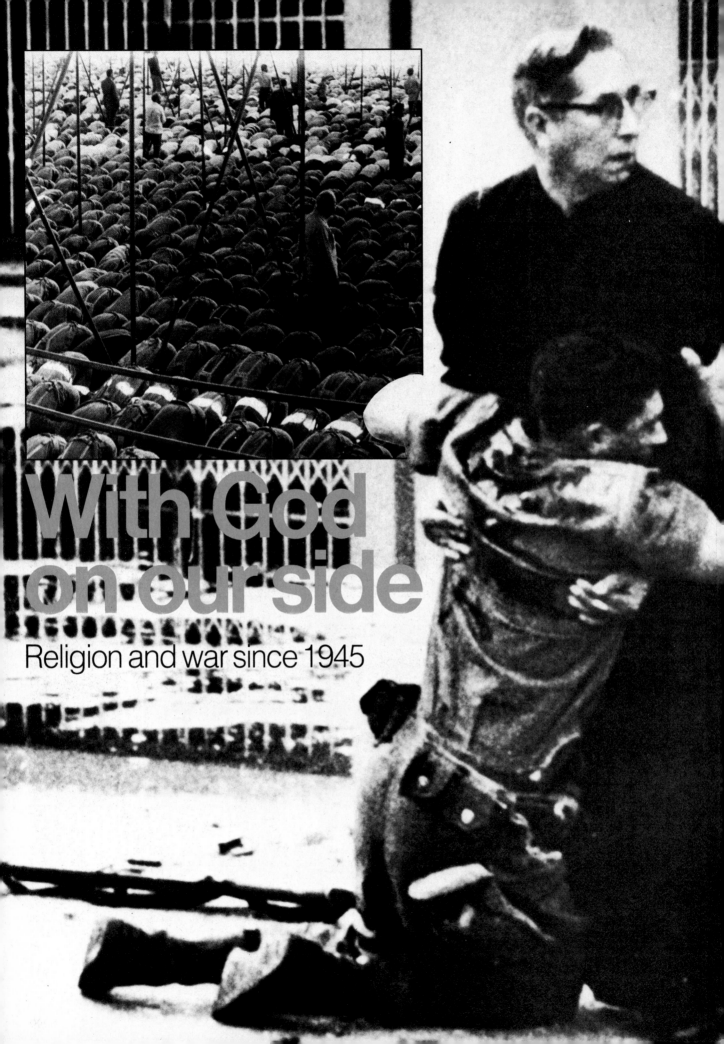

With God on our side

Religion and war since 1945

Of all forms of warfare, wars of faith are often the bloodiest. When one group finds the beliefs, traditions or practices of another group intolerable, the resultant warfare can be fierce and merciless. The conviction that the enemy represents an evil to be extirpated removes all formal inhibitions on viciousness and cruelty.

Yet most wars between groups professing different religions are not of this nature. Although the people may be identified as Jewish or Muslim, Protestant or Catholic, the essence of the war will lie elsewhere – in territorial disputes, national aspirations or economic conflicts of interest. Religion may bring a sharp edge to the conflict, clarifying differences and deepening hatred, but it will not in itself be the ground of the dispute, which will be at root a purely secular power struggle.

In the 20th century the West has become accustomed to the notion of religion as a private matter, playing only a marginal role in public affairs. Other divisions between men – their allegiance to a nation or a political system – have superseded religion. Christianity has remained a part of the ideological armoury of the West against atheistical communism, but it is often played down to avoid alienating non-believers in the Western camp. As if to emphasise this withdrawal from the practice of warfare, Christian spokesmen have been prominent in pacifist and anti-nuclear movements, despite support for Western defence policies from the major Church organisations.

Christianity has always been committed to peace in principle, whatever its practice may have been. But Islam was from its outset a fighting religion. Mohammed, the founder of Islam, was a warrior prophet who led his followers in battle. In its early years Islam expanded through religious war, the Jihad. Since World War II, while Christianity has declined, Islam has been increasingly influential, with both a religious revival among believers and a constant stream

Opposite page: In South America the Catholic Church has increasingly come into opposition with the state; the vanguard of the movement being led by the lower clergy – such as this Venezualan priest (left) holding a dying protester. In Iran, by contrast, Islamic fundamentalism has acted as a mobilising force for the policies of the state: Iranian soldiers (inset) bow down in prayer before an offensive. Above right: Lebanese Phalangists kneel at an altar but with M16 and AKMS assault rifles at the ready. Centre right: Muslims lead away a Maronite Christian priest taken hostage during the Lebanese Civil War. Right: A few of the many victims of religious fanatacism – Muslims slaughtered by Sikhs in the Punjab, 1948.

of new converts, notably in West Africa. Since the colonial powers in Asia and Africa were Christian, anti-colonial revolt and national self-assertion could often be identified with Islam.

Islamic militancy in the post-war period found its first major expression in the founding of Pakistan in 1947. The partition of the Indian sub-continent into Hindu-dominated India and Muslim Pakistan was a triumph for Mohammed Ali Jinnah and his Muslim League. Opposing the influence of Mahatma Gandhi, who advocated independence for a united India in which Muslim and Hindu would live harmoniously, Jinnah persuaded the British to back partition.

The new Muslim state, born amid scenes of riot and massacre that were in a sense a spontaneous religious war between communities, made no territorial sense – East and West Pakistan were separated by 1600km (1000 miles) of Indian territory – and the act of partition left a legacy of disputed territory with India which soured relations between the two states. From this situation flowed border incidents and tension until, in 1971, open war between India and Pakistan resulted in independence for East Pakistan as Bangladesh. Yet that war could not be described as religious – Hindu India's allies in the war were the Muslim Bengalis of East Pakistan.

In the Middle East, the religious lines of conflict are more clearly drawn. Jewish Israelis have faced Muslim Arabs in repeated conflicts. Yet the idea of a Jewish homeland in Palestine, although rooted in religious fundamentalism, found its expression in a secular and initially largely socialist state. Jews had for many years been among the most enthusiastic supporters of left-wing, and often atheistic, movements. Although the Jews were identified by their religion, as the Arabs by Islam, Arab-Israeli conflict grew out of the confrontation of two nascent nationalisms over a fundamental territorial dispute: who were the rightful inhabitants of Palestine?

After 1967 Israel's takeover of the holy places of Islam in Jerusalem gave a new impetus to Muslim hostility. Orthodox Jews, with an aggressive attitude to Islam, have caused disturbances by sacrilegious acts against Muslim holy places.

Yet the role played by religion in the wars between Israel and its neighbours highlights the complexity of the issues. Within Israel itself, it is possible to draw a rough line equating expansionist Zionism – the call for Jewish settlements on the West Bank, for example – with more orthodox or fundamentalist religious groups; but in the Arab world, this simple equation breaks down. For those states that conform most rigorously to the precepts of Islamic law – such as Saudi Arabia – are politically conservative, and have always been afraid of the consequences of the radical nationalism that Israel's most implacable opponents – Nasser of Egypt, Assad of Syria or Gaddafi of Libya – have sought to unleash.

Civil war in the Lebanon

Middle Eastern religious conflict is at its most confusing to the north of Israel, where the Lebanon is riven by social and political divisions along religious lines. The country's constitution at independence in 1946 established an elaborate balance between Christians and Muslims, who are themselves divided into often mutually hostile sects. The Christians' slender numerical predominance was threatened through the 1950s by the higher Muslim birthrate, and in the 1960s the emergence of the PLO in Palestinian refugee camps in the Muslim south challenged Christian military superiority. In the 1970s, only external pressures prevented a Muslim takeover of the government, and civil war now seems established as a permanent way of life.

Yet even in the Lebanon a religious interpretation

Above: a rabbi conducts a service in the field for men of the Israeli Army; the Israeli Defence Force maintains a strong association with the Hebrew religion. Above right: Spraying fire from their assault rifles, diehard Islamic fundamentalists carry out the assassination of Egypt's President Anwar Sadat. For the fundamentalists Sadat had not only betrayed Egypt's leading role in the Arab world by coming to an agreement with Israel, but he had also compromised the Islamic religion by his decidely 'occidental' lifestyle.

of the conflict is inadequate. The divisions between Christian and Muslim sects in the country are always reinforced by political and cultural factors. The Maronite Christians have normally been commercially prosperous and politically right-wing (to the extent of supporting an important neo-fascist element), whereas the Muslim leaders have been largely identified with the left. The situation is complicated by the Druze who inhabit the hills in the south of the country, and whose religion is associated with Islam, but who are traditionally separate from 'other' Muslims. The United States has consistently supported a Christian government as part of its strategic policy for the region, while the Israelis have armed and trained Christians as their allies in the Lebanon, despite the religious difference between Christian and Jew.

Muslims and Christians have confronted one another in several other parts of the world. In the Philippines, the communist-dominated Hukbalahap movement which was mainly supported by the Muslim minority, fought against the Catholic-dominated central administration from independence in 1946 until 1954. The victory of the government forces was only partial, and the Muslim minority has remained in a state of smouldering rebellion ever since.

In a swathe across Africa from the Sudan through Chad to Nigeria, the colonial powers created territories in which a Christian (or sometimes animist) south was yoked with a Muslim north. After independence conflict resulted. In the Sudan, Christians and animists revolted against an Islamic central government; in Chad a lengthy civil war resulted in the replacement of a Christian by a Muslim government; and in Nigeria massacres of Christian Ibos by northern Nigerian Muslims precipi-

Below: A Jewish soldier prays at the Wailing Wall following the capture of Jerusalem during the Six-Day War of 1967.

A Protestant slogan in Northern Ireland. Like the many visual references to William III's victory over the Catholics at the Battle of the Boyne in 1690, the red hand of Ulster has become a symbol of the Protestant ascendancy in the Six Counties.

tated the 1967 Biafra War. In none of these cases was religion the crucial issue, although it was a contributory factor. The Chadian civil war has continued with Muslim against Muslim. The Biafran question involved fundamental issues about the nature of Nigeria's federal regime and the special position of the Ibos in the country's administration. Nowhere did one group try to impose its beliefs on the other.

Both Islam and Christianity are, of course, divided within themselves by internal scissions with deep historical roots. The Iranian revolution in 1979 brought to prominence Islam's ancient division between Shi'ia and Sunni. Iran's successful revolt against the Shah was led by Shi'ia ayatollahs, but many of Iran's Arab neighbours are Sunni Muslims. Since 1980 Iran has been locked in war with its neighbour Iraq, a state with a Shi'ia majority but ruled by an elite professing the Sunni faith, and its relations with other Sunni states in the region such as Saudi Arabia have been very poor. But the differences between Iran and neighbouring countries are far more than religious; there are territorial disputes and conflicting political perspectives, since the Saudis suspect the Iranians of being politically disruptive. There is also a difference of nationality: the Iranians are not Arabs like the Iraqis and Saudis.

Still, it would be difficult to exaggerate the importance of religion in Iran's internal affairs, and this Shi'ia upsurge is a major fact of modern political life.

Its example has given a fresh impetus to the Islamic revival throughout the Middle East.

The major example of conflict between Christian sects is the fighting in Northern Ireland since 1969. As elsewhere in the world, the religious divide also marks a social divide. Catholic hostility to the dominant Protestants has been fed by years of social injustice, and the appeal of Irish nationalism carries more weight with Catholics than religious fervour. Insults to the Pope and Catholic 'superstition' play a large part in the rhetoric of Irish Protestantism, but the true cause of the conflict is the fearfulness of an embattled community.

Communism and the church

Religion has played its part in national revolts against Soviet communism. In eastern Europe, and most notably in Poland since the accession of the first Polish Pope, the church is a focus for traditional nationalism against unpopular communist governments and Soviet influence, while in central Asia Afghan rebels resisting Russian intervention since 1979 have asserted their traditional Islamic beliefs in the face of attempts to modernise the country by force.

In Latin America, by contrast, many Catholic priests have sided openly with left-wing revolutionaries. They have identified the left-wing concern with the living conditions of peasants and workers with their own Christian beliefs. International Christian organisations also support anti-racist guerrilla movements in southern Africa.

Some observers have considered communism itself a modern religion, with its church (the party), its Pope (Stalin, but probably not Andropov?), its heretics (Trotsky), its saints and martyrs (Lenin, Che Guevara). Certainly the hopes and the fears involved in the confrontation between East and West seem to have many parallels in the religious wars of the 16th and 17th centuries, in that many on both sides feel that they can never rest until the whole world is converted to their beliefs.

As we have seen, although religion has featured in many recent conflicts, it has been in a local and subsidiary role. Religion has functioned as one of those features, like nationality or social class, which defines a group and distinguishes it from its neighbours; the problems, or aspirations, of such distinct groups living in close proximity cause most wars – not religious beliefs in themselves.   **R.G. Grant**

Divided Islam

The Muslim world is split between Sunnites and Shi'ites with the former constituting the majority. The split dates back to the seventh century, and a dispute over who should succeed the prophet Mohammed: the Shi'ites preferred his son-in-law, Ali, while the Sunnites turned instead to the prophet's father-in-law, Abu Bakr. Shi'ites constitute majorities in Iran, Iraq, North Yemen and Bahrain, and form substantial minorities in Lebanon, Syria, Turkey, Pakistan and Afghanistan, but most Muslim countries tend to be governed by Sunnites.

This religious divide is a source of constant division and rivalry in the Muslim world and has recently assumed great importance.

The Shi'ites believe in the possible or actual existence of an Imam, or leader of the Muslim community, who is appointed by God and divinely inspired. Their tradition encourages a fusion of the separate functions of religious and political leadership. The Shi'ite Ayatollah Khomeini is Iran's spiritual leader, but can also lay down the law on matters of state. Shi'ia claims to divine insight into political matters can be uncomfortable for secular or Sunnite rulers.

Key Weapons

ANTI-TANK ARMAMENTS

The radical improvements in tank design that took place during World War II led, not unnaturally, to counter-developments in the field of anti-tank weaponry. The high-velocity anti-tank gun came into general service as the surest means of dealing with the massively armoured tanks that dominated the battlefields of World War II. And yet that war saw the first developments in a new class of anti-tank weapon – the anti-tank missile. Initially primitive hand-held devices, they were to be transformed into a range of electronically-sophisticated guided weapons capable of extraordinary degrees of accuracy; and while the gun has remained a potent anti-tank weapon, the most dramatic advances made in this field since 1945 have come about through progress in ATGWs (anti-tank guided weapons).

The anti-tank gun's main advantage over the ATGW is its ability to fire all three types of anti-tank ammunition – AP (armour-piercing), HESH (high-explosive squash-head) and HEAT (high-explosive anti-tank) – and while the gun itself is an expensive item the rounds of ammunition are relatively cheap and plentiful, especially when compared to the projectile costs of the more advanced ATGWs.

Ranged against the anti-tank gun are its weight and size which make it an unwieldy object on the battlefield, rendering it and its relatively exposed crew highly vulnerable to small-unit infantry support weapons as well as to standard counter-battery fire.

Following on from the experience of World War II the Soviet Union continues to place faith in anti-tank guns and today has two principal types in service. The 85mm D-44 gun is a conventional World War II design – and has seen extensive use on the battlefields of the Middle East – while the larger 100mm T-12 is a smooth-bore weapon capable of firing the latest high-velocity APFSDS (armour-piercing fin-stabilised discarding-sabot) rounds. With a muzzle velocity of 1500m/sec (4920ft/sec), the T-12 is effective against thick armour up to a range of 1500m

Page 803: A Hughes 500 MD Defender armed with a mast-mounted sight (above the rotor blade) fires a TOW anti-tank missile. The mast sight allows the helicopter to engage enemy armour at low-level while remaining hidden by undulations in the ground. Left: Based on the M113 APC (armoured personnel carrier) an Emerson ITV (improved TOW vehicle) lets loose its TOW missile. Below left: Soldiers of the British Army set up a 120mm Wombat recoilless rifle.

(1640yd). On the other side of the Iron Curtain, West Germany, Belgium and Switzerland deploy self-propelled 'tank destroyers', armed with 90mm quick-firing high-velocity guns based on the success of the German Jagdpanther of World War II. The other Nato armies, while not employing the conventional high-velocity anti-tank gun, ensure that their field artillery batteries can be used in a direct-fire anti-armour role, which, for example, in the case of the US 105mm M101 howitzer enables it to penetrate 100mm (4in) of armour plate up to a range of 1500m (1640yd).

At the infantry level, the lightweight recoilless rifle has been brought into service. By allowing some of the propellant gases to be vented directly through the breech on firing, it eliminates the need for the heavy recoil-absorbing buffer recuperator system which makes conventional artillery so unwieldy. The British Army employs the 120mm Wombat recoilless rifle, capable of firing a HESH round to a distance of 1000m (1100yd), which can be mounted on an infantry-manned two-wheel trailer, a long wheel-base Land Rover or the FV432 armoured personnel carrier. Apart from a somewhat limited armour-piercing capability, the recoilless rifle suffers from the problem of a large back-blast which gives away the firer's position – a potentially fatal situation for the advanced and supposedly well-hidden recoilless-rifle crew. Possessing no significant advantages over the modern anti-tank missile, the recoilless rifle is now being phased out in favour of the ATGW.

The simplest anti-tank missiles on offer today are shoulder-launched weapons, termed LAWs (light anti-tank weapons), which utilise the lightweight HEAT warhead. The LAW operates on either the rocket-launched or recoilless system. The US Bazooka was one of the first and best known of the rocket-launched systems; although even modern versions have a range limited to around 200m (220yd) its lightness makes it attractive to the over-burdened infantryman. The Soviet RPG-7 combines a light

Above: An Iraqi soldier prepares to fire his Soviet-designed RPG-7 rocket launcher, supported by comrades armed with AK assault rifles.

Right: A soldier of the Royal Irish Rangers aims his 66mm LAW which features a disposable launch tube. Below: While needing a crew of two men the 84mm Carl Gustav LAW has a more powerful warhead than the lightweight 66mm LAW.

launcher with a relatively large warhead by adopting a two-stage launch system: the first is a small charge which propels the rocket clear of the launcher after which the main rocket is fired to carry the warhead to the target. The RPG-7 has its drawbacks, however, most especially a lack of flight accuracy caused by the mid-air ignition knocking the moving – and potentially unstable – missile off course.

Of the recoilless LAWs the Carl Gustav FV550 launcher has an improved range of 700m (765 yd) but its complicated sights increase its weight to 15kg (33lb) and two men are needed to operate the weapon. In an attempt to solve the weight problem, the French Strim recoilless launcher uses a novel system of firing the projectile from within a discardable package tube which absorbs most of the recoil, thereby allowing the launcher to be built of lightweight materials.

Beating the LAW

Whether the LAW incorporates the rocket or recoilless system has begun to seem less relevant, however, for improvements in MBT (Main Battle Tank) protection – especially the Chobham compound armour – have rendered sophisticated tanks virtually immune to light anti-tank weapons. While LAWs can be usefully employed against softer targets such as MICVs (Motorised Infantry Combat Vehicles) and APCs (Armoured Personnel Carriers), for use against MBTs they need to be replaced by more complex and heavier ATGWs which can send a powerful warhead to ranges considerably in excess of the anti-tank gun's shell.

In the short history of the ATGW three generations of missiles have been developed. The first – including the Soviet Sagger, the British Vigilant and the French SS 11 – are all wire-guided missiles using 'command to line-of-sight guidance' which entails an operator using a joy-stick to relay signals down the command wire and by simple optical means to guide the missile directly onto the target. The second generation is more complex, though by using a semi-automatic guidance system the operator's task is in fact made simpler; his function is to track the enemy vehicle by keeping his sights aligned to the target for the time it takes the self-correcting infra-red homing, wire-guided missile to hit it. The Franco-German HOT (high-subsonic optically-tracked tube-launched) missile and the US TOW (tube-launched optically-tracked wire-guided) missile are the two most important semi-automatic ATGWs in the Nato armoury and, while they both have excellent maximum ranges of 4000m (4375yd) and 3750m (4050yd) respectively, their bulk forces them to be taken away from the foot soldier and to be set on vehicle mountings. Less heavy is the Franco-German Milan (*missile d'infanterie légère anti-char*) which is just man-portable and has equipped a number of European armies.

At long ranges the ATGW missile can take some time to hit its target – 17.5 seconds at 3000m (3280yd) for the West German Mamba, for example – and under stressful battlefield conditions it has been found that the longer the flight duration the less accurate the missile: it is not easy to hold a target in your sights for 17 seconds when you are under fire. Allowing the operator to use a 'fire-and-forget' system improves matters considerably, as has been suggested by the semi-active Hellfire missile. The Hellfire can be fired from either a helicopter or from behind cover and guides itself to the target by picking up the laser beams

Above: Well-sited in a prepared position a Vigilante anti-tank missile team lines up a potential target.

Like its TOW counterpart, the HOT anti-tank missile can either be launched from a helicopter – such as the West German MBB Bö105 (right) – or from a ground vehicle (above).

Above: The technologically advanced AH-64 Apache attack helicopter is armed with 16 Hellfire anti-tank missiles. Left: The Soviet Army's wire-guided anti-tank missile, the AT-3 Sagger, is highly portable. Right: German and French anti-tank helicopters are now fitted with TOW or HOT missiles as, for example, the four TOW tubes on this Bö105.

reflected off the target by a well-concealed, forward laser operator.

The more advanced systems need to be mounted on tracked vehicles which because of their size and vulnerability on the battlefield need to be so well armoured that they begin to resemble the armoured vehicles they are set against. Somewhat ironically many armoured warfare theorists regard this as a logical consequence of the fact that the tank itself is the best anti-tank weapon. Armed with a large-calibre high-velocity main gun, the modern MBT is superior to the ATGW in the short-range engagements that make up most modern tank versus anti-tank encounters. The introduction of compound armour on the latest MBTs has lessened the effect of the chemical-action HEAT and HESH rounds and as a result the armour-piercing kinetic energy round has regained much of its former importance. The latest high-velocity tank guns fire a sub-calibre (discarding-sabot) solid shot (either tungsten carbide or depleted uranium) held on course by fin-stabilisers, so that on contact the hardened shot has a very high specific gravity which allows it to pierce a tank's armour.

While the kinetic energy APFSDS round is the most important anti-armour weapon of the MBT, HEAT and HESH chemical-action projectiles have been most successfully deployed in the latest attack helicopters. Although exaggerated claims were made for the anti-tank attack helicopter, both HOT and TOW missiles have been fitted to Nato helicopters thereby providing them with the opportunity of attacking large armoured formations at relatively safe distances. In many ways the highly manoeuvrable attack helicopter is the ideal weapons platform for the anti-tank missile. The advanced US AH-64 Apache anti-tank helicopter is fitted with electronic devices to suppress hostile ground fire and numerous other built-in survival features, while at the same time being capable of launching 16 laser-guided Hellfire missiles according to a flexible tactical plan that ensures a very high number of direct hits. On the Soviet side a similar interest in anti-tank helicopters has been shown. The introduction of the Mi-24 Hind attack helicopter in the early 1970s caught many Western observers by surprise. A powerful if cumbersome aircraft, the Hind's first role in a European war would be to provide an extra cutting edge to the otherwise blunt instrument of the Red Army; and with the introduction of the Hind-F – able to carry six Spiral laser-guided fire-and-forget anti-tank missiles and a 30mm armour-piercing gun – the Soviets have an advanced and very specialised anti-tank weapon.

In its different way the fixed-wing aircraft can be highly effective against tanks. Of the many munitions that can be used against armoured vehicles, one of the most potent is the cluster bomb, a collection of hollow-charge mini-bombs that break away from the parent weapon to form a scattered spread of destruction over a wide area. Of the latest improved conventional munitions the most cost-effective has been the anti-tank mine, which in the case of the German Medusa and Pandora series can be sown quickly and efficiently from helicopters. Although such mines are unlikely to knock out an MBT they can cause sufficient damage to both crew and vehicle to halt its progress.

As military planners in both the West and the East regard the tank as the most important single element in the land forces' armoury, the efforts made to counter this threat will be correspondingly great. The dramatic improvements in conventional weapons accuracy that began to take effect in the late 1960s and 1970s have now been fully extended to anti-tank weapons. In the future it seems likely that the range and application of anti-tank weapons will continue to expand so that the MBT will be faced by a concerted all-arms offensive ranging from the simple hand-held LAW, through land-based ATGWs to the latest electronic guidance systems for shells and 'smart' bombs.

Top: The Hellfire ATGW. Above: The Hellfire sight is slaved to the helmet-mounted optical unit of the gunner. Below: A T55 in flames, victim of a Hellfire.

Index

A